Scenic Routes & Byways™
MONTANA

S. A. SNYDER

gpp®

travel

Guilford, Connecticut

All the information in this guidebook is subject to change. We recommend that you call ahead to obtain current information before traveling. Globe Pequot Press assumes no liability for accidents happening to, or injuries sustained by, readers who engage in activities described in this book.

Editor: Kevin Sirois
Project Editor: Heather Santiago
Layout: Casey Shain
Maps: Tim Kissel © Morris Book Publishing, LLC.

ISBN 978-0-7627-7954-3

Printed in the United States of America
10 9 8 7 6 5 4 3 2 1

CONTENTS

Scenic Routes & Byways

ABOUT THE AUTHOR

In 1878 **S. A. Snyder**'s great-great-grandparents homesteaded in Montana. Their small farmhouse in the Bitterroot Valley still stands occupied today. An inveterate traveler, Snyder has journeyed throughout many countries and across much of the United States. Her college education in biology and journalism, along with her work in, and dedication to, conservation, provide the fodder for both her personal and professional writing.

Today Snyder is a freelance writer, editor, and voice actor.

ACKNOWLEDGMENTS

I am grateful to Paul Dumond for his help with the first edition of what was then *Scenic Driving Montana,* first researched in 1994. As my chauffeur he navigated many an unmarked road, always maintaining a sense of humor and adventure, while I took notes on these drives. Thank you to the many outstanding photographers who shared their work with me, even if their photos didn't make it in the book: Pam Arroues; Heidi Beck-Heser, Philipsburg Chamber of Commerce; Ariel Bleth; Brad Christensen; Kathie DeWitt; Paul Dumond; Roxanne Escudero; Amy Falcione; Craig Flentie, BLM; Joanne Girvin, Gallatin National Forest; Tom Kilmer; Michael Lynch; Chris McGowan; James N. Perdue, WildAndScenicPhotos.com; Andrea Pipp; Jane Ruchman, Gallatin National Forest; Donnie Sexton, Montana Office of Tourism; and Dusti Thompson, Libby Area Chamber of Commerce.

A special thank you to one of my best friends, Ariel Bleth, who helped with this third edition. Another big thanks to Craig Flentie, with the Bureau of Land Management Lewistown Field Office, for his detailed updates to, and photos of, remote Scenic Route 20.

For all my family and friends, past and present,
who made this book possible. And to the people of Montana.

INTRODUCTION

WHAT WE [MONTANANS] ARE NOT IS OFTEN MORE COMPELLING THAN WHAT WE ARE. THE FACT OF OUR EMPTINESS IS IN ITSELF IMMENSELY SIGNIFICANT.

—K. ROSS TOOLE, *MONTANA: AN UNCOMMON LAND*

Few Western states conjure up images of leathery cowboys, unscrupulous outlaws, Native Americans, dusty trails, unforgiving mountains, endless wilderness, and old-fashioned lawlessness like Montana does. Throw in a few explorers, trappers, settlers, lots of wild animals, and some cattle and sheep, and you have the state as it once was. This young state, which joined the union in 1889, couldn't have a richer history if it were left to simmer for a few hundred more years.

Montana is the fourth largest state, after Alaska, Texas, and California, and its more than 147,000 square miles are still sparsely populated in relation to the rest of the country. In 2010 the population was just under 1 million people, although between 2000 and 2010, the population grew by 9.7 percent. Still, cattle outnumber people here three to one. Of all the states, Montana ranks 48th in population density (after Alaska and Wyoming), with nearly 7 people per square mile, if they were spread out evenly. But most residents live in western Montana; in eastern Montana—roughly two-thirds of the state on the Great Plains—many neighboring towns are separated by 2-hour drives. In such communities, the landscape overshadows the people.

Montana borders 3 Canadian provinces and 4 other US states. Within its boundaries lie 2 national parks, 10 national forests, 7 Indian reservations (representing 11 tribes), more than 40 state parks, nearly a dozen wilderness areas, more than 15 national wildlife refuges, dozens more state-owned wildlife management areas, and several national monuments and historic sites.

Huge and diverse, Montana has more than 22 million acres of forest. The rest of the state is a mix of grasslands, "badlands," cultivated crops, rocky mountains, sagebrush flats, glaciers, and water. The name Montana was derived from either the French or the Spanish word for "mountain," although only the western third of the state is mountainous. The eastern part, with scattered bumps, bulges, and canyons, is relatively flat, and agricultural plains and grasslands are dominant features. "Island" mountain ranges add relief to Montana's wide spaces, rising in great lumps, seemingly out of nowhere.

The Beartooth Plateau is pockmarked with thousands of lakes and ponds. TOM KILMER

Overview

The Florence Carlton Church was built in 1884. S.A. SNYDER

This variable landscape is one reason for Montana's weather extremes—many are record breaking. In 1954 the lowest recorded temperature in the Lower 48 states was registered at Rogers Pass north of Helena at a brisk -70 degrees Fahrenheit. The largest temperature drop was 100 degrees in 24 hours near Browning in 1916. Montana has the lowest average monthly temperatures in the contiguous United States for 6 months of the year, including the month of August, which has seen a low of 5 degrees. West Yellowstone, on Montana's southern border, is consistently the nation's cold spot year-round. Conversely, the state's hot, dry summers can bake the life right out of the land. In northeastern Montana Medicine Lake holds the state's record for the highest recorded temperature: 117 degrees.

Since I first wrote this book in 1994, Montana has seen dramatic changes. In some places, the landscape remains unchanged since 19th-century settlement. In other places, the landscape would be unrecognizable to 19th-century time-travelers, having been altered by human development as well as natural events like wildfire and flooding. Climate change has created new landscapes, as have people. Glaciers are receding, wildfires and droughts are more frequent, the pine beetle has taken its toll on forests, and floods have altered riparian habitats and in some cases the course of streams and creeks. On a positive note, more multiuse paths

The Big Hole River drains the Beaverhead and Pioneer mountain ranges. TOM KILMER

for cyclists, pedestrians, joggers, inline skaters, and cross-country skiers have been built, many on reclaimed land once scarred by mine tailings and timber mills.

It seems ironic, therefore, that this book promotes scenic driving in vehicles fueled by oil. Personally, I prefer my bike to my car. But Montana is too vast to see efficiently from the seat of a bicycle, and not all that safe for riding in some places. So instead, opt for a hybrid car or a motorcycle to explore the drives in this book.

Montana Past & Present

Some anthropologists believe the Kootenai Indians were the first native inhabitants of Montana. The tribe's oral traditions say they have been here for several thousand years. The Kootenai were followed by the Salish, Crow, and Pend d'Oreille peoples, who arrived a few hundred years ago, and shortly thereafter were joined by the Blackfeet, Sioux, Assiniboine, Gros Ventre, Cheyenne, Chipewyan, and Cree.

The first whites to come to the region were probably French trappers, but close on their heels were Meriwether Lewis, William Clark, and the other members of the Corps of Discovery. When the United States bought the city of New Orleans and environs in 1803, the French government threw in an extra chunk of land—the Louisiana Purchase—totaling 838,000 square miles of what is now the American West. Anticipating this acquisition, President Thomas Jefferson planned to send an expedition to the region and asked Congress for money to fund it, even before its purchase was finalized. Upon congressional approval the Corps of Discovery set out from St. Louis in 1804 with orders to map the United States' new holdings and record its plants, animals, and minerals. The explorers were also asked to make contact with any human inhabitants they came across as well as make celestial observations. Most important, Lewis and Clark were hoping to find a passage to the West Coast and the Pacific Ocean.

The expedition covered more than 8,000 miles in 2 years, 4 months, and 9 days, and the journals that the team kept remain some of the world's most detailed and meticulous. The leader of the expedition, Meriwether Lewis, was only 29 years old when the Corps of Discovery set off (and 4 years younger than Clark). Lewis made scientific observations and kept records, while Clark acted as diplomat and negotiator with Native Americans. Only one of the expeditionary party died on the whole trip, reportedly from a ruptured appendix, and there was only one fatal encounter with Native Americans, in which two Blackfeet were killed. The expedition was considered a grand success by Jefferson and other officials. Montana historian K. Ross Toole attributed the success to Lewis's and Clark's intelligence and ability to command.

The explorers initially made their way across what would later become Montana by following the Missouri River. In the 1840s and 1850s, this wide waterway became Montana Territory's first "road" of sorts, bringing more trappers and explorers, such as John Colter (who had accompanied Lewis and Clark), Jim Bridger, and Manuel Lisa (who established the first fur-trading post) to the territory. Jesuit priests, called "black robes" by Native Americans, arrived around the same time and tried to convert Native peoples to Christianity.

This relatively quiet period in Montana Territory came to an end when gold was discovered in the early 1860s. Strikes in Grasshopper Creek (Bannack), Alder Gulch (Virginia City), and Last Chance Gulch (Helena) made news back East, and the rush to Montana was on. Trappers and explorers were joined by miners, enterprising settlers, and merchants who served their needs. Steamers and keelboats brought more gold seekers up the Missouri River, and wagons streamed across the continent in long trains, bringing dreamers and hopefuls to a seemingly endless land for the taking.

The wave of Montana's agricultural pioneers, known as "honyockers," began flowing during the 1880s (including my ancestors), although the peak of the homestead era in Montana came later in the dryland farming days from 1914 to 1918. The Homestead Act of 1862 entitled anyone who could make a go of it to 160 acres. All you had to pay was a $10 filing fee! More land was homesteaded in Montana than in any other state. Although many of the honyockers were seasoned, determined, and tenacious, most were nevertheless defeated by geography—Montana's dry and severe climate, combined with natural disasters, eventually broke their spirits. My own great-great-grandparents sold their Bitterroot ranch and moved to Missoula to work for the railroad after the devastating floods around the turn of the 20th century.

With the arrival of European peoples to Montana Territory, Native Americans and their traditional lifestyles were soon threatened. Long-used hunting grounds and sacred sites weren't respected by land-hungry settlers or gold-greedy miners who believed it was their manifest destiny to use these "empty" spaces. Increasing settlement caused more and more conflicts with Native Americans. Miners wanted access to tribal lands, under which lay vast mineral riches. Settlers demanded land and water rights, and they sought protection from the US Army, especially in the days following the Civil War. Most Indian nations depended on bison for the bulk of their protein, shelter, tools, and clothing, only to see commercial hunters exterminate bison herds by the millions. Many Native people starved. In an effort to control "unruly" Natives and "civilize" them, the government decided to move them onto reservations, lands often deemed unsuitable for crops, livestock, or mining. Reservation boundaries were often redrawn if minerals proved to be rich there.

The history of the relationship between the US government and Native Americans was one of broken promises. As K. Ross Toole wrote in *Montana: An Uncommon Land:*

> Our "policy" toward the Indian has been no policy at all. It has run an extraordinary gamut from extermination to impractical Christian humanitarianism, but has always been a "policy" which ignored the Indian himself and his peculiar heritage.

Conflict was inevitable when the two cultures clashed. The most famous battle between the US Army and Native Americans in Montana took place on the Little Bighorn River in 1876. The bloody fight killed many on both sides and brought General George Armstrong Custer to his end. Just days before the confrontation, Sioux and Cheyenne warriors had defeated General George Crook at Rosebud Creek, an event that affected the outcome of the Battle of the Little Bighorn.

A year later another series of battles involved the Nez Perce tribe. In 1860 gold was discovered on the Nez Perce Reservation in Idaho, and for several years the Nez Perce had lived in peace with the miners. But when the US government drew up new boundaries for the reservation, shrinking it to about one-tenth of its original size, five bands of Nez Perce refused to sign any more treaties. These bands were considered hostile and ordered onto their new reservation nevertheless. Somewhere in the course of the story, a Nez Perce warrior was killed; his friends retaliated by killing some whites, and the saga of the 1,170-mile Nez Perce march began.

Quake Lake was created when debris from a 1959 earthquake dammed the Madison River. USDA FOREST SERVICE

Under the leadership of five chiefs, the nontreaty Nez Perce—as they were called—fled their homeland in search of a new home free from US government inter-ference. Chief Joseph, the Nez Perce spiritual leader, led the entire crew of 800 people, including 125 warriors, and 2,000 horses. During their 4-month journey across Mon-tana, the Nez Perce entered from Lolo Creek, went south up the Bitterroot Valley, crossed into the Big Hole, headed south again into Idaho, cut east through Yellow-stone Park, re-entered Montana passing west of Billings, and headed north toward Canada, where they surrendered just shy of the border. In all, nine skirmishes were fought between Nez Perce and US military forces before Chief Joseph's poignant sur-render in the Bears Paw Mountains. Scenic Routes 4, 6, 20, 21, and 24 in this book cross parts of the Nez Perce National Historic Trail (Nee-Me-Poo Trail).

As Montana's Native Americans were driven onto reservations, the tide of miners, loggers, and agricultural settlers continued to advance. It wasn't long before railroads crisscrossed the state, hauling livestock, minerals, wool, grains, and furs from the commodity-rich West to population centers in the East. Many boomtowns choked and died after just a few short years; many others sprang up to take their places. One of the more successful towns was Butte, atop "the rich-est hill on earth," considered the copper-mining capital of the world. Its mines yielded gold, silver, copper, and abundant minerals. Mining continues in Butte to this day.

Two figures in Montana's history, Marcus Daly and William Clark, are synonymous with mining. Known as the "copper kings," both Daly and Clark owned extensive mining claims, mills, and smelters in Butte and Anaconda, as well as their own newspapers. After falling out over territorial delegate elections, Daly and Clark saw fit to destroy each other through slander and other dirty tricks. They fought over the designation of the newly created state capital: Clark won with his pick of Helena. Later he also won the race for US Senate, but Daly's relentless pursuit to get him evicted over allegations of bribery proved fruitful. Clark was forced to resign from the Senate, although he later served a full term. The "war of the copper kings" became worldwide news.

Butte's streets witnessed other mining wars. Horrible working conditions in Montana mines motivated laborers to form unions—among the first workers' unions ever created in the United States. Violent and bloody clashes between union members and anti-unionists were frequent in Butte during the latter part of the 19th century and the early days of the 20th century.

Not all of Montana's history was violent, though. In fact, one of the state's more famous legislators was known for her pacifism. In 1916 Jeannette Rankin became the first woman elected to the US Congress—before most women in the United States could vote. She served two separate terms and was the only member to vote against entry into both world wars. In 1941 she announced, "As a woman, I can't go to war, and I refuse to send anyone else." Her congressional career ended after she refused to declare war on Japan, but that didn't stop her from promoting peace. She died in 1973, but the Jeannette Rankin Peace Resource Center in Missoula still carries out her mission.

Montana's present is deeply ingrained with mythic cowboys and Indians, cattle drovers, miners, vigilantes, and mountain men, but its future will most likely be marked by tourists and small-business owners who need only cell phones and computers to conduct business. Today, the state's "gold" lies in its scenery, wildlife, and outdoor recreational opportunities. Towns boomed again in the 1990s as newcomers sought quieter, slower lifestyles in safer, friendlier communities.

Yet many native Montanans have soured on the arrival of too many neo-Westerners, many of whom have been perceived to threaten the values and lifestyles from which Montana evolved. Like Montana's Native Americans, ranchers, miners, and loggers have felt as if they were targets of Montana's latest heritage assault. Battles continue to be fought over how much wilderness is necessary, how many trees can be cut before destroying habitat and watersheds, how much public land should be allowed for grazing livestock, and how many mountains should be

The Gallatin River was named for President Jefferson's Secretary of the Treasury, who had refused to finance the Lewis & Clark Expedition. Michael Lynch

bulldozed for minerals and precious metals. Montana is still thought by some to be full of limitless natural resources for the taking. Battles over the consequences of such takings have been waged in courtrooms and in Congress. Their outcomes may change Montana by a magnitude that it hasn't seen in more than a century.

Natural History

Most of Montana's native trees are conifers, and many native hardwoods are only shrubs. Forest types vary from wet to arid and comprise pines, spruces, firs, larches, hemlocks, cedars, Douglas firs, and junipers. Cottonwoods, aspens, box elders, ashes, and elms are dominant along rivers and streams. Native herbs, grasses, and shrubs number more than 300. Montana is home to 107 native mammals, from the tiny shrew to the awesome grizzly bear. All of our nation's native large hoofed mammals, except caribou, can be found roaming Montana's mountains or eastern prairies. Mountain lions prowl the forests and, lately, many urban areas. The endangered black-footed ferret was reintroduced to Montana, and wolves—once exterminated from the state—have made a dramatic comeback such that hunting of wolves is on the table again.

Nearly 380 bird species have been recorded here, and about 250 of those birds nest in Montana or are year-round residents. Our largest bird is the trumpeter swan, weighing in at 40 pounds; the smallest is the calliope hummingbird, a whopping 0.1 ounce. Reptiles and amphibians are few because of the cold climate, although 33 species (17 reptiles and 16 amphibians) live in the state's forests, water sources, and arid plains. Montana lakes, rivers, and streams harbor more than 80 fish species. About 55 are native, while 32 have been introduced.

Hidden in Montana's bowels are the remains of much earlier flora and fauna. Montana is one gigantic dinosaur-and-fossil bed, where some of the world's most important (and only) finds have been made. Most of the world's *Tyrannosaurus rex* skeletons have been unearthed in Montana (more than 30 to date), the first discovered in 1902 and the most complete dug up in the first decade of the 21st century. Even soft tissue of dinosaurs has been discovered in Montana recently, including that of a T. rex. One of the world's few discovered dinosaur nesting colonies was found along the Rocky Mountain Front as recently as the 1970s. And one species of dinosaur uncovered in eastern Montana, a type of *Hadrosaurus*, is the only specimen of its kind.

Fossils of marine plants and animals tell us that a much different landscape once existed in what is now eastern Montana. A gargantuan Cretaceous-era sea covered this portion of the state about 75 million years ago. Montana's rich coal deposits and scattered oil fields are the biggest legacies left by ancient creatures and the sea.

Scenic Routes & Byways Montana gives you just a taste of what the Big Sky Country has to offer. I encourage you to explore the many places not mentioned in this book and meet Montana's people. Montanans are not ostentatious, nor do they make apologies for who they are. They are proud to be hardworking and grounded to the land, and they are painfully honest about the way life is. The best way to get to know Montanans is to go to county fairs, rodeos, powwows, and museums; hire guides for fishing, hunting, or backpacking; or hang out in local cafes and bars. In many cases, saloons were the first establishments to be erected in every Montana boomtown and the last to close their doors when a town went bust. Even today Montana bars are gathering places for members of small communities of all ages. I once saw a hand-printed sign hanging behind the bar in a small-town saloon that read, PLEASE WATCH YOUR LANGUAGE. THIS IS A FAMILY BAR. Considerate, unapologetic, and honest. Welcome to Montana.

Before You Begin

From east to west and north to south, Montana's highways are adorned with occasional white metal crosses. These sad reminders of lives lost on the road are also warnings to others: slow down, be watchful of wildlife and other users of the road (not just high-speed motorized vehicles), and use common sense regardless of driving conditions. Most Montana roads are unimproved gravel or dirt tracks, which are rarely or never maintained. In many counties, even secondary paved roads receive little attention. If you were to have an accident in such rural country, help might not arrive for several hours—if at all—in the most remote places. Many steep, narrow mountain roads have no guardrails, so go easy on those turns.

In addition, officials report that all roads on the routes in this book are passable, although flooding in 2011 did cause damage in some areas. Wildfires also frequent the state, forcing road closures not only from fire damage and hazards but also from subsequent landslides. As with all the remote drives in this book, especially those that are mostly unpaved, check local conditions before heading out.

And finally, winter can occur during any month in Montana, and severe conditions can pop up faster than a tick dropped in a hot frying pan. Be prepared for all driving conditions, regardless of geography and season. Winter is a spectacular time in Montana, but if you venture into the Treasure State during this time, check travel conditions before heading out on any long-distance drive.

For the latest road report, call the Montana Highway Department at (800) 226-7623 (TTY call 800-335-7592), or listen to local weather radio. This website reports all road closures and other road information: www.mdt.mt.gov/travinfo/map/mtmap_frame.html. Also, you can contact local chambers of commerce, ranger districts, or parks offices for more specific information and updates.

Notes About Montana Attractions

Before setting your heart on visiting any of the funky little museums and backroads sites mentioned in this book, remember that many attractions in Montana, especially outside of major urban areas, are open only from Memorial Day to Labor Day. So call ahead for the latest information if you're unsure. In some cases, a local docent will open a museum upon request, and in such cases you might find a sign on the door with someone's phone number. Call it; they'd be happy to let you in, and you can often get an earful of local history and stories. If you find yourself in Glasgow in October and you really want to see that pioneer museum, you can also stop by the chamber of commerce and ask about it. Don't be surprised to hear, "I know Bob, the owner. I'll give him a call and he can pop on down to let you in." If Bob does open up the place for you, have the courtesy to take your time there and chat with him. He'll have a ton of great stories to tell and may even point you in the direction of some really cool place that got left out of this book! Also, give him a small donation to help keep the place running.

As of 2010 all of Montana's state parks managed by the Department of Fish, Wildlife & Parks are free to Montana residents (if you've paid the $4 tax on your vehicle registration). If you're not a resident (or snubbed the tax), you will be charged a minimal user fee—up to $5 per visit—to access some of the parks. Camping fees are usually additional, and please don't begrudge paying them. They are negligible and necessary for the maintenance of these beautiful places.

As you drive throughout western Montana, you may notice thousands of acres of burned forest. Since the original edition of this book in 1995, the state has experienced many years of severe drought and accompanying wildfires just about everywhere. Also, there have been recent floods, especially in eastern Montana. It's impossible to keep up with, so some of the descriptions in this book may describe an area that has since been burned or flooded. Keep in mind that fires are necessary for rejuvenating forests, though due to suppression over many decades, some fires have burned wildly out of control and have proved deadly to more than just trees. Don't despair if you see lots of charred forests; they'll soon recover, and with caution you can still enjoy a walk among the standing dead. Just be careful with those matches.

Watch for Wildlife

Some visible victims of the highway are wildlife of every species, from small reptiles recharging on hot pavement to huge moose eyeballing succulent willow shoots on the other side of the road. Even in the best of situations, a collision with a large animal will damage your vehicle and likely kill the animal. In the worst case, both you and the moose could die. Please be alert for wildlife near all Montana roads during all seasons and at all times of the day, but especially from dusk to dawn. Slow down whenever you see wildlife near the road. I like to pull over to a safe spot and move turtles out of the road, too. They often don't stand a chance against high-speed vehicles. If you follow suit, remember to pull over where it's safe to do so and take care when venturing into the road. Move turtles to the side of the road in the direction of turtle travel, rather than taking them back to where they came from.

Access on Indian Reservations

Both private property and tribal lands can be found on Montana's 7 Indian reservations. Because most tribal lands are off-limits to nontribal members, you must ask permission before using many of the areas for hiking, fishing, hunting, or other outdoor activities. Permits may be required for any activity, and regulations differ from place to place, so check with tribal headquarters at each reservation for details. Contact information is listed in For More Information.

Montana's Speed Limit

For a few short years in the late 1990s, the speed limit on Montana's highways was "reasonable and prudent." In case you missed the opportunity to drive your Ferrari at 120 mph across the Big Sky, well, I'm sorry. The speed limit is now 75 mph for most vehicles on the interstate and 70 mph on other public highways. Please be reasonable and obey the generous limit with prudence.

Because of severe winters, road construction usually can take place only from May through September, depending on when the snow flies. And because of severe winters, road construction is usually *necessary* to repair ice- and snowplow-damaged roads. That's another good reason to follow all posted speed limits.

So, bearing all this in mind, enjoy your travels, drive safely, watch out for wildlife, take only memories away with you—and please don't litter. Thanks!

Map Legend

Interstate Highway/
Featured Interstate Highway

US Highway/
Featured US Highway

State Highway/
Featured State Highway

Paved Road/
Featured Paved Road

Bureau of Indian Affairs/
Featured Bureau of Indian Affairs

Unpaved Road/
Featured Unpaved Road

Trail

Building/Structure	■	Route Number	24
Campground	⚠	Small State Park, Wilderness or Natural Area	
Campsite	▲		
Dam	—	Scenic Area/Overlook	
Falls		Ski Area	
Historic Site		Visitor, Interpretive Center	?
Lodge		Wildlife Management Area	
Point of Interest	◘		

Mountain, Peak, or Butte

▲ Deseret Peak
   11,031 ft.

River, Creek, or Drainage

Lake or Reservoir

Swamp

State Line

MONTANA

National Park

National Forest

Wilderness Area

Indian Reservation

Wildlife Refuge

1

Yaak River Country

Libby to Yaak to Eureka Loop

General description: A 175-mile drive through the damp spruce and fir forests of northwest Montana, following rivers, traversing a steep mountain pass, and hugging the shores of finger-like Lake Koocanusa.

Special attractions: Kootenai Falls, Yaak River Falls, Lake Koocanusa, Libby Dam, Ross Creek Cedar Grove Scenic Area; Tobacco Valley Historical Village; museums; skiing, snowmobiling, hiking, backpacking, boating, fishing, wildlife viewing, camping.

Location: The extreme northwest corner of Montana between the Idaho and British Columbia borders, beginning and ending in Libby.

Drive route numbers: US 2, CR 508 (Yaak Valley-Libby Dam Road), Yaak County Road 92/Upper Ford Road, West Kootenai Road, Highway 37.

Travel season: Year-round. FR 228 (west shore of Lake Koocanusa) is closed in winter. Snow and ice conditions make winter travel hazardous. Be mindful of log truck traffic along the entire route.

Camping: There are several campgrounds in Kootenai National Forest. More campgrounds border Lake Koocanusa.

Services: Full services in Libby and Eureka. Limited services in Troy, Yaak, and Rexford.

Nearby attractions: Cabinet Mountains Wilderness.

The Route

Both this drive and Scenic Route 2 course through Montana's wettest habitats, where forests of spruce, fir, hemlock, and western red cedar dominate the plant community. Hundreds of square miles of hiking trails make **Kootenai National Forest** a great place to play if solitude is your goal—or you'd like to commune with grizzlies, moose, and wolves. Large blocks of forest and riverine ecosystems, though fragmented from logging, provide great habitat for all of Montana's charismatic megafauna. The wildlife management area near Kootenai Falls is home to bighorn sheep, best seen during fall through winter, as well as black bears, mountain lions, bobcats, and deer, among others. Several other wildlife areas across the state's northwest corner are worth a visit, too. Unlike the rest of Montana's "big sky," this region feels more like "big woods" and, sadly, in places "big clear-cuts."

Evidence of human habitation in the Kootenai River valley dates to at least 8,000 years. Back then the elevation of the Kootenai River was higher, and the river channel was wider. Archaeological finds include spear points and evidence of campsites along what would have been the banks of the river at that time. These historic finds, combined with the colorful past of white settlers and a rich collection of wildlife, make for a well-rounded tour.

Yaak River Country

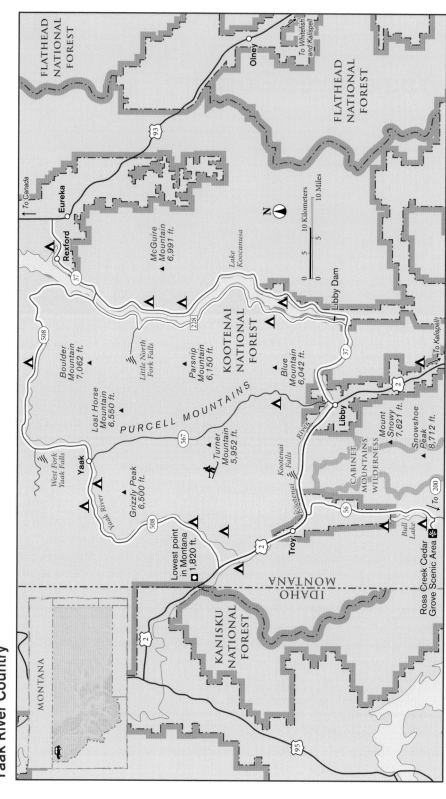

Libby

The drive begins on US 2 in **Libby,** originally a gold-mining camp founded in 1886. When word reached the miners that a railroad had been proposed for the area, the tent camp—cobbled together on Libby Creek—transformed into a real town. Given Libby's location, bung in the middle of hundreds of square miles of virgin forest, a seemingly endless supply of timber provided all the buildings the town needed. In 1906, however, a fire destroyed a whole business block and damaged several others. Take a historic walking tour of the town; self-guided pamphlets are available from the chamber of commerce. If you want to learn more about the town's history, visit the **Heritage Museum** (www.libbyheritagemuseum .org), open June through August only, exhibiting artifacts and telling the history of the people who lived in the area: miners, loggers, trappers, and Native Americans. Local wildlife (albeit stuffed) are also on display. You can tour several buildings on the grounds, such as a miner's cabin, forestry cookhouse, and wagon barn. You'll find the museum just east of Libby on US 2.

In July celebrate the **Two Rivers Rendezvous,** where mountain men and women can test their outdoor skills. Also during summer, **Montana Shakespeare in the Parks** comes to Libby. The troupe is composed of professional actors that travel the state bringing the Bard's works to life for the public to enjoy free. **Nordicfest,** the second weekend in September, wraps up summer with concerts, music, the arts, and food.

Libby to Yaak

From downtown Libby follow US 2 about 11 miles west to **Kootenai Falls,** which overlooks the vertical bluffs of the Kootenai River. Named for the Kootenai Indians, who are said to be Montana's earliest Native people, the falls are considered a sacred place, traditionally used for meditation and vision quests. They're also the largest undammed falls in the Northern Rockies. Park in the wide area between the road and the river and take the short, paved trail through a copse of western red cedar and grand fir, where you'll find picnic tables and barbecue pits. The trail continues over the railroad tracks to the river. The walking is easy, although to get to the falls you do have to go along an uneven rocky terrace; watch your footing. From the bank you can see the series of spectacular rocky ledges—about 2 miles long—adding zip to the river's course during high water. You can also view the spectacle from a suspended bridge downstream. Signs will direct you to both bridge and falls. This stretch of Kootenai River made its screen debut in the 1994 film *The River Wild*, starring Meryl Streep and Kevin Bacon. Unless you're a highly skilled whitewater boater, however, you might want to skip this section on your next float trip.

A kayaker rides the "superwave" below Kootenai Falls. DUSTI THOMPSON

US 2 meets Highway 56 about 5 miles west of Kootenai Falls (about 15 miles west of Libby). Take Highway 56 south about 17 miles to **Ross Creek Cedar Grove Scenic Area,** a 100-acre preserve of giant western red cedars. Turn west at the entrance and follow the road to the parking lot, where you'll find a trailhead. The winding, narrow road has some turnouts, but be sure to take the corners slowly to avoid oncoming traffic. You can camp a few miles from the scenic area on the south end of Bull Lake. Signs will direct you.

Ross Creek Scenic Area was set aside in 1960 to preserve these rare, old-growth cedars. The larger trees are as big as 12 feet in diameter and tower above to 175 feet high. A 1-mile-loop trail leads you on a self-guided nature tour, complete with interpretive signs. It's an easy walk on flat terrain. Take time to stand inside the cavity of one of the dead cedars; it can be a humbling experience. Understory plants here include wild ginger, trillium, queen's cup bead lily, devil's club, Rocky Mountain maple, and several species of fern. Western white pines and grand firs mix with red cedars to form a high canopy, allowing only filtered sunlight to reach the forest floor. Take a deep breath and smell the richness of the soil. You can picnic in the lush green array along Ross Creek, which tumbles over moss-covered rocks in moist years but is bone dry in times of drought. For a longer hike (4.5 miles) take Ross Creek Trail 142 through the forest.

Back on Highway 56 you'll find additional recreation sites where you can camp, fish, and boat on Bull and Spar Lakes or boat and fish on Savage Lake. On the third week in August the Halfway House on Bull Lake hosts the annual **Big Sky Rendezvous.** Enjoy live country music and home-cooked food while camping. On the east side of the highway is the 94,000-acre **Cabinet Mountains Wilderness,** which you can access via trails along Highway 56. Refer to the Kootenai National Forest map for more details.

To continue Scenic Route 1, retrace your route back to US 2, then turn west and pass through the mining and timber town of **Troy.** This outpost was once a base for railroaders and freight trains on the Great Northern Railway, as well as the headquarters for silver miners working in the Cabinet Mountains. Learn more at the **Troy Museum and Visitor Center** (www.troymtchamber.org/node/166) on US 2 at the east end of town.

About 14 miles past Troy, the Yaak River Road (CR 508) heads northeast. Follow the road, and about 6 miles after the turnoff is a small set of falls on the Yaak River, just above a campground. Though much smaller than the ones on the Kootenai River, the **Yaak River Falls** are worth the stop. They're most impressive during early summer when snowmelt from the surrounding mountains cascades over the exposed rock, which geologists estimate to be 800 million to 1.5 billion years old.

The next 73 miles through "the Yaak," as locals call it, is heavily forested and, in places, heavily clear-cut. Take care as you drive the wildly twisting road, which is narrow with little shoulder. You needn't go fast through here anyway; dozens of side roads offer opportunities to pull over for a mountain bike ride, a hike, or to cross-country ski in winter. You'll also find several Forest Service campgrounds.

Why call this a scenic drive when it traverses thousands of acres of clear-cuts scarred by hundreds of miles of timber roads? Fortunately, you can't see most of the roads and clear-cuts until you approach the top of the pass northeast of Yaak. Because of the region's high precipitation, trees grow quickly, and some of the logged-over areas are recovering nicely. You can explore hundreds of trails and a dozen or more lookout towers here. As you gaze across the clear-cuts, keep in mind that some cutting is necessary to thwart the spread of the mountain pine beetle, which has been munching its way through much of Montana's—and the West's—forests.

Most of this section of the drive follows the Yaak River corridor. After skirting Abe Lincoln Mountain, where Seventeenmile Creek spills into the Yaak, you will come to the tiny ghost town of **Sylvanite,** named for the gold-bearing ore found here. It was once a small mining community complete with a brewery, hotels, restaurants, saloons, general stores, and its own newspaper. Those who bothered to bathe were able to do so three nights a week with advance notice to

The Kootenai River along US 2. Dusti Thompson

the barbershop-bathhouse. When massive forest fires blazed through Idaho and Montana in 1910, Sylvanite was destroyed and, except for a few buildings, has never been rebuilt to its full splendor.

Watch for moose as you approach the town of **Yaak,** about 30 miles up the Yaak River Road. Named for an Indian word meaning "arrow," Yaak is a scattering of houses and a bar, and its claim to fame, apart from its remoteness, is that it's Montana's northwesternmost town.

Yaak to Eureka

Just west of mile marker 30 in the center of Yaak is the turnoff to CR 567 (the South Fork Road), which flows along the South Fork of the Yaak River and cuts right through the **Purcell Mountains.** Take this route for an interesting side trip. The rounded hills you see were sculpted by glaciers scouring the continent south from what is now British Columbia. The sharply hewn peaks of the Cabinet Mountains are made of the same Precambrian sediments but were spared complete suffocation by ice and so appear vastly different. CR 567 has a maddening twist as it makes its way to Libby, about 38 miles south. After spiraling along for several miles, you might want to stop and explore some of the small lakes. Several trails provide ample hiking along the way, and Turner Mountain will appeal to downhill skiers in winter.

The main loop of Scenic Route 1 continues on the main Yaak River Road, CR 508, from Yaak. The road is also called Yaak CR 92. As you head northeast from town, pay attention to road signs directing you to Lake Koocanusa and the community of Rexford. If you're here during fall, you will be treated to the cottonwoods, aspens, and larches turning gold against the dark green backdrop of the surrounding forest. Roll down your windows and listen to the fallen leaves scutter across the road. Smell the spruce and fir, their fragrant scent a mixture of autumn's rotting leaves and a hint of the holiday season to come.

About 9 miles beyond Yaak, take a right at the Y in the road and follow the signs toward Rexford. (If you go left at the Y, you can view both the upper and lower North Fork Falls.) The road traces many curves, and the dense forest on each side makes you feel like Theseus in the Labyrinth, the paved road your only thread. A few small lakes to the east are accessible by trail from Vinal Lake Road, about 6 miles after the Y turn. At the wildlife viewing area here—marked with signs—look for pileated woodpeckers, barred owls, goshawks, common loons, and great blue herons, as well as ungainly moose in the bottoms and squeaking pikas on the rocky slopes. Follow Vinal Creek Trail to Turner Falls and Fish Lakes. Refer to the detailed Kootenai National Forest map for more information and directions to specific trails.

Around mile marker 43, the road begins to climb to a pass. If you follow the signs to **Boyd Mill Cemetery,** you'll find that chainsaws replace the usual cherubs on stone markers here, attesting to the livelihood of the men they memorialize. Here, you are only about 3 miles from the Canadian border—if you were a flying crow.

At Porcupine Creek, you reach the top of the pass where the road heads down into spruce forest. This is FR 92, also known as Sullivan Creek Road. Keep following the signs to Rexford and **Lake Koocanusa.** The 90-mile-long lake, a dammed portion of the Kootenai River, gets its name by combining *Kootenai, Canada*, and *USA*. It's a popular fishing spot for anglers seeking kokanee salmon, rainbow and cutthroat trout, and whitefish.

At the lake the road intersects with FR 228, which is closed in winter. When it's open, you can follow this road south to Highway 37 or cross the only bridge over the American portion of Lake Koocanusa and head south to continue on the scenic drive loop. The bridge is purported to be the tallest and longest in Montana. You can turn north and head toward the town of Eureka as well as to recreation areas with campgrounds and boat launches along the eastern shore of the lake at **Rexford.** The town of Rexford is situated about 2 miles from its original location along the

Lake Koocanusa is named for Kootenai, Canada, and the United States. Dusti Thompson

Kootenai River. With no flood insurance, the 2-block village had to pull up stakes and move when the Libby Dam was built. An Amish auction here in June draws people from all over the West to buy handmade goods put on the block.

Eureka to Libby

Eureka is built on a little hill along the banks of the Tobacco River. Learn all about its history at the **Tobacco Valley Historical Village** at the south end of town (Memorial Day to Labor Day). In July, take in the Tobacco Valley rodeo, complete with "mutton bustin'" (that's sheep riding for the kiddies, in case you're wondering) and ladies' breakaway roping. In September you can celebrate the annual salmon run on the Tobacco River, with casting contests, fishing derbies, and a cook-off of the honored anadromous guests: salmon.

The landscape surrounding Eureka is wide open, with the Whitefish Range bearing down on the northeast and the Salish Mountains to the southwest. South of town and near Lake Koocanusa, you can explore several small lakes along the Tobacco River. Many offer fishing, and a few have campgrounds. You can enter Canada just north of Eureka, though you won't find many towns near the border.

The 422-foot Libby Dam holds back 90 miles of the Kootenai River to create Lake Koocanusa. Dusti Thompson

Continuing on the main scenic drive route, head south from the Lake Koocanusa bridge, following Highway 37 around the lake for 53 miles to Libby Dam.
The road winds along rock cliffs and the eastern shore of the long and narrow
lake. Watch for bighorn sheep on the rock faces in late fall and winter. You might
also spot spandex-clad rock climbers of a different species during summer, as this
is a minor mecca for them as well.

South of Sutton Creek, Peck Gulch Campground has a boat launch. The next
nearest boat launch is Koocanusa Marina and Resort (http://koocanusaresort
.com), about 22 miles farther on; the resort includes a restaurant and fuel station,
as well as cabins and a campground. There is also a recreation area below **Libby
Dam,** 17 miles northeast of Libby. Stop at the visitor center and tour the dam, a
420-foot-high wall of concrete holding back the 370-foot-deep reservoir. Completed in 1975, the dam took 9 years to build and backs up the Kootenai River well
into Canada for 42 miles. Exhibits at the visitor center walk you through the dam's
construction and operation. A 1.5-hour guided tour of the dam and powerhouse
are available during summer.

At the south end of the lake, you can either drive across the dam or access the
other shore a few miles south of the dam. A paved road along the west shore of

Lake Koocanusa offers access to more campsites, boat launches, and wildlife viewing areas. A wheelchair-accessible trail to the **Little North Fork Falls** is located 11 miles south of the bridge on the west shore of the lake. Follow signs to the trailhead on FR 336. You may see bald eagles near the lake and Alexander Mountain from October through mid-December (the dam visitor center has an eagle web cam). Cross the bridge over the Kootenai River and head north on FR 228 for about 7 miles to the Alexander Creek Picnic Area for more eagle viewing.

Take Highway 37 back to Libby. You can pick up Scenic Route 2 due west of Libby, though you must take the circuitous US 2 south and east through Kalispell before heading north again to West Glacier.

Glacier National Park

West Glacier to St. Mary

General description: A spectacular 50-mile mountain drive that switches back up and over the Continental Divide along glacial river canyons and over an alpine mountain pass.

Special attractions: Glacier National Park, Logan Pass; wildlife watching, hiking, boating, fishing, camping.

Location: Glacier National Park in northwest Montana, from West Glacier to St. Mary.

Drive route number: Going-to-the-Sun Road, aka Logan Pass Road.

Travel season: From late spring or early summer until the snow flies. The road is closed to vehicle traffic beginning the third Monday in October, depending on snow conditions. Check with Glacier National Park offices for specific open dates each year.

Camping: There are several campgrounds in and around Glacier National Park, but these fill up early in the day during summer. You will need reservations for some.

Services: Full services in West Glacier, at Lake McDonald Lodge, and in St. Mary. Full services are also available outside the park in Columbia Falls, Kalispell, and Browning. Limited services in Apgar, Babb, and Kiowa.

Nearby attractions: Bigfork, Big Sky Waterpark, Blackfeet Indian Reservation, Museum of the Plains Indian, John L. Clarke Western Art Gallery & Memorial Museum, Kalispell, North American Wildlife Museum.

The Route

Not only are there no adequate words to describe the splendorous Going-to-the-Sun Road, but mere description pales against driving the real deal. This is one of those drives where you must get out of the car at every opportunity to take in the smells, feel the weeping rock walls, listen to the haunting wind, and scan for incredible wildlife: mountain goats, harlequin ducks, pine martens, grizzly bears, and raptors.

Even by today's standards, the road is an engineering masterpiece. Twelve years of construction were finally completed in July 1933 at a cost of $3 million. Crews risked their lives to dynamite the road from sheer cliffs, in some places thousands of feet high. No wonder the employee turnover rate was 300 percent! The road was listed on the National Register of Historic Places in 1983 and was designated a National Historic Civil Engineering Landmark in 1985.

Even though it's closed for a good portion of the year, you can still drive the road as far as the first switchback ("The Loop") above the north end of Lake McDonald into late fall and again during early spring. From here I recommend parking and walking up the road as far as you're able (when the rest of the road is

Glacier National Park

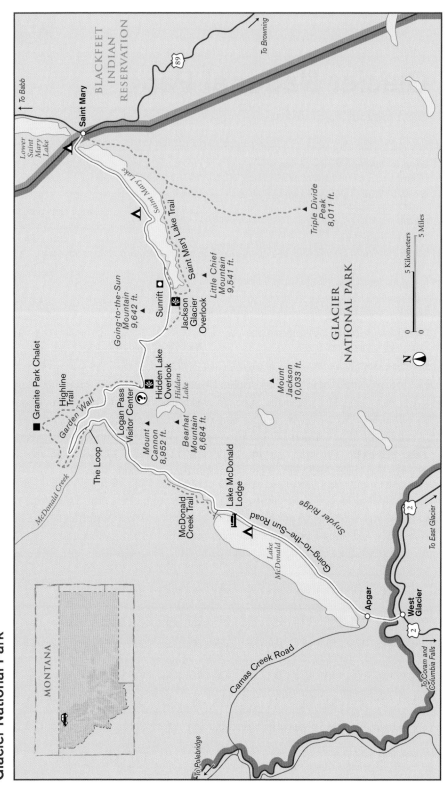

MONTANA

BLACKFEET INDIAN RESERVATION

To Browning

89

To Babb

Saint Mary

Lower Saint Mary Lake

Saint Mary Lake

Saint Mary Lake Trail

Going-to-the-Sun Mountain 9,642 ft.

Sunrift

Jackson Glacier Overlook

Little Chief Mountain 9,541 ft.

Triple Divide Peak 8,011 ft.

GLACIER NATIONAL PARK

Granite Park Chalet

Highline Trail

Garden Wall

Logan Pass Visitor Center

The Loop

McDonald Creek

Hidden Lake Overlook

Hidden Lake

Mount Cannon 8,952 ft.

Bearhat Mountain 8,684 ft.

Mount Jackson 10,033 ft.

McDonald Creek Trail

Lake McDonald Lodge

Lake McDonald

Going-to-the-Sun Road

Snyder Ridge

Apgar

West Glacier

2

2

To East Glacier

To Coram and Columbia Falls

Camas Creek Road

To Polebridge

5 Kilometers

5 Miles

N

closed). Without the string of summer traffic, your senses are heightened, and the experience is much grander for taking in the wildness around you.

Summer is the only season when repairs can be made on Going-to-the-Sun Road, and the road crews don't always know where repairs will take place until after the snow is cleared. For information on traffic delays due to major repairs, call (406) 888-7800, or view current conditions at: www.nps.gov/glac/planyour visit/conditions.htm. Also, in order to keep traffic flowing during peak visits in July and August, you may not be allowed to stop along the way.

West Glacier to Avalanche Creek

Just off US 2, West Glacier is a small community located at the west entrance to Glacier National Park. From the village, turn north to Apgar—named for a family who homesteaded here in 1895. After a stop in Apgar, follow signs for Going-to-the-Sun Road. On a clear day you can see Stanton Mountain, McPartland Mountain, Mount Cannon, and Mount Brown across Lake McDonald. From the south shore of the lake in Apgar, you can trace your route: The drive will take you along the farthest point visible, a long arête called the Garden Wall. This sharp ridge forms the Continental Divide as it splits Glacier National Park's waters between the Atlantic and Pacific Oceans. If visibility is low, or it's raining, your chances are slim of seeing the deeply gouged canyon of McDonald Creek or the full effect of cataracts on the Garden Wall, Bird Woman Falls, or other magnificent views along this route. You may want to postpone this scenic drive for a day when skies are relatively clear. However, if you are dressed for it, hiking in the cool mist here can be just as spectacular, and Glacier Park wrapped in fog has a unique charm.

In the 1980s the south end of **Lake McDonald** was a popular stop along the flyway for migrating bald eagles. They came to feed on kokanee salmon that choked McDonald Creek during their spawning. The eagles, numerous as sparrows in the spruce trees, attracted late autumn visitors, steam from excited whispers swirling around people's heads as they watched the eagles feed and perch. But due to changes in the complex food web of the Flathead River Basin, salmon populations began to decline in 1987, and the eagles moved on to other food sources. Today some bald eagles still make the stopover during autumn and winter.

On still days Lake McDonald is a sheet of reflective glass. Rent a boat in Apgar and explore the cold, clear waters for yourself. From the pebbly shores you can skip rocks or sit quietly, reflect, and write in your journal. Though the water clarity tempts swimmers, unless you have a sufficient layer of blubber—your own or a wetsuit—you're better off leaving the swimming to the fish.

From Apgar head north along the east shore of Lake McDonald. For the first 8 miles, you will see a snarl of spruce, fir, and hemlock forest on the right side; on the left, the lake shimmers between scattered trees. Across the lake you'll notice

Going-to-the-Sun Road is an engineering marvel through awesome scenery.
CHRIS MCGOWAN

the evidence of one of several wildfires that burned in Glacier Park in 2003. Dozens of pullouts along the way allow access for brief walks along the east shore, across from the burn. The lake was formed when a large slab of ice settled into a depression during the last ice age, preventing glacial sediment from filling up the basin that is now the lake. On windy days the lake can seem like an inland sea, with whitecaps breaking on the gray, cobbled shore. At 9.5 miles long and 1.5 miles wide, the lake is the largest in the park. It is more than 400 feet deep and has little plant life to speak of, which allows you to see several feet below the surface. Despite the nutrient-poor conditions, some fish make their home here, including cutthroat trout and mountain whitefish.

Nearly 11 miles up the road from West Glacier at the north end of the lake, you'll find **Lake McDonald Lodge,** built in 1913 and originally called the Lewis Hotel. The National Park Service bought the lodge in 1932. It's a large, yet not imposing, heap of timbers with balconies that overlook the lobby inside, adding to its rustic charm. Inside you can view mounted animal heads of all the species that are found in the park, though I hope you can catch a glimpse of the live versions during your visit. Boat tours of Lake McDonald leave the dock, located behind the lodge, several times daily.

In winter Going-to-the-Sun Road is plowed to only about 2 miles north of the lodge. Here you can park and cross-country ski farther up the road or into the woods on a trail. The snow is usually in good condition, and venturing this far in winter, whether on skis or on foot, is a great way to experience the park during a season when few tourists clog the roads. I recommend a midnight cross-country ski during a full moon. If you listen carefully, you may hear the ghostly cries of wolves guiding members of their pack to a rendezvous. A short road heading west from the northern tip of Lake McDonald leads to private holdings and a ranger station. Several trails are accessible from this road also; consult a park map for further details. Just under 1 mile up the main road from the ranger station junction, a bridge crosses McDonald Creek. You may want to park here and get out to take a closer look at the creek. The water has carved holes in the bedrock and smoothed the rock surface, giving the creek bed a soft, buffed appearance. On the other side of the creek, a trail leads through the woods and back to the ranger station road. It's a soothing, 2-mile walk through hemlock and grand fir forest, relatively flat, with only one steep incline.

Continuing on the main Going-to-the-Sun route, the road winds around curves and narrows north of Lake McDonald, following McDonald Creek, where harlequin ducks dabble from spring to fall. Get out at any one of the turnouts along the creek and search with binoculars for these steel-gray, white, and rust-colored ducks quietly bobbing in the ice-blue riffles. These tiny ducks spend their winters along the West Coast, tossing about in the surf, a world away from the quiet flow of Glacier Park's icy creeks.

Farther up the road take your chances and stop at the turnout marked Moose Country. I've seen a moose here only once in the dozens of times I have traveled this route, but you may get lucky, especially in early morning or evening. If nothing else, you can read the interpretive signs and learn all about these ungainly members of the deer family. Remember, moose can become aggressive when people invade their space. Always observe wildlife from a distance.

About 4 miles north of Lake McDonald, near Avalanche Campground, the **Trail of the Cedars** is a popular and worthwhile walk. This short boardwalk tour leads you through a western red cedar and hemlock forest, where interpretive signs teach you about the ecology of this magnificent ecosystem. The ground is carpeted with ferns and devil's club, and a moss-covered rock wall weeps spring water year-round. The 200-foot-high trees block out light so well that you need a flash for pictures. The boardwalk crosses Avalanche Creek, where you can take pictures of probably one of the most photographed sights in the park. Here the creek tumbles over slick, green boulders into a narrow gorge. After crossing the bridge, the boardwalk ends and the way becomes a trail. You can return to your car by going through the Avalanche Campground on the asphalt road, or carry on along the trail 2 miles to Avalanche Lake.

The Avalanche Lake trail is gentle and takes you through a thick forest to the lake, where you might see mountain goats on rock ledges around the shoreline. Grizzly bears also use the trail, but warnings will be posted at the trailhead if bears have been spotted recently in the area. In Glacier National Park it is probably wise to hike with a companion and make plenty of noise, though that seems anathema to enjoying a walk in the woods. Talking is usually warning enough for bears to hear your approach and move out of your way. If they feel like it. For extra precaution, carry bear repellent—a pressurized can of red pepper spray has proved effective for warding off bears, but use it only if you really have to. Remember, red pepper spray is no substitute for commonsense safety precautions when hiking in bear country. Believe it or not, a friend gave an eyewitness account about a couple who brought bacon into bear country to cook over a camp stove for BLTs. They were actually surprised when a bear showed up for lunch. Don't let this be you.

Across the main road from the Trail of the Cedars is the **Avalanche Picnic Area.** If you decide not to head up to the lake, you can sometimes see mountain goats from this vantage point as well. With binoculars scan the ridge to the east. Mountain goats have sharp hooves and spongy foot pads, much like a dog's, allowing them to skip along precipitous ledges with ease. At times they appear to taunt you with their penetrating gazes and the flippant way they bounce along the bluffs. You will likely have a chance to see them at close range near Logan Pass.

Avalanche to Logan Pass

Shortly after you leave the Avalanche area, the road begins its ascent. Vehicles longer than 21 feet and wider than 8 feet (including side-view mirrors) are prohibited beyond the Avalanche parking lot. From here travel will be slow going during summer when traffic is heaviest.

The first big hairpin turn you come to is called "The Loop." A severe fire burned across the road here in July 2003. You can park here and look south across the valley below to the 8,987-foot Heaven's Peak. A trail from here leads up to Granite Park Chalet, open around July 1 through mid-September for overnight guests (by reservation only) and day visitors. Granite Park and Sperry chalets are the only remaining of the seven chalets built in Glacier backcountry between 1910 and 1917. For overnight stays you must make reservations and pay in advance. In years of heavy snow, the chalets, along with some backcountry camping sites, may not open at all. Visit the Glacier National Park website (www.nps.gov/glac/index .htm) for details.

The Granite Park area is heavily used by grizzlies, especially in autumn. Again, warnings will be posted if bears have been seen in the area for extended periods, but take extra precautions in any case. *Bears have mauled and killed hikers on this*

Mountain goats often hang out at Logan Pass. Chris McGowan

trail. These unfortunate events affect the bears as well; when a bear kills or seriously injures someone, it is trapped and usually euthanized. You can save your own and a bear's life by using common sense while hiking. Never approach a bear even if it appears uninterested in you. Upon entering the park, the ranger will hand you a leaflet on how to avoid bear attacks. Please heed the instructions.

Should you decide to hike the Loop Trail, once you get beyond Granite Park Chalet, the **Highline Trail** continues along the Garden Wall to Logan Pass. It's a spectacular hike—mostly level once you are beyond the chalet—and you are just about guaranteed mountain goats, bighorn sheep, mule deer, hoary marmots, and pikas (little furballs related to rabbits but without the long ears and cotton scut). You can also see stromatolites, formations of fossilized sea creatures left behind in boulders strewn along the trail.

Continuing on the main scenic drive from The Loop, Going-to-the-Sun Road gains quite a bit of altitude as you approach **Logan Pass.** To one side is a sheer rock wall, to the other, several hundred feet of vertical drop. *Drive slowly.* Several cars have taken unplanned plunges over the edge. Because you must keep your eyes on the road the whole time, you will benefit by getting out of the car at designated pullouts to take in the valley as it unfolds below. Or opt for a chauffeured drive in one of the park's old classic red buses.

A couple of miles before you reach Logan Pass, you can look for mountain goats at Haystack Bend, which has the only big parking area between The Loop and the pass. In all but the driest of years, water pours seemingly out of the grassy mountainside over Haystack Falls and seeps from the moss to dribble down the Weeping Wall.

Logan Pass, at the Continental Divide, was the meeting point for two glaciers scouring rock in opposite directions. The result was the low, saddle-like cut of the 6,680-foot-high pass. You can see scrape marks in the cliffs above the road. From the Logan Pass Visitor Center, hike up the boardwalk over another low pass to the **Hidden Lake Overlook,** keeping your eyes open for mountain goats along the way. They sometimes graze on grasses right next to the boardwalk, unbothered by the streams of people. Goats are inquisitive and sometimes follow people. They've been known to lick hikers' urine for the minerals, but please keep it zipped while on this well-used trail. Although mountain goats are cute and fuzzy, and appear tame, they are wild animals. Resist the temptation to approach or feed them and other wild animals. Frequent contact with people can make wild animals aggressive because they lose their fear of people. Aggressive animals are sometimes euthanized. Don't be responsible for destroying your nation's wildlife.

In wet years Logan Pass is often covered with snow year-round. The weather here can change by the minute, so if you venture out on the boardwalk, dress appropriately or bring some extra clothes in a daypack. When the snow does recede, about July or August, the grassy valley at the top of the pass is blanketed with fragile alpine plants, some only blooming one day a year. Monkey flowers and all shades of Indian paintbrush also color the grassy meadow, turning it into a painting Monet himself could have created. The plant community here, called krummholz, is characterized by gnarled pines, deformed by the intense winter weather. These stunted trees add to the otherworldly feeling of Logan Pass. Step inside the visitor center to read more about the flora and fauna of Glacier.

Snowmelt from high peaks cascades down the mountain sides along the drive. CHRIS McGOWAN

Logan Pass to St. Mary

Continuing on the main scenic drive from Logan Pass toward St. Mary, 18 miles away, you will notice that the terrain and plant communities change dramatically. The west side of Glacier Park is wet and often rainy throughout spring and into midsummer. East of the Continental Divide, moisture is more scarce. Notice the change in vegetation, from the tall cedars, spruce, and hemlock at Avalanche to the stunted pines at Logan Pass to dryland pine toward St. Mary.

About 2 miles beyond Siyeh Bend is **Jackson Glacier Overlook,** a good place to see remnants of the massive glaciers, some 4,000 years old and some still carving the park's terrain. According to the US Geological Survey, when Glacier National Park was established in 1910, there were about 150 glaciers. By 2010, the estimate was about 25 glaciers larger than 25 acres remaining. Climate change, it seems, has taken over as the most predominant landscaping tool.

Just below the turnout are trails leading to Gunsight Lake, Gunsight Pass, and Twin Lakes. A few more pullouts and trailheads along the way give you ample opportunity to explore Glacier on foot for a much more intimate experience.

The drop down to St. Mary Lake is nothing short of stunning. At the north end of the lake you will find a trailhead for St. Mary and Virginia Falls. At this point you can also walk along both shores of the south and west portion of St. Mary Lake. Just below these trailheads on Going-to-the-Sun Road is **Sunrift Gorge.** Park on either side of the bridge and go have a look at this unique feature, just a short walk from the road. The gorge is referred to as a geologic curiosity because it was not formed by erosion. Interpretive signs describe the likely processes that helped shape it.

St. Mary Lake is 9.5 miles long by just under 1 mile wide at its widest point. It's not as deep as Lake McDonald, only 300 feet, and has a much greener hue owing to "glacier flour," that is, powdered rock ground down by glaciers and leached into the streams that feed the lake. **Wild Goose Island,** another one of the most photographed features in the park, was named for a pair of geese that for years had built their nest there.

When you reach the area around Rising Sun, you will have dropped to an arid bunchgrass ecosystem, vastly different from the cedar-hemlock forests of Glacier's west side. At the Triple Divide turnout, you can see the only place in the country (and one of two on the continent) where water flows to three different drainage systems: the Gulf of Mexico, the Pacific Ocean, and Hudson Bay. During summer, the St. Mary Visitor Center periodically hosts traditional drumming and dancing by members of the Blackfeet Nation. At St. Mary you can either turn around and return to West Glacier over Logan Pass or drive southeast on US 89 to Kiowa, then take Highway 49 south to US 2, which follows the south and east borders of the park.

As you travel through Glacier National Park, you may want to keep in mind the sacredness of this place to the Blackfeet people, both past and present. The US government purchased the lands from the Blackfeet for a mere $1.5 million in the late 19th century, during a time when Indian peoples were starving and completely dependent on the federal government for support. Until 1910, when these lands became a national park, the Blackfeet were allowed to use the area for hunting and fishing as well as for spiritual rituals. You can learn more about the Blackfeet Nation at the Museum of the Plains Indian in Browning, Montana, where you can pick up Scenic Route 22. If you head back to West Glacier, you can pick up Scenic Route 3 in Big Fork (where the drive ends) or follow US 2 south and west then north again to Libby for Scenic Route 1.

Seeley Lake & the Swan Valley

Clearwater Junction to Bigfork

General description: A 91-mile trek through the Swan Valley, flanked by the Swan and Mission Mountains and following the Clearwater and Swan Rivers through a chain of glistening lakes. Surrounding larch, spruce, and pine forests offer great hiking opportunities.

Special attractions: Blackfoot-Clearwater Wildlife Management Area, Swan River National Wildlife Refuge; numerous lakes, boating, fishing, camping, wildlife viewing, hiking, backpacking, skiing, snowmobiling, ice skating.

Location: Northwest Montana, from Clearwater Junction, 33 miles east of Missoula on Highway 200 to near Bigfork at the north end of Flathead Lake.

Drive route number: Highway 83.

Travel season: Year-round. Snow and ice make winter travel hazardous.

Camping: You'll find many Forest Service and private campgrounds along most of the route. There is also unlimited camping off many Forest Service roads and in the wilderness areas.

Services: Full services at Seeley Lake, Condon, Swan Lake, and Bigfork. Limited services at Clearwater Junction and various places along the way.

Nearby attractions: Flathead National Forest, Garnet Ghost Town and Coloma mining camp, Lolo National Forest, city of Missoula, Bob Marshall and Mission Mountain wilderness areas.

The Route

This drive begins at Clearwater Junction, 33 miles east of Missoula at the junction of Highways 200 and 83. Sandwiched between the Swan Range and the Mission Mountains, the Swan Valley is largely a recreation area for hikers, boaters, hunters, cross-country skiers, and other outdoor sports enthusiasts. In recent years the valley has seen a boom in development, largely in the form of retirement villages, as much of the public and private forested land has been logged over in the past several decades and the timber industry has scaled back considerably. If you do any off-road exploring at all, you'll witness the extensive clear-cuts, especially on the east side of the highway. And many of the forest roads provide access for recreationists of all pursuits.

Generally speaking, the Swan Valley has retained much of its character despite major development, especially since the 1990s boom. Take advantage of the scores of hiking trails throughout the valley on both the Lolo and Flathead National Forests. If you're not keen on noisy powerboats that skim the numerous lakes on the main chain, there are plenty of minor water holes within the national forests, many of them reasonably accessible by car or foot. You're likely to see lots

Seeley Lake & the Swan Valley

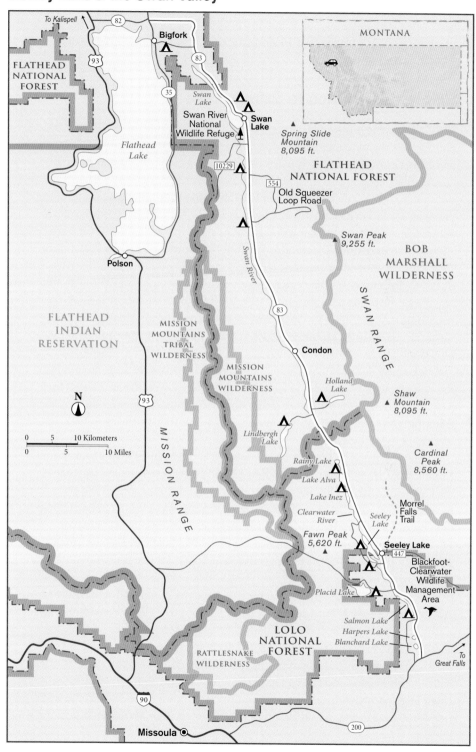

of wildlife, too. Watch for deer all along the road throughout this scenic drive, especially at dawn and dusk.

Clearwater Junction to Salmon Lake

From Clearwater Junction (Highways 83 and 200), head north on Highway 83. Shortly after the junction, there's a turnoff on the left leading to tiny Harpers and Blanchard Lakes, where you can fish, boat, and swim. Because of its small size, Harpers Lake warms up quickly in the summer and is one of the few lakes in Montana where you can swim comfortably without turning blue. It's ideal for paddling around in a small raft or canoe, especially for kids. No motorboats are allowed, and the lake is always calm. Another short way up the road you'll see signs for the **Blackfoot-Clearwater Wildlife Management Area,** a 77,000-acre refuge for elk, mule deer, white-tailed deer, and other wildlife, including grouse, ducks, eagles, and bears. You can access the refuge from mid-May through mid-November; turn east onto the gravel East-West Road around the 3-mile marker from Highway 83 (May 15 to mid-November). Several roads traverse the game range, as well as several more on which you can hike or ride your mountain bike or horse.

Beginning in December, about 1,400 elk migrate from the high mountains of the Bob Marshall Wilderness to winter on these sage-covered hills. The elk then head back to high country sometime in April. With binoculars you can view them from the road in early winter into late March, before they trek back to their summer range in the mountains.

Farther north, Highway 83 begins to wind and narrow as it approaches Salmon Lake, the southernmost in the series of watery jewels strung together by the Clearwater River. The lakes were created as flood depressions in the glacial moraine, which filled with meltwater from giant chunks of ice. At **Salmon Lake** motorboats are permitted, and summer weekend warriors ski until nightfall. There is a state park along the southeast shore with a boat launch and fishing access. Just north of that is a campground. The lake is set in a basin surrounded by conifer forest, as are all of the lakes in the Clearwater chain. These lakes get a lot of weekend use during summer, but on weekdays you might find some quiet time. Also found here are bald eagles, red-necked grebes, great blue herons, and yellow warblers that migrate in spring and fall.

Common loons nest on the shores of Salmon and Seeley Lakes and Lake Alva. This region supports the largest nesting population of loons in the western states, with an estimated summer population of more than 200. You can learn more about loons at a wildlife viewing area and roadside interpretive sign on the west side of the road. Loons use at least four basic sounds: wails, tremolos, hoots, and yodels. One of the loon's most identifying characteristics is its wailing call, which can pierce the most dense spruce-fir forests. The birds' haunting cries can shatter tranquility, evoking images of the truly wild. The loon's tremolo, also called a laugh, is a warning cry to others that intruders are near. Loons are tremendous divers, too, and adults can dive deeper than 200 feet, though typically dive from 6 to 120 feet. Chicks less than 1 week old have been filmed diving as deep as 15 feet. Loons are also able to swim submerged for a few hundred yards and sometimes even streak beneath boats.

If you want to look for loons, go to the northeast shore of Salmon Lake, the western shore of Seeley Lake at Seeley Lake Campground (and the northeast shore near the ranger station), and the northeast shore of Lake Alva. These incredible divers nest from May through mid-June, so please keep your distance while they're raising babies. Loons will readily abandon their nests if disturbed by people coming within 200 to 300 yards, whether by boat or on foot. Even anglers can unknowingly fish too close to nesting loons, forcing the birds to abandon their two-egg nests.

Salmon Lake to Seeley Lake

Northwest of Salmon Lake you can turn left to find **Placid Lake** and a state park, a haven for boating, fishing, and camping. As the name suggests, it's usually quieter than Salmon Lake, though not always. Anglers may want to try for trout and kokanee salmon in this basin surrounded by forested, rolling hills. Many private cabins dot its shores. Follow the signs to the park. This is open range, so be mindful of cattle along the gravel road.

Back on Highway 83, north of Placid Lake and south of the town of Seeley Lake (named for the first white man to live there), this scenic drive passes through more open range, allowing for great views of the Swan Mountains to the east and the Mission Mountains to the west. The Swan Mountains have been heavily logged and are sliced with forest roads, which don't always bode well for wildlife, especially grizzly bears. The best way to explore this country without disturbing wildlife is on foot, skis, or mountain bike. Mountain bikers should stay on the main forest roads and avoid adding to the erosion of sensitive hiking trails.

The town of **Seeley Lake** thrives on both winter and summer recreation, serving boaters, anglers, hunters, snowmobilers, and cross-country skiers. Each year in January, **Winterfest** takes over the town for a long weekend, featuring broomball games, Nordic skiing races, a snow sculpture competition, biathlon, entertainment, and more. Stop by the Historical Museum and Visitor Center, a restored barn that houses exhibits depicting the livelihoods of those who settled the area. You won't want to miss "Gus," a 1,000-year-old Western larch tree in the

Girard Grove along Seeley Lake; ask at the visitor center for directions. Gus's tree neighbors ain't no spring chickens, either; many of them are 500-plus years old. Imagine the stories they could tell. Learn about fire ecology at the grove, too, with an interpretive display sponsored by the Forest Service.

Just north of town is the road to **Morrel Falls National Recreation Trail.** This relatively flat trail, about 2.5 miles long, will guide you through the forest to a set of tiered waterfalls that tumble over high rock bluffs. Two small lakes (ponds, really) catch the water streaming in from the falls. It's a great hike if you don't like steep trails, and the falls at the end are worth the walk. More adventurous types can carry on via a steep trail along the falls to another tier. Keep going and you will find smaller and smaller tiers as you head up the mountainside.

To get to the trailhead, take FR 477 (Cottonwood Lakes Road) heading east just north of the town of Seeley Lake. Follow it for about 1 mile until you get to a left-hand turn; you're still on FR 477. In about 2 miles take West Morrell Road 467 (north) for another 7 miles. Take Pyramid Pass Road for a quarter mile and continue north on Morrell Falls Road 4369 about 1 mile to the trailhead. The route is well marked with Forest Service signs, and there's ample parking at the trailhead, as well as some campsites. Watch for other traffic on the narrow road.

Continuing on the main scenic drive on Highway 83, you'll find the Seeley Lake Ranger Station at the north end of Seeley Lake, where you can get information and directions for boating the **Clearwater Canoe Trail.** This gentle, 3.5-mile float along the Clearwater River connects the southern chain of lakes in the Swan Valley and is a great way to spend a couple of hours. Watch for muskrats, beavers, turtles, warblers, common loons, wood ducks, kingfishers, snipes, and other shorebirds and waterfowl. This float is especially nice if you have only one vehicle, because you can park it at the ranger station and take a short walk (1.5 miles) back to the put-in point. During winter take advantage of cross-country ski trails south of the ranger station, which offer both easy and difficult routes. You can also ice skate on this and many of the other lakes in the chain when conditions are right.

North of the ranger station, Highway 83 is heavily forested on both sides, mostly with larch, Douglas fir, and lodgepole pine. In autumn the larch—our country's only deciduous conifer—turns gold before dropping its needles.

Several Forest Service roads allow access for a drive through the forest off the main road. Some of these drives are loops and clearly marked with signs. I recommend getting a Lolo National Forest map for more details about forest road driving. These roads will give you a better vantage point for viewing the Swan and Mission Mountains and can provide access for hiking or mountain biking.

The Mission Mountains from the western edge of the Swan Valley. Tom Kilmer

Seeley Lake to Bigfork

North of Seeley Lake you'll find another short chain of lakes—Inez, Alva, and Rainy Lakes—all providing opportunities to boat, fish, and camp. These are the larger of the northernmost lakes in the Clearwater chain, while several smaller lakes to the north and west also trickle into the Clearwater River. Dense forests along both sides of the road allow you to catch only glimpses here and there of the mountains on each side of the road, which are most stunning when snowcapped.

North of Lake Inez, the West Fork of the Clearwater Road leads to several small lakes in the foothills of the Mission Mountains. In order to hike in the **Mission Mountains Tribal Wilderness,** you need to buy a tribal permit. For information contact the Confederated Salish and Kootenai Tribes at the Flathead Reservation; details appear in For More Information.

At about mile marker 29 on Highway 83, the trees clear from the road for a moment for a staggering view of the Swan Mountains. Pull over and have a look. Just over 1 mile up the road at Summit Lake is a turnout on the west side where the sharp peaks of the Mission Mountains come into view. A mile north of that, Beaver Creek Road leads to Lindbergh Lake and the Mission Mountains

Wilderness. From this road the lake is accessible only by trail. A few miles farther up Highway 83, you'll find another turnoff to Lindbergh Lake and a campground, accessible by vehicle.

Lindbergh and Holland Lakes are the southernmost lakes in the Swan River chain. About 2 miles north of Lindbergh Lake Road is the turnoff to **Holland Lake** on the east side of Highway 83. You can boat, camp, fish, and swim here, as well as enjoy many hiking trails, including the Holland Falls National Recreation Trail. Holland Lake has a guest lodge, and campers can use showers there for a small fee. This is a great place from which to enter the 1-million-acre **Bob Marshall Wilderness** complex, known locally as "the Bob," just east of Holland Lake.

Bob Marshall was an avid outdoorsman with a keen interest in preserving remote national lands of scenic significance. He founded the Wilderness Society, which helped pass the 1964 National Wilderness Preservation Act that today protects millions of acres of wildlands from development. In 1930 Bob Marshall wrote an article for *Scientific Monthly* in which he stated that there was only "one hope of repulsing the tyrannical ambition of civilization to conquer every niche on the whole earth. That hope is the organization of spirited people who will fight for the freedom of the wilderness." If you have the chance, experience Bob's one hope that repulses the tyrannical masses. Information is available from the Flathead National Forest (see For More Information).

North of Holland Lake, Highway 83 flows past meadows and copses of trees. In early morning or evening, you may want to pull over where it is safe to do so and look for wildlife. You will likely see small groups of white-tailed deer and possibly hear coyotes getting ready for their evening hunt. Grizzly and black bears also use these meadows to forage for food. Remember to keep your distance from all wildlife.

Continuing on Highway 83, just north of Condon you enter the **Swan River State Forest.** At the forest headquarters building, you can take the Old Squeezer Loop Road to a couple of short loop trails through the conifer forest and add a few birds to your "life list." You may see hairy woodpeckers, warblers, Swainson's thrushes, and hummingbirds. Take FR 554 (Goat Creek Road) for 1.5 miles, then turn right onto Squeezer Creek Road. The trails are about 2 miles farther up the road. You can also follow FR 554 to the north and back out onto the main highway. Consult a Flathead National Forest map for more details.

About 1 mile south of Swan Lake is the **Swan River National Wildlife Refuge** (www.fws.gov/bentonlake/swanRiver), a collection of marshland and meadow. This 1,568-acre refuge supports at least 170 bird species as well as moose, elk, bears, bobcats, and river otters. Turn west off the highway and go down a narrow dirt track to watch for black terns, bald eagles, great blue herons, tundra swans, wood ducks, and yellowlegs. You can paddle a canoe through the water and get a better view of these birds and more. Except for a few wildlife viewing platforms, the refuge is closed from March into mid-July to protect nesting birds. Fishing is also prohibited on Spring Creek during this time. Put your boat in at the bridge on Porcupine Road (FR 10229) south of the lake and float the 3.5 miles to a boat ramp on the southeast shore of Swan Lake.

The small town of Swan Lake lies at the southern end of its eponymous lake. There are a few campgrounds here and fishing and boating access. You'll also find full services and many trails and Forest Service roads leading into the foothills on both sides of the lake. From here you can pick up the **Glacier Country Recreation Trail,** open year-round and extending between Bigfork and Seeley Lake. Cross-country skiers will enjoy the 50 miles of Nordic backcountry trails; pick up a trail map at the Laughing Horse Lodge (www.laughinghorselodge.com), right on Highway 83 in Swan Lake. For one Saturday in August you can celebrate with town residents the delights of all things huckleberry at the Swan Lake Huckleberry Festival. Come see why this little berry is like purple gold to Montanans.

Back on the main scenic drive, Highway 83 skirts the entire east shore of Swan Lake before making its way toward the town of Bigfork. Look for signs for the turnoff to the west. **Bigfork** was once described as a "huddle of little gray houses in a hollow" but has now become a trendy tourist town with coffeehouses, art galleries, and gift shops. It's also a popular place to retire. Situated on the northeast shore of Flathead Lake, Bigfork hosts art fairs and theater during summer. Flathead Lake, by the way, is the largest natural freshwater lake west of the Mississippi and happens to be one of Montana's most gorgeous. There are several events happening throughout the year in Bigfork too plentiful to list here. For more information, contact the chamber of commerce or log onto Bigfork's website (http://bigfork.org).

From Bigfork you can further explore the Flathead Lake area or head northwest to Scenic Route 1 or northeast to Scenic Route 22. Missoula, where Scenic Route 4 begins, is about 2 hours south.

4

The Bitterroot Valley

Missoula to Lost Trail

General description: A 95-mile drive up the Bitterroot Valley to the Idaho border, from the urban setting of Missoula south through the Bitterroot Mountains.

Special attractions: Fort Missoula, the University of Montana, USDAFS Aerial Fire Depot and Smokejumper Visitor Center, Lolo Hot Springs Resort, International Wildlife Film Festival, Ravalli County Museum, St. Mary's Mission, Daly Mansion; wildlife refuges, urban and mountain trails, hot springs, theater, concerts, museums, art fairs, county fairs, farmers' markets, lecture series; skiing, bicycling, floating, fishing, shopping.

Location: West-central Montana from Missoula to the Idaho border. Drivers may elect to loop back to Missoula via the East Side Highway.

Drive route number: US 93.

Travel season: Year-round. Snow and icy conditions make winter travel hazardous.

Camping: There are several Forest Service campgrounds in the Bitterroot Mountains and unlimited camping (undeveloped) in the national forest surrounding the valley. Missoula has a few commercial/private campgrounds and RV parks.

Services: Full services in Missoula, Lolo, Stevensville, Hamilton, Sula, and Darby. Most services and limited lodging in other towns along the route. Numerous private guest ranches and lodges.

Nearby attractions: Frenchtown Pond State Park, Lolo Pass, Nez Perce Trail, Ninemile Historic Remount Depot, Skalkaho Pass, Threemile Wildlife Management Area, Selway-Bitterroot Wilderness Area, Welcome Creek Wilderness Area.

The Route

This drive begins in Missoula, one of Montana's largest cities set in a relatively small valley surrounded by mountains. Like many places in the state, Missoula has grown dramatically since the 1990s, with even more development happening in the first decade of the 21st century. Though I no longer live in Montana, I count Missoula as my hometown. On visits, I stop by the cemetery in the Bitterroot Valley where my ancestors are buried. Their homestead in Florence and their houses in Missoula still stand, occupied, but the old folks wouldn't recognize the place today. And sometimes I don't either. The foothills and plains once covered in sagebrush and knapweed now sport subdivisions and ranchettes. Some of these developments are visible from the road and many more aren't, which means the scenic quality of the drive hasn't been hampered by unsightly development—that is, until you go off the main road.

This is the most urban of all the drives in this book, but despite any biases you might have against urban sprawl, development in the Missoula and Bitterroot

The Bitterroot Valley

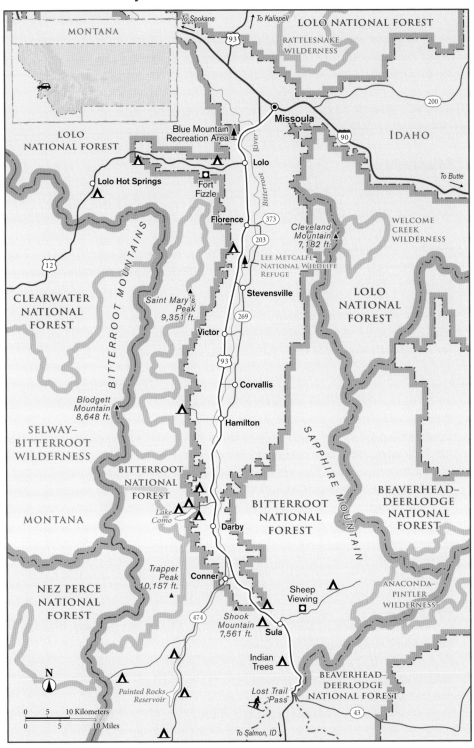

MONTANA

To Spokane

To Kalispell

LOLO NATIONAL FOREST

RATTLESNAKE WILDERNESS

93

200

Missoula

IDAHO

90

LOLO NATIONAL FOREST

Blue Mountain Recreation Area

River

To Butte

Lolo

Lolo Hot Springs

Fort Fizzle

Bitterroot

Florence

373

Cleveland Mountain 7,182 ft.

WELCOME CREEK WILDERNESS

12

203

LEE METCALF NATIONAL WILDLIFE REFUGE

CLEARWATER NATIONAL FOREST

BITTERROOT MOUNTAINS

Saint Mary's Peak 9,351 ft.

Stevensville

LOLO NATIONAL FOREST

269

Victor

93

SELWAY– BITTERROOT WILDERNESS

Blodgett Mountain 8,648 ft.

Corvallis

Hamilton

SAPPHIRE MOUNTAIN

MONTANA

BITTERROOT NATIONAL FOREST

Lake Como

BITTERROOT NATIONAL FOREST

BEAVERHEAD– DEERLODGE NATIONAL FOREST

Darby

NEZ PERCE NATIONAL FOREST

Trapper Peak 10,157 ft.

Conner

Sheep Viewing

ANACONDA– PINTLER WILDERNESS

474

Shook Mountain 7,561 ft.

Sula

Indian Trees

BEAVERHEAD– DEERLODGE NATIONAL FOREST

43

N

Painted Rocks Reservoir

Lost Trail Pass

0   5   10 Kilometers
0   5   10 Miles

To Salmon, ID

Valleys has also brought some positive changes. For one thing, no matter where you are along US 93, you're not far from a good cup of designer coffee and a decent meal, which was not the case pre-1990. And there's so much to do—both indoors and out—that the scenic quality of the Bitterroot Mountains to the west and the Sapphire Range to the east is really just the scoop of freshly churned ice cream on the huckleberry pie.

Missoula

Historians disagree on the original meaning of the name *Missoula*, but the most commonly accepted theory tells us it's Salish for the "river of awe" or "by the chilling waters." Whatever its origin, there is no doubt that the river passing through Missoula, the Clark Fork, is both awesome and chilly.

Missoula is home to the **University of Montana,** which hosts a variety of events and activities year-round. Theater performances, art shows, concerts, lectures, and sporting events will keep you busy in town. During summers, many special music and entertainment events take place in downtown parks and on the university campus. Once a single farmers' market took place every Saturday morning and Tuesday evening at Circle Square at the north end of Higgins Avenue. Today, there are a few markets that operate from about May through October. One popular market can be found on Saturday mornings under the Higgins Street Bridge by Caras Park. If you go, look for the man selling scrumptious delights, both sweet and savory, wrapped in a soft waffle—to die for! On Wednesday during summer, "Out To Lunch" features a food fair in Caras Park, with entertainment starting at noon. For a list of all the year-round events and activities, contact the chamber of commerce or log onto Missoula's website (www.ci.missoula.mt.us).

The **Historical Museum at Fort Missoula** (www.fortmissoulamuseum .org) has a permanent exhibit detailing the city's 100-plus-year history and some great old photos of downtown dating back to the turn of the 20th century. Some of those images were used in the opening montage of the 1992 film *A River Runs Through It*, based on the short story of the same name by Missoula's own Norman McLean. The film helped launch this fair city into the hearts of people across the country and no doubt contributed to the influx of newcomers to all parts of the state in the 1990s. Changing exhibits at the museum document various trades in which Missoulians have thrived. Visit the USDA Forest Service's **Aerial Fire Depot and Smokejumper Visitor Center** (www.fs.fed.us/fire/people/smoke jumpers/missoula) near the airport and learn about the people who risk their lives twice in one go: first by jumping out of airplanes and second by fighting forest fires. Even if you don't understand why these brave men and women do what they do, you will at least gain some appreciation for it.

Scores of miles of trails both in and out of town provide a wonderful way to explore Missoula on foot or bike. Anglers, floaters, skiers, and wildlife watchers will find plenty of water, snow, and habitat in which to ply their hobbies. If you visit in spring, the weeklong **International Wildlife Film Festival** (late April or early May) showcases the best wildlife films of the year from all over the world and features film workshops and demonstrations, some of which are open to the public. If you enjoy walking or biking, Missoula has several unique urban trails where you can watch for interesting birds, discover some of the city's colorful people, or enjoy a picnic. If you want a less urban setting without going too far out of town, three major national recreation areas just minutes from the valley—Rattlesnake, Pattee Canyon, and Blue Mountain—should have what you're looking for.

Missoula to Stevensville

From Missoula head south on US 93 toward Lolo. You'll pass **Blue Mountain Recreation Area** for access to hiking, mountain biking, motorbiking, and folfing. Turn right at the Montana Athletic Club, a round building that looks like it landed here from outer space. There are three major places along Blue Mountain Road to park your car; all are adequately marked. You can sled at Blue Mountain in winter or visit a fire lookout in summer. A small observatory near the lookout opens its telescope to the public for stargazing on certain Fridays during summer. Check the local newspaper for details.

South of Missoula, US 93 skirts the flanks of the Bitterroot Mountains, affording nice views of the Sapphire Mountains to the east. The low, grassy hills of the Sapphires provide a stark contrast to the higher, forested peaks of the Bitterroots. Composed of sedimentary rocks that in places oozed granite, the Sapphires were never molded by glaciers like their valley neighbors, which were heavily glaciated. The route between Missoula and Lolo is the windiest section of road until you get to Darby. A word of caution: Even though much of this route is straight, US 93 has a lot of traffic, and many deer have bit the asphalt crossing the highway. Pay particular attention at dusk and sunrise.

The small town of **Lolo** is about 8 miles south of Missoula, and like its neighbor to the north, the name's origin is disputed. Some think it was an Indian corruption of the word for Lewis, one half of the explorer duo Lewis and Clark, or for Lawrence, a French trapper. Others tout a Nez Perce word meaning "muddy water." At the south end of town, US 12 heads west into Idaho. Traveler's Rest, near here, is where Lewis and Clark camped September 9–10, 1805, and again on their return from the West Coast June 30–July 3, 1806. This spot was so named because it was an ideal place for the gang to rest before continuing on their journey. It was here, too, that the Lewis and Clark party split up on their return trip;

Clark headed southeast to explore Yellowstone country, and Lewis went northeast to the Sun and Marias Rivers.

The expedition's passage through Lolo Creek proved to be the most difficult portion of their entire journey. Today US 12 seems like a breeze for the team to have negotiated, but much of the canyon had to be blasted to build the highway, and the route was much narrower then. Instead the explorers took the high road, crossing ridge after ridge after ridge. The weather was cold, the mountain travel strenuous, and the food scarce. To get an idea of the approximate trail Lewis and Clark took through the Lolo Creek drainage, look for the red dotted line on a Lolo National Forest map and try to follow it. You can also take a guided hike along part of this route; visit Lewis & Clark Trail Adventures at www.trailadventures.com.

About 5 miles west of Lolo on US 12 is another historic site. **Fort Fizzle,** as it was later dubbed, was a blockade built by Captain Charles Rawn of the US Army infantry from Fort Shaw. Built in 1877, it was intended to stop advancing nontreaty Nez Perce Indians from entering the Bitterroot Valley as they fled Idaho toward Canada. But the blockade . . . well, fizzled. The Nez Perce, who were camped near the hot springs 20 miles upstream, got wind of the plans to stop them. They sent a small delegation to negotiate with the soldiers, and while the party parleyed, Nez Perce scouts led the main band of 800 people up and over a hill past the army undetected. A fire burned what remained of the "fort" in the 1930s. Lolo Hot Springs (www.lolohotsprings.com) is a small resort now, with a hot pool for soaking, a warm pool for swimming, a restaurant, a bar, lodging, and camping year-round. It makes a nice stop for cross-country skiers, snowmobilers, and hikers returning from a day at Lolo Pass.

South of Lolo on the main drive, the Bitterroot Valley opens up wide. As the chain of Sapphire Mountains continues south, the mountaintops become more fully dressed in Douglas fir and ponderosa pine. At the turn of the 20th century, apple orchards blossomed across the valley; at one time Montana was a leading producer of this fruit. My great-great-grandfather owned an orchard in Missoula, and some of his trees still stand more than 100 years later. Apples were shipped east by rail; some of the orchards were so productive, they filled more than 500 rail cars per season. But the apple boom was short-lived. Better fruits could easily be produced in other parts of the country, sending many of the Bitterroot orchards out of business. Remnants of these orchards can still be found on the benches above the valley floor, and a few relict orchards still produce commercially.

Soon you come to **Florence,** one of several tiny burgs in the Bitterroot Valley. At one time sporting a cheese factory, creamery, and greenhouse, the town was named for Florence Hammond, the wife of prominent Missoula businessman A. B. Hammond. From here you can access the East Side Highway, a left-hand

The Bitterroot Valley has much to offer even in winter. KATHIE DeWITT & PAUL DUMOND

turn off US 93 as you head south. If you are driving from Missoula and returning there at the end of this drive, the East Side Highway makes a nice loop. Save it for the trip back.

Continue on the main US 93 route, following the Bitterroot River (east of the highway) as it carves a winding path north to Missoula where it joins the Clark Fork. Floaters enjoy the gentle Bitterroot, although spring thaw often brings down large cottonwoods along the banks, making some spots a bit hard to maneuver around. If you like to drop a line, there are several fishing access sites along the Bitterroot, most marked clearly with signs. One interesting spot 2.5 miles south of Florence is called the "car pool," so named for the rusted bodies of 1940s and '50s cars intentionally imbedded in the banks. Several other rivers in Montana have "car pools," a plan promoted by Lady Bird Johnson to prevent stream-bank erosion. Fortunately, the plan is no longer practiced, but its legacy remains in steel. Today the cars provide pools and hiding cover for fish. Pull off the highway where you see a Forest Service sign indicating the Charles Waters Campground, just 0.25 mile farther. The "car pool" is a short walk down the dirt road beyond the closed gate.

The Bitterroot River cuts a sinuous ribbon through its namesake valley.
KATHIE DEWITT & PAUL DUMOND

Hikers have countless opportunities to explore just about every drainage in the Bitterroots, with easily accessible trails leading into the mountains. Most lead directly to lakes, and many feature waterfalls in the creeks along the trails. Refer to a Bitterroot National Forest map or read about the trails in the Falcon Guide *Hiking Montana*, also published by Globe Pequot Press. The 9,351-foot **St. Mary's Peak** is a popular spot. You can hike to the top of the peak via a 4-mile trail, at times steep and often covered in snow until July. From the top of St. Mary's, or any other peak in the Bitterroots, you can appreciate the vast mountain wilderness to the west into Idaho. There are no settlements for hundreds of square miles, so if you want to get lost, this is the place to do it.

Stevensville is the next town along this scenic drive, but you'll have to drive east off the highway to access "downtown." Stevensville is said to be the oldest community in Montana, established in 1841 with the founding of **St. Mary's Mission** (www.saintmarysmission.org). (It was actually authorized as a town in 1864 and called Stevensville after its founding father, Isaac Stevens.) Father Pierre Jean de Smet, a Jesuit priest, was sent to the valley with a Bible and mandate to convert the Flathead Indians. The mission is believed to be Montana's first church, and it may be where the first oats and wheat were harvested in the state. You can tour the tiny mission village and some of the outbuildings from April to October. To get there from Stevensville, turn west onto 4th Street and go to the end of the block. At the southern end of Main Street on the west side of the street, you'll find the Stevensville Museum, which complements the mission with exhibits about the valley's history (open during summer only).

In 1850 St. Mary's Mission was sold to John Owen, who eventually opened a trading post just north of the grounds. **Fort Owen** (http://fwp.mt.gov/parks/visit/fortOwen/) is said to be the first permanent white settlement in Montana. Flathead Indians, miners, settlers, and fur traders all did business here. Some remains of the original fort lie northwest of Stevensville and are well marked with signs. Period furnishings and artifacts are displayed in the restored rooms of the east barracks. The fort is located on CR 269 just east of US 93. You will pass it going to and from the main town of Stevensville from US 93. Fort Owen may very well be the state's smallest park, at only 1 acre.

Lee Metcalf National Wildlife Refuge (www.fws.gov/leemetcalf) is just northeast of Stevensville. From Main Street turn onto the East Side Highway, right near the Forest Service ranger station. Large signs clearly point the way to the refuge. There are several wonderful walking trails through the cottonwood forest and along the Bitterroot River. There is also a nice new visitor center near the big lake and another walking trail that heads toward the large marshes. You can expect to see white-tailed deer, muskrats, and many species of waterfowl most of the year. Other commonly seen species include pileated, hairy, and downy woodpeckers; flickers; great-horned owls; bald eagles; ospreys; wood ducks; ruddy ducks; and teal, in addition to many other waterfowl during spring and fall migrations. In summer you may see a tireless beaver, a turtle basking on a fallen log in the water, or a porcupine napping on a ponderosa pine limb—the only place I've ever heard a snoring porcupine.

Stevensville to Hamilton

South of Stevensville US 93 continues a straight course through ranchland and growing subdivisions. The view of the Bitterroots becomes more spectacular through this stretch. Sharply defined peaks with chiseled ridgelines—covered in snow much of the year—look as if they were recently carved from raw granite. The granite makes for some nice rock climbing in some of the drainages. If you're interested in watching climbers, a good spot is just a short way up the North Kootenai Creek trail. Watch for the two-legged mountain goats on the low bluffs just off the trail to the right. The north end of the Bitterroots is largely composed of metamorphic rock not conducive to climbing.

Lee Metcalf National Wildlife Refuge provides an important habitat for migrating and resident birds, among other wildlife. S.A. SNYDER

Continuing south on US 93, you come to the little town of Victor, just west of the highway. Stop by the tiny Heritage Museum in the old railroad depot on Blake and Main Streets (summer only) for a little glimpse into local history. Browse through the few antiques shops here, too. Nine miles farther south is the community of Pinesdale, and east of US 93 (take CR 373) lies the little burg of Corvallis, named for the town in Oregon from which people had come to settle in Montana. If you take CR 373 from US 93 to Corvallis, pick up CR 269 (East Side Highway) and go south a few miles to the **Daly Mansion** (http://dalymansion.org). Marcus Daly, one of Montana's "copper kings," built this summer house among his thousands of acres of ranchland where he raised cattle and horses.

Daly's wealth was dug from the ground by fellow Irishmen who sweated their lives away in his copper mines and smelter in Anaconda. The mansion has 24 bedrooms, 15 bathrooms, and a sprawling lawn shaded with maples and cottonwoods. Professional ghost hunters even periodically monitor the old house for signs of ectoplasmic life. You can tour the mansion for a fee (May–October), and you might find it entertaining to do so during special events that take place throughout the summer on the grounds. Daly's horses lived a posh lifestyle, too. Their barn (across the East Side Highway from the mansion) was more like a miniature estate than a stable and was called Tammany Castle. It's since been converted into a luxury residence.

From Daly Mansion continue south on CR 269 to Hamilton, the largest community in the Bitterroot Valley. Or continue south to Hamilton from the main scenic drive route, US 93. The town was named for J. W. Hamilton, from whom the Northern Pacific Railroad gained its right-of-way to build track through here. Hamilton is now a popular retirement area because of its small-town atmosphere, low crime, and wonderful scenery.

Stop by the **Ravalli County Museum** (http://brvhsmuseum.org) run by the Bitter Root Valley Historical Society and housed in the old county courthouse, with intriguing permanent exhibits, rotating collection, and extensive archives. The museum hosts special programs throughout the year, including the Annual McIntosh Apple Day in October, with music and arts, crafts, baked goods, and of course, all-things-apple for sale. To get to the museum, turn west off US 93 onto Bedford Street. The museum is on the second block on the left just behind the county government building.

Like Missoula, Hamilton hosts a number of events throughout the year, from powwows to microbrew festivals, street dances, and art fairs. Check with the Bitterroot Valley Chamber of Commerce for more details; see For More Information.

Hamilton to Lost Trail

Continuing south of Hamilton, US 93 becomes a twisted ribbon on its way to Darby, where the valley narrows. To the southwest lie the tallest and most pointed peaks of Montana's Bitterroots: El Capitan, Como, North Trapper, and Trapper. Only **Trapper Peak** breaks the 10,000-foot level, by just over 150 feet, and only the hardiest of hikers can make it to the tops of these peaks and back in 1 day.

About 9 miles south of Hamilton is the turnoff for **Lake Como Recreation Area,** a popular spot for locals because of its scenery and proximity to Hamilton. It has a boat ramp and a few campgrounds. You can fish and swim in this artificially created lake also. Take a hike around its shores or explore two additional trails that lead to higher mountain lakes much farther up the drainage.

Just south of Lake Como, **Darby** springs up in a narrow passage between the mountains. Darby grew out of the mining and fur trade, with a little boost from a minor timber industry boom. Today it relies more on agriculture and cattle ranching with some timber interests. The Pioneer Memorial Museum houses collections of artifacts from the pioneer families who settled in the area. Hunting outfitters, fishing guides, and numerous guest ranches cater to outdoor enthusiasts.

You may have noticed that west of Darby the mountain vegetation appears dense compared to the east side. East of the Bitterroot River the scrubby hillsides are covered with sagebrush and scattered with dryland ponderosa pine. You can travel up both the East and West Forks of the Bitterroot River and the difference in vegetation is much the same. This is because storms moving from west to east usually dump their wet loads on the Bitterroots, leaving little for the drier—and lower—Sapphires. You'll find the turnoff to the West Fork of the Bitterroot River 3 miles south of Darby. If you take this road about 20 miles southwest, you come to **Painted Rocks Reservoir,** a flooded, narrow canyon where you can boat and, in places where it is warm enough, swim. The well-developed campsites are often full on summer weekends.

Back on US 93 south of Darby, you'll see the effects of severe wildfires that burned through this area in the summer of 2003. Soon you reach the town of Sula, named for Ursula Thompson, the first white child born here. This town, also called Ross Hole after a man who was trapped in an 1824 snowstorm here, is the background depicted in a Charles M. Russell painting that hangs in the state capitol in Helena. The painting captures Lewis and Clark meeting with Flathead Indians during their expedition.

From Sula you can take the East Fork Road to view bighorn sheep near the Broad Axe Lodge and Restaurant (www.broadaxelodge.com). The East Fork Road heads east just before you cross the bridge. Follow the wildlife viewing signs (binoculars symbol) 5.5 miles to the sheep viewing site. A few interpretive signs along the road tell you a little about bighorn sheep and where to look for them. The best time to see sheep is during winter. You may even see them grazing along US 93—use caution, as sometimes you find them crossing the road in the most inconvenient places.

South of Sula on US 93, Indian Tree Campground is laid out among large ponderosa pines. Turn west and follow the gravel road to the campground near the Lost Trail Hot Springs Resort. Look for the giant ponderosa pines with long, wide scars in their bark. Early Native Americans peeled the bark to eat the inner portion, called the cambium. The sweet sap and soft cambium of ponderosas were considered delicacies. Although quite large and visible, the scars don't appear to have harmed the trees.

Just south of the campground, drop by **Lost Trail Hot Springs** (http://lost trailhotsprings.com/index.html) for a soothing and cozy finish to a day of downhill skiing at Lost Trail Powder Mountain (on the Montana-Idaho border), after cross-country skiing on the trails at Chief Joseph Pass, or after a long day of hiking. The hot springs are open year-round and there is lodging here. From here you can retrace your tracks to Hamilton on US 93 and then pick up the East Side Highway—an alternative route—emerging at Florence. Or take Highway 43 (Chief Joseph Pass) at Lost Trail Pass to the Big Hole Valley and Scenic Route 6. Not far from Missoula you can pick up Scenic Routes 3 or 5.

5

Pintler Scenic Route

Anaconda to Drummond

General description: A 63-mile drive from Anaconda, one of Montana's most historic towns, past Georgetown Lake and Philipsburg and up to Drummond.

Special attractions: Historic Anaconda, Georgetown Lake, Philipsburg, Granite ghost town; gem mining, fishing, skiing, camping, hiking, boating, biking, wildlife viewing.

Location: Southwestern Montana east of Missoula, from Anaconda to Drummond.

Drive route number: Highway 1.

Travel season: Year-round. Snow and icy conditions can make winter travel hazardous.

Camping: You'll find several public campgrounds in nearby national forests, especially around Georgetown Lake. There are some camping sites near Anaconda at Lost Creek State Park.

Services: Full services at Anaconda, Georgetown Lake, Philipsburg, and Drummond.

Nearby attractions: Beavertail Hill State Park, Fairmont Hot Springs Resort, Garnet ghost town, Grant-Kohrs Ranch National Historical Site, Missoula, Butte, Southern Cross ghost town.

The Route

This scenic drive is a great alternative to I-90 if you're traveling between Butte and Missoula and would like to get off the beaten path. You'll find full services along the way, as well as the chance to delve into Montana's European settlement history. The Anaconda and Butte areas were once the largest mining and smelting operations for copper in the country, and many of the state's early settlers gave their lives to cash in on the riches—which, of course, made only a few rich and many die young.

The scenery you'll encounter is my favorite: rolling foothills scattered with pine parkland forest overlooking grasslands and with higher mountains for a backdrop. This part of Montana isn't as touristy as other parts, and even though you'll no doubt find some crowds at Georgetown Lake during summer, they're bearable. There are plenty of opportunities to get out of the car and explore. Or if you prefer, just make it a scenic drive on your way to somewhere else.

Anaconda to Philipsburg

Begin in **Anaconda** off I-90 about 15 miles west of Butte. Take the exit to Anaconda and follow the signs marked for the Pintler Scenic Route. You will drive

Pintler Scenic Route

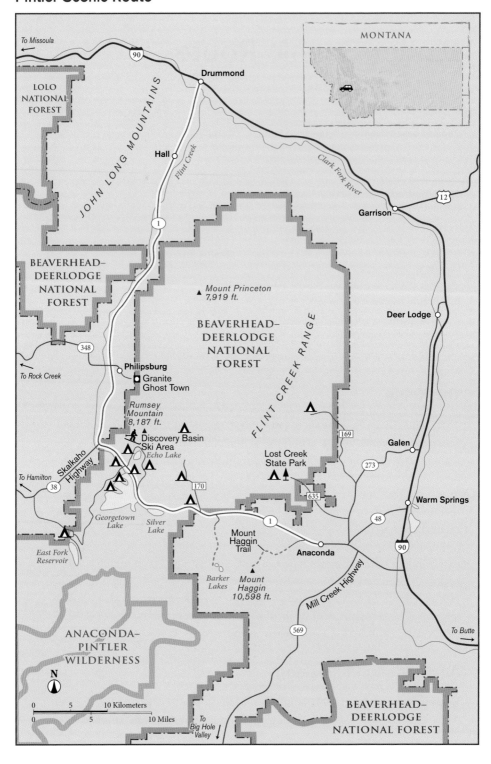

through Anaconda's downtown, a sizable place with a history as rich as the precious metals ripped from its hills. Named for the giant South American snake, Anaconda was originally called Copperopolis for the teaming veins of the metal uncovered in the surrounding mountains. But the name Copperopolis was already claimed by another Montana town, so Anaconda's first postmaster chose the frightful reptile as the community's moniker. It's anyone's guess whether his choice was meant to describe the snaky veins of copper that would eventually put Anaconda on the map or as a warning to other Montana burgs that Anaconda would one day reign supreme.

Anaconda was the dream town of mining giant Marcus Daly (see Scenic Route 4), who opened up shop as the Anaconda Copper Mining Company's Washoe Smelter. Because of its plentiful water supply, Daly picked this site to process ore from his mines in nearby Butte. The smelter closed in 1980, but its 585-foot smokestack—still looming over the town—is one of the tallest free-standing brick structures in North America. In fact, it's now a state park, though you'll have to take your photos from a distance. The stack's diameter is 86 feet at its base; the Washington Monument could fit inside its core. You can see ruins of Anaconda's first smelters, built in the 1880s, along the hillsides north and east of town. If you want to swing some wood or iron, play a round at the Old Works Golf Course, designed by Jack Nicklaus on reclaimed smelter ruins and formerly a Superfund cleanup site!

Anaconda hosts an annual chocolate festival during 1 weekend in February. The festival includes a bake-off and window decorating contest. Local shops hand out free chocolates to visitors, and "fines" are issued to businesses that fail to hand out chocolates to clients (I vote we "fine" all Montana businesses year-round for such a failure). Anaconda hosts several art, music, and celebratory events throughout the year. You'll find contact details in For More Information for the Anaconda Chamber of Commerce. I highly recommend the city bus tours, during which you can learn colorful tidbits of Anaconda's early days. You can also take a walking tour of downtown; inquire at the chamber for details. Peek your head inside what the Smithsonian Institution has called the fifth most beautiful theater in the country, the Washoe Theatre, built in 1937. Silver, copper, and gold leaf accentuate its WPA-era murals, and hand-carved rams' heads stand guard on the ceiling. In September, drop by the Wildlife Expo, an annual event featuring many award-winning artists from across the state.

About 2 miles north of Anaconda you can see live bighorn sheep and mountain goats at **Lost Creek State Park** (http://fwp.mt.gov/parks/visit/lostCreek) as they perform death-defying leaps across the steep limestone cliffs. The best times to see the mountain acrobats are winter and spring; during summer you may be able to see sheep in Olsen Gulch, 4 miles west. You can usually see mountain goats from a pullout by the entrance to the park. Be sure to visit **Lost Creek Falls** via a short hike along a trail. You can also ride your bike along a closed portion of road here and look for moose in the creek bottom. To get to Lost Creek Park, take CR 273 (east of Anaconda off Highway 48) north about 2 miles; take a left and continue about 7 miles to the end. The road is paved for the first few miles and then becomes gravel.

To continue this scenic drive, stay on Highway 1 from downtown Anaconda. Soon you'll be among forested foothills as you approach Mount Haggin on your way to Georgetown Lake. The valleys here were carved by immense glaciers, which left their calling cards of debris in the moraines and granite boulders that give this area its bumpy texture. There is a trail leading to several lakes below Mount Haggin, south of the highway. You might also want to explore **Mount Haggin Wildlife Management Area,** but you will have to backtrack to Mill Creek Highway (CR 569) off Highway 1 just east of Anaconda. Chert spearheads mined from ancient pits found here are evidence that people used the Mount Haggin area for more than 10,500 years. If you decide to explore the area on foot, remember that arrowheads and other artifacts are protected under the Antiquities Act, so resist the temptation to bring any home. Mountain bikers will find it a pleasant place to ride. Farther west on Highway 1, and to the south, is another set of trails in Barker Creek, leading to Barker Lakes.

As you head west, the road winds through a canyon and arrives at a small body of water called **Silver Lake.** From here a few Forest Service roads head into the mountains above the lake, where you'll find several smaller mountain lakes and a few nice meadows. This is the Anaconda Range; the Anaconda-Pintler Wilderness lies just beyond it. A portion of the Continental Divide National Scenic Trail passes through here as well. Check a Beaverhead-Deerlodge National Forest map for details on hiking trails.

Just past Silver Lake, artificially created **Georgetown Lake** is a year-round mecca for Anaconda residents. The lake has all the standard recreational opportunities—boating, fishing, swimming, waterskiing, camping, and hiking. During winter little huts on the frozen lake surface house those who find pleasure in ice fishing. A road circles the entire shoreline, providing access to several campgrounds. In recent years the lodgepole pine around Georgetown Lake and Anaconda have been killed from mountain pine beetle. As a result, more logging to remove infected trees has taken place. Warming temperatures mean that the bugs are better able to survive what were once harsh Western winters. Beetles are able to survive, and their appetites are ravenous. Montana's—and other Western states'—thickets of pine have been keeping the pine beetles well fed.

Georgetown Lake was created in 1885 when the outlet of Flint Creek was dammed. Beneath the waves are the remains of an old cattle ranch. The dam

Flint Creek courses through the Beaverhead-Deerlodge National Forest. Tom Kilmer

provided power for the Bi-Metallic Mining Company located in Philipsburg and the now ghost town of Granite.

Discovery Basin (www.skidiscovery.com), a downhill ski area with beautiful, long, open runs for both beginners and experts, overlooks Georgetown Lake. From the top of Discovery you can view the Anaconda-Pintler Mountains to the south, spectacular when covered by snow. This area prides itself on having plenty of sunshine, so even during the winter you have a good chance of sunny ski days.

From Georgetown Lake, Highway 1 turns north toward the mining town of Philipsburg. The road goes over a short pass then descends through a narrow canyon into the Philipsburg area. As you head up to the pass, look up at the rock walls to see ruins of an aqueduct running along the side of the bluffs. Many of the wooden flumes are now gone, but they once carried water from Georgetown Lake to generate power for the Bi-Metallic Mining Company. In winter snowmelt sometimes accumulates in the flumes' remains, dribbling from the structure and freezing to form beautiful aqua blue ice sculptures on the rock faces.

During summer you can take an alternate route through the mountains to the west on the Skalkaho Highway/Route 38 (Skalkaho is Salish for "beaver"). The turnoff is 6 miles south of Philipsburg. Most of it is unpaved, and it's quite curvy, with sheer drops down a canyon in places. The road emerges just south of the town of Hamilton in the Bitterroot Valley, where you can pick up Scenic Route 4. There are several hiking trails along the way and a beautiful set of waterfalls right along the road. If you like off-road driving and exploring, this will be a fun route for you. Otherwise continue on the Pintler Scenic Route to Philipsburg.

Philipsburg to Drummond

Like many western Montana towns, **Philipsburg** began as a mining camp in the 1860s. Soon the population reached 1,500, and with other camps and settlements in the surrounding areas, Philipsburg served as many as 8,000 people in the late 19th century. Then the boom crashed in the 1870s. The town has survived; its schoolhouse, built in 1895, is now a living museum (www.oldbutte.com/joe template.html) open for tours by appointment. It also houses an antiques dealer and auction. Discover more of the region's past with a visit to the **Granite County Museum and Cultural Center** (http://philipsburgmt.com/museum), which features the Ghost Town Hall of Fame and the Granite Mountain Mining exhibit. During summer enjoy live theater given by **The Opera House Theatre Company** in one of Montana's few remaining historic opera houses (www.operahouse theatre.com). You can also "mine" your own gems when you buy a bucket of rocks at the **Sapphire Gallery** (www.sapphiregallery.com) on Broadway, washing the gravel to find sapphires from the local mountains. This is probably about as close as you will ever get to experiencing the livelihood of early miners—and it's a much easier way to dig for precious gems. For other events in Philipsburg, check the chamber listed in For More Information.

About 5 miles southeast of Philipsburg you'll find the ghost town of Granite, dug into a mountainside in the Flint Creek Range. In the mid-1880s Granite boasted the largest silver-producing mines in the world, with $20 million worth of silver coming from its bowels in just a few short years. As quickly as it boomed, it died; the silver panic of 1893 drastically reduced the price of silver and emptied the town of its 3,000 residents in less than 2 days. Today you can explore what little is left of the town because most of it burned in the 1950s. Unfortunately, some of the few remaining buildings have been burned and vandalized in recent years, including the Miner's Union Hall, once a magnificent structure and no doubt witness to many a good time. The remaining buildings are rickety and dangerous, so use caution when exploring.

To get to Granite from downtown Philipsburg, head south on Sansome Road, then east on a rough dirt road (across from Center Street). The road to Granite can be rough and is steep in places, so don't drive it unless you have a vehicle with good clearance—no trailers. Consult a Beaverhead-Deerlodge National Forest map or ask at one of the shops in town about road conditions. Many other ghost

Flint Creek Valley Days Car show in Philipsburg. PHILIPSBURG CHAMBER OF COMMERCE

towns, some with only a few buildings, litter the hillsides around Philipsburg and Georgetown Lake. Several are on private property, are relatively inaccessible, and are not worth exploring unless you happen upon them while hiking. Please observe all PRIVATE PROPERTY and NO TRESPASSING postings.

To continue this scenic drive from Philipsburg, head north on Highway 1 toward I-90 again, cutting between the Flint Creek Range and the John Long Mountains. The road passes through a somewhat narrow canyon north of Philipsburg for about 9 miles before entering open sagebrush cattle range south of Hall. When you come out of this low canyon, you will see large granite boulders littering the fields. The boulders were left behind from a mudflow that raged down Boulder Creek sometime after the last ice age.

About 70 million years ago the Sapphire Mountains just west of the John Long Mountains moved east out of Idaho, shoving the Flint Creek Range out of their way. As a result, the western portion of the Flint Creeks are crumpled and folded. Magma oozed into the crevices of the folds to eventually form granite. It was in these granite intrusions that ore deposits were found. The drive ends in Drummond at I-90. Though small, the community of **Drummond** has a couple of events you might enjoy during summer, including a mule show, an

6

Big Hole Valley

Divide to Bannack Loop

General description: A 125-mile drive meandering through the Big Hole Valley to the ghost town of Bannack, returning via the Pioneer Mountains Scenic Byway to Wise River.

Special attractions: Big Hole Battlefield National Monument, Bannack and Coolidge ghost towns, Crystal Park, Elkhorn and Jackson hot springs; hiking, camping, boating, fishing, backpacking, mountain biking.

Location: Southwestern Montana from Divide, off I-15, circling the Pioneer Mountains and returning through the Pioneers to Wise River a few miles east of Divide.

Drive route numbers: Highway 43, CR 278, Pioneer Mountains Scenic Byway.

Travel season: Year-round. Snow and ice conditions make winter travel hazardous. Portions of the road may close in severe weather.

Camping: There are several Forest Service campgrounds along Highway 43 and many along the return route through the Pioneers. You can camp at Bannack State Park.

Services: Full services in Wisdom, Wise River, Jackson, and nearby Dillon. Limited services in most other towns along the way.

Nearby attractions: Beaverhead-Deerlodge National Forest, Butte, Clark Canyon Reservoir, Dillon, Fairmont Hot Springs Resort, Nez Perce Trail.

The Route

Ghost towns, hot springs, and great hiking opportunities make this a drive you'll want to savor. Spend a few days or a long weekend to really take in this remote part of Montana. Though some of the places along this route see a fair number of visitors during summer, you won't find the large crowds that you get at other state attractions. If you decide to visit Bannack State Park, expect to spend most of the day there, especially if you love exploring ghost towns.

Divide to Wisdom

Begin the drive in Divide, just off I-15 about 18 miles south of Butte, an open landscape with scattered buttes and a long sight of vision. Look for the slender pillar of Maiden Rock on the ridge north of town. From Divide follow Highway 43 toward Wisdom, as you wind around the Big Hole River, passing through a narrow canyon. Just a few miles west is Divide Ridge Recreation Area, with camping and fishing access on the Big Hole River. The road continues to follow the river to the 1-block-long town of Dewey, which has a cafe and lodging as well as fishing access and fishing guide service. Wise River is a slightly larger town 5 miles

Big Hole Valley

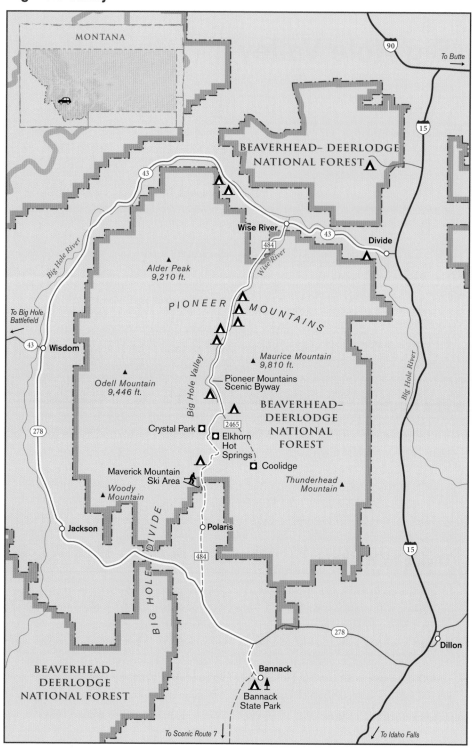

MONTANA

To Butte

90

15

BEAVERHEAD–DEERLODGE
NATIONAL FOREST

43

Wise River

43

Divide

484

Wise River

Alder Peak
9,210 ft.

Big Hole River

PIONEER MOUNTAINS

To Big Hole
Battlefield

Maurice Mountain
9,810 ft.

43

Wisdom

Big Hole Valley

Odell Mountain
9,446 ft.

Pioneer Mountains
Scenic Byway

Big Hole River

BEAVERHEAD–
DEERLODGE
NATIONAL
FOREST

278

Crystal Park

2465

Elkhorn
Hot
Springs

Coolidge

Maverick Mountain
Ski Area

Thunderhead
Mountain

Woody
Mountain

DIVIDE

Jackson

Polaris

484

BIG HOLE

278

15

Dillon

BEAVERHEAD–
DEERLODGE
NATIONAL FOREST

Bannack

Bannack
State Park

To Scenic Route 7

To Idaho Falls

farther along Highway 43. It caters mostly to anglers and was named for the river that flows into the Big Hole River here. The route between Dewey and Wise River is somewhat pastoral, traversing sagebrush rangeland with the Anaconda-Pintler Mountains rising to the north.

Continuing on to Wisdom, you will see a landscape of mostly wide open hills and rangeland covered with sage. Beyond that are the dry pine forests of the Pioneer Mountains to the southeast and the higher, moister Anaconda-Pintlers to the northwest. The road makes a few twists and turns while following the contours of creeks, sloughs, and rolling hills.

The openness of this valley, where there are seemingly more haystacks per square mile than anywhere else in the universe, is how this area got its name: "the Big Hole." Geologists believe it was created by a block of rocks, now called the Pioneer Mountains, that slid off the top of another block about 70 million years ago. Moving from Idaho, the rocks pushed east, creating the gap that is now the Big Hole Valley. To literally top it off, the valley has something on the order of 14,000 feet worth of sediment and fill covering bedrock, making it not only the largest but also the deepest valley in the region.

A character in Ivan Doig's novel *English Creek* called the **Big Hole Valley** the "front parlor of heaven." Many who have spent much time here agree. Because the Big Hole Valley isn't overdeveloped, like the Bozeman and Missoula Valleys, traffic is usually sparse—although anglers from all over the country descend on the Big Hole River during fly hatches, adding a noticeable presence at certain times of year. A few pullouts along the route, with roadside picnic tables by the river, offer the only places to stop and look around.

Near Fishtrap Creek the Anaconda-Pintlers come into view, and the Big Hole starts to look even larger, the immense valley looming before you. The forested folds of the Pioneer Mountains close in, while the higher peaks that separate Atlantic from Pacific waters at the Continental Divide can be seen in the distant northwest.

As the road turns south toward Wisdom (14 miles north of town) and crosses the river, a gravel road to the west follows the west side of the Big Hole River. The river branches quite a bit here, and other creeks flow into it from the mountains. Take this gravel road, passing through private ranchland, to enjoy the valley views. You will miss the town of Wisdom but hit Highway 43 again in 20 miles, near Wisdom, so you can backtrack to the town easily.

Wisdom to Jackson

Wisdom has one main road with an art gallery, a few bars and cafes—serving buffalo burgers—and about a half dozen places where you can hole up for the night. And if you need to fill up your gas tank, Wisdom is the best (and only) place to

The Big Hole Valley was a hard place to scratch a living in past centuries. Ariel Bleth

do so for miles around. Despite the trendy art gallery, this ranching town still appears well worn, which is part of its charm and helps make the Big Hole what it is: a ranching haven held together with cowboys whose weather-chiseled faces speak volumes about Montana ranch life in this 6,000-foot-high valley. So even during summer the valley weather can be harsh at times. A Wisdom cowboy once told me, "Yeah, we get summer in the Big Hole, and on that day everybody gets together for a picnic."

Wisdom was originally called Crossings and later derived its name from the river that passes through. The river was originally named by Lewis and Clark, who also named two others in this area after the virtues of their president, Thomas Jefferson—Wisdom, Philosophy, and Philanthropy. Somewhere along the way the rivers' names were changed to the Big Hole, Beaverhead, and Ruby.

A 15-mile side trip from Wisdom on Highway 43 west toward Chief Joseph Pass takes you to the **Big Hole Battlefield National Monument** (www.nps.gov/biho/index.htm). Here 163 soldiers of the US Seventh Infantry, along with 33 civilian volunteers, attacked about 800 men, women, and children of the Nez Perce tribe on August 9, 1877. The Nez Perce had already journeyed several hundred miles from their homeland in Idaho in search of a new home where they could live in peace. The soldiers mounted a surprise attack that lasted for 36

The Big Hole River drains the Beaverhead and Pioneer mountain ranges. TOM KILMER

hours and ended when Colonel John Gibbon's troops were forced to retreat. In all, between 70 and 90 Nez Perce were killed, most of them women, children, and elderly men. Dead US soldiers numbered about 20.

Today the battlefield is silent and sorrowful. Tepee poles stand like skeletons scattered about the meadow where the Nez Perce camped more than a century ago. In the forest overlooking the campsite, shallow pits in the ground have slowly filled with forest debris. Dug by soldiers for shelter from flying bullets, the pits evoke an eerie and sad feeling for the tragic conflict between newcomers to the land and those who had lived here for centuries. The howitzer on the mountain above looks out over the battlefield like a guard dog, a cold reminder of what happened here. Take a self-guided tour of the battlefield's three walking trails, with a pamphlet that gives an account of the events that took place. The visitor center shows a short film about the Nez Perce and their flight.

To reconnect with the main scenic drive, head south from Wisdom on CR 278 toward Jackson. The road is fairly straight with a few turns, but watch out for low-flying aircraft taking off and landing from the baseball field and picnic area. The Bitterroot Mountains, now to the west, contrast sharply with the softer Pioneers in the distant east. The Big Hole River continues to meander as if someone took a giant wad of string and dropped it from the clouds. Tangled willows bind the water's edge, and ranches and hayfields blanket the valley floor. In late summer and autumn, large loaves of hay pimple the mown fields. The hay is stacked with a large wooden contraption called a beaver slide. The device was invented and built in the Big Hole Valley around 1907 and patented in 1910; it can stack about 20 tons of hay as high as 30 feet.

Just thinking about all that hay stacking makes you hanker for a soak in Jackson, the next town south, at the **Hot Springs Lodge** (www.jacksonhotsprings.com). The pool is drained and cleaned once a week, the food is great, and the log cabin accommodations are quite comfortable. A gravel road southwest of town will take you to several lakes and hiking trails with fishing and camping access in the Bitterroot Mountains. You can hike up to the Continental Divide, which draws the line between Montana and Idaho through here.

Jackson to Bannack

South of Jackson, CR 278 heads due east for a bit and climbs up Big Hole Pass into the grassy and pine-dotted foothills. The 7,000-foot pass is not a difficult climb, since the valley floor is already more than 6,000 feet above sea level. At the crest of the pass, the peaks of the Pioneer Mountains come into view. To the south, thick conifer forests cover the hills. Aspen groves on both sides of the road complement the green forest in autumn when the leaves turn gold. The bald mountain to the east in front of you, appropriately named Baldy Mountain, is 10,568 feet high.

About 7 miles from the top of the pass is the northbound turnoff to Polaris, Maverick Mountain, and Elkhorn Hot Springs. This is your optional return route, but don't take it now. First head south to **Bannack State Park** (www.bannack.org), another 7 or 8 miles along CR 278.

From the Bannack turnoff follow the signs and the gravel road to this well-preserved ghost town. The road is fairly wide and smooth. It heads into some dry, scrubby hills that probably look much the same today as they did about a century ago when Bannack was a bustling, rough-and-tumble gold town and Montana's first territorial capital. The town's name was derived from the Bannocks, Native Americans who lived in the area. Like many Montana towns, Bannack began with a gold strike, this one in Grasshopper Creek in 1862. By 1863 it drew more than 3,000 people. At the time, Montana was just a territory, and the strike was the first major claim within its boundaries.

Bannack was as rough as any frontier gold town at the end of the road to nowhere, and it had more saloons than churches. As noted in the Montana Department of Fish, Wildlife and Parks publication the *Bannack Free Press*, one resident at the time wrote: "There was nothing visible to remind a person in the slightest degree that it was Sunday. Every store, saloon, and dancing hall was in

Baldy Mountain rises more than 10,000 feet in the Pioneer range. Tom Kilmer

full blast. Hacks running, auctioneering, mining and indeed every business, is carried on with more zeal than on week days."

No doubt that's also how many folks of decency felt in the 1860s when Bannack's sagebrush hills echoed gunshots, mining machinery, and sounds of your basic debauchery. Even the town's notorious sheriff, Henry Plummer, had better things to do than protect his citizens. Legend has it that Plummer and his henchmen, a gang known as the Road Agents, kept busy by relieving people of their gold and cash, often not sparing lives in the process. Many thousands of dollars and more than a hundred lives later, the Vigilantes formed, giving the old "California collar" to every thug they caught. One of the Vigilantes' first acts was the hanging of Road Agent George Ives in Nevada City. Eventually they caught up with Plummer and the rest of his gang, too. All but three were hanged or banished. Three cheers for Western justice. Or so it would seem. A few historians claim that Plummer was wrongly implicated and have attempted to exonerate him.

In the wake of their clean sweep, the Vigilantes left a mysterious mark on the cabin doors and tent flaps of known Road Agents. The mark, 3-7-77, struck fear in those who were targeted, knowing they were marked for a one-way ticket to the gallows. Although its meaning is still a mystery (many theories abound), the numbers adorn the badges of Montana sheriffs to this day.

In its heyday the ghost town of Bannack had fewer churches than saloons. Tom Kilmer

Plan on spending several hours at Bannack. With remnants of more than 60 preserved buildings, a cemetery, and mine works, there's plenty to keep you busy. Bannack Days, the third weekend in July, is a two-day event with music, food cooked the pioneer way, wagon rides, old-time crafts, black-powder shooting events, and live drama in the dusty streets. Some years, local Masons perform a play about the Vigilantes. During these festival days church services are held in Bannack's only remaining church. On the Friday and Saturday nights before Halloween, The Bannack Ghost Walks will entertain you with spooky reenactments of significant events in the history of Bannack. On weekends during winter, park officials flood a dredge pond for ice skaters, weather pending. (Skates are available free of charge.) A warming hut is an added attraction for both skaters and skiers.

From Bannack you have three choices for continuing this scenic drive. You can return to CR 278, where you can continue east to I-15, emerging near Dillon. Or you can head south from Bannack on the gravel road to CR 324 and pick up

Scenic Route 7, Big Sheep Creek Road, through the Tendoy Mountains. A third alternative is to return to CR 278 and take the drive through the Pioneer Mountains. That's the route we'll follow here.

Bannack Through the Pioneer Mountains & Back to Divide

From Bannack, retrace your route to CR 278 and turn left toward Polaris. You'll reach the right-hand turnoff for Polaris about 10 miles northwest. Polaris, a one-time mining camp, was originally about 2 miles north of where the town now sits. With a single-digit population, the community consists of a few buildings (including a post office), the Grasshopper Inn and RV Park, and the Polar Bar, supposedly moved here from Bannack and the place where Sheriff Plummer gulped his last drink. Not much is left of the original silver-mining camp in the hills.

Continuing north from Polaris, the road traverses sagebrush country, cutting a swath through the rolling hills of the Pioneer Mountains. The forests of the Pioneer Mountains are managed by the Beaverhead-Deerlodge National Forest; you'll find a few hiking trails leading to high mountain lakes between Polaris and Elkhorn Hot Springs to the east. There are developed campgrounds scattered about, too, but you can camp just about anywhere in the national forest.

Maverick Mountain Ski Area (http://skimaverick.com) is in the western Pioneers near **Elkhorn Hot Springs** (www.elkhornhotsprings.com). Check out the hot springs resort for a nice soak and a good meal year-round, as well as lodging. In winter, you'll find groomed trails for cross-country skiing and snowmobiling. Near Maverick Mountain, the road passes through thick spruce-fir forest and a small community of vacation cabins. Grasshopper Creek flows near the road and is the same creek that bled gold for the 19th-century residents of Bannack.

From Elkhorn Hot Springs north, the road is part of the Pioneer Mountains National Scenic Byway. It climbs to a pass through the forest to a place called **Crystal Park,** about 6 miles from the hot springs. At Crystal Park you can dig for crystals and keep whatever you find. Be mindful of the posted rules, though. The forest here is pockmarked with small craters from people digging for the clear stones, formed from molten rock intruding through limestone. Some of the lodgepole pines have fallen over and others look unsteady from people digging under the roots. *Such digging is not allowed.* The dig sites and parking lot, built to accommodate RVs and trailers, are to the west.

The elevation at the top of the pass near Crystal Park is around 7,000 feet. The air is cool and the scenery delightful: somewhat flat on top with grassy meadows on both sides of the road. The high peaks of the Pioneers form the backdrop. Several trails take off from the road, and many lead to high mountain lakes.

Just below Crystal Park, a gravel road to the east will take you to the ghost town of **Coolidge**—named for the former president. Heed the warning signs if there is logging going on. Sometimes log truck drivers like to go as fast as negotiable on these narrow, winding Forest Service roads (unpaved). The route to Coolidge is rough and rocky in spots and not suited for RVs and cars pulling trailers. If you want to make the trip, go slowly and carefully. Better yet, take a not-too-grueling mountain bike ride to the town. A campground up this road is nicely situated in the woods.

From a small parking area below Coolidge, it's about a 0.75-mile walk to the town. Coolidge sits in a narrow, high mountain valley sliced down the middle by Elkhorn Creek, which drains the steep ridges that face it. The town is mostly in shambles but there are a few standing buildings you can explore. The schoolhouse now rests in the middle of Elkhorn Creek. The main mine site is still intact but very dangerous to explore. I do not recommend it. The mine works were constructed in the 1870s, and the ore was sent to Wales for processing. Remains of a narrow-gauge railroad, perhaps one of the last built in the country, can be found here.

Back on the main route through the Pioneers, you will find plenty more hiking opportunities and a few more campgrounds. The road winds down from the top of the pass near Crystal Park for another 25 miles to the town of Wise River. The trees close in again as you head down, so drive carefully. About 5 or 6 miles before you get to Wise River, the landscape opens up and the Anaconda-Pintler Mountains rise sharply to the north. From here you can head back to I-15 where you began the drive and pick up Scenic Route 5 to the north or Scenic Route 7 to the south.

7

Big Sheep Creek Back Country Byway

Dell to Clark Canyon Reservoir

General description: A 55-mile gravel road with a short section of one-lane dirt surface—sometimes quite rough—traversing arid country cut by vein-like creeks and dry washes. The road glides through the grassy meadows of the valley between the Tendoy and Bitterroot Mountains.

Special attractions: Clark Canyon Reservoir; wildlife viewing, fishing, hiking, mountain biking.

Location: Southwest Montana from Dell, off I-15, to Clark Canyon Reservoir 19 miles south of Dillon on I-15.

Drive route number: Big Sheep Creek Road.

Travel season: Late spring through autumn; many sections are impassable during wet conditions.

Camping: Clark Canyon Reservoir has a few campgrounds. Camping at undeveloped sites is available on Bureau of Land Management (BLM) and Forest Service lands; camping on private land with owner permission only. There is one semi-primitive campground (outhouse only) near the beginning of the drive on BLM lands, called Deadwood Gulch.

Services: Full services at Dillon. Limited services in Dell and at Clark Canyon Reservoir.

Nearby attractions: Bannack ghost town, Beaverhead-Deerlodge National Forest, Calf A restaurant, Red Rock Lakes National Wildlife Refuge.

The Route

The Big Sheep Creek Back Country Byway is one of a few covered in this book that takes place off-road (read: not paved) through a not-oft-traveled section of the Big Sky. Its remoteness is, of course, part of the charm, yet it can also lead to trouble if you're not careful or if your vehicle isn't well suited to long drives on unpaved surfaces (and in some places the road can develop deep ruts). *A word of warning: Do not attempt this drive if it looks like rain.* With the slightest moisture, these soils can turn from dusty clouds to slick as ice faster than you can say, "We should have heeded the author's warning." I recommend bringing extra food and water, and waiting out the weather, in case you do get stuck in a sudden rainstorm. Do not attempt to drive out if your vehicle starts slipping on the freshly wetted road surface. The Bureau of Land Management claims that large RVs and vehicles towing trailers can make the trip in dry weather only, but I wouldn't do it. Four-wheel-drive is not necessary but could be helpful if you get stuck or if the

Big Sheep Creek Back Country Byway

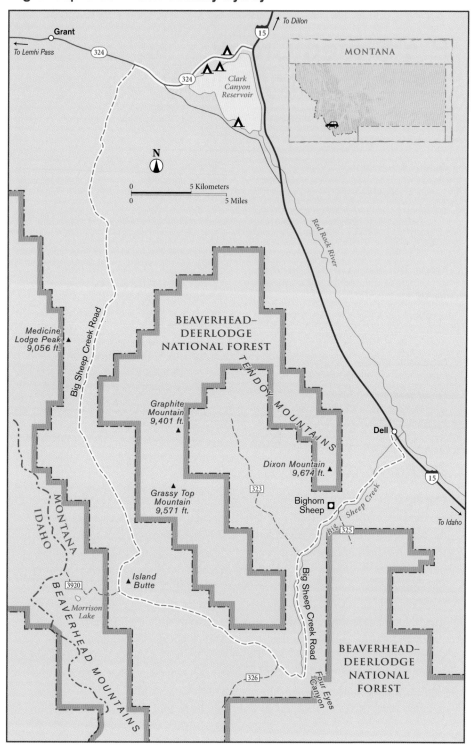

Grant

To Lemhi Pass

324

324

To Dillon

15

Clark
Canyon
Reservoir

MONTANA

N

0   5 Kilometers
0   5 Miles

Red Rock River

Medicine
Lodge Peak
9,056 ft.

Big Sheep Creek Road

BEAVERHEAD–
DEERLODGE
NATIONAL FOREST

TENDOY MOUNTAINS

Graphite
Mountain
9,401 ft.

Dixon Mountain
9,674 ft.

Dell

15

Grassy Top
Mountain
9,571 ft.

323

Bighorn
Sheep

Big Sheep Creek

325

To Idaho

MONTANA
IDAHO

Island
Butte

3920

Morrison
Lake

BEAVERHEAD MOUNTAINS

Big Sheep Creek Road

326

Four Eyes Canyon

BEAVERHEAD–
DEERLODGE
NATIONAL
FOREST

road hasn't been recently graded. If you have any doubts about road conditions or local weather, call the BLM office in Dillon.

I hope this caveat hasn't frightened you away. This scenic drive is truly delightful, with lots of opportunities to pull the mountain bike down from the rack and go for a spin or to drop a line into Big Sheep Creek or Clark Canyon Reservoir.

Dell to Island Butte

Begin the drive south of the town of **Dell.** Exit I-15 at Dell and head south on the frontage road for about 1.5 miles. Turn west (right) onto Big Sheep Creek Road, which is clearly marked with small, brown signs. Pay attention to these signs, as the road forks in quite a few places, so you will have to read the signs carefully to know which direction to go. In general, the gravel road is in fair shape but quickly develops a washboard surface when freshly graded. Watch for potholes all along the route. At the start the road is wide and winds quite a bit. Later the road narrows, so though you're unlikely to see many other vehicles, watch for them and pass with caution. On the drive, you may pass through three or four gates; please remember to leave each one as you found it. If the gate is closed and latched, close and latch it again behind you.

As you begin the drive, the Tendoy Mountains rise ahead, taking their name from a chief of the Lemhi, a band of Shoshone Indians who lived in Idaho and this part of Montana. Dixon Mountain, at 9,674 feet, stands guard to the west and rangeland dominates the foreground.

The road follows Big Sheep Creek, where alder and willow thickets seem to hold the banks in place. There is a spot or two to camp along the creek, or you can stop to drop a line or swim. Keep your eyes on the rocky hillsides along the road for bighorn sheep. Sheep were prolific in the area until disease nearly wiped them out in the early 1990s. The population is recovering, so if you watch carefully you may see a few ewes or rams. The best place to look is about 4.5 miles up the road, where the canyon narrows and becomes quite rocky. You might also try a hike up Hidden Pasture Trail near Deadwood Gulch or along Muddy Creek for both scenery and sheep.

Many trails along the route provide hikers with a chance to explore this arid country. If you venture out, take plenty of water since there is not much cover; you may want to hike in the cooler hours of morning or evening. Also remember that much of this scenic drive passes through leased rangeland and a few private ranches, so respect all NO TRESPASSING signs.

About 10 miles up the road, you will pass the mouth of a gulch called Four Eyes Canyon. Three miles past it you will come to a major fork in the road. Bear to the right. Shortly after you turn, there should be a sign confirming that this is the Sheep Creek route. If you take a left onto FR 326 at this junction instead, you can hike part of the Continental Divide Scenic Trail, which takes you into the hills to the southwest.

Continuing on the main Sheep Creek road after the right turn, the country opens up quite a bit to wide, flat land with buttes and the Beaverhead Mountains in the background to the west. The Beaverheads are actually a continuation of the Bitterroot Mountains. Eighteenmile Peak, rising to 11,141 feet in the south, is the highest point on the Continental Divide between Banff, Alberta, and central Wyoming. The Beaverhead moniker comes from a rock formation near Dillon that supposedly resembles a beaver's head. It was recognized by the Shoshone as such, although you might have to use your imagination. Sacagawea, the Lemhi Shoshone woman and guide for the Lewis and Clark Expedition, recognized the rock when the explorers happened upon it. At the sight of the familiar outcropping, Sacagawea knew she had returned to the land of her ancestors. Her affiliation with the homeland proved to be a windfall of luck. At this point in their journey, the Corps of Discovery desperately needed horses. Sacagawea knew her people were near and that the expedition team could count on the Shoshone to supply them with the animals. For this reason **Beaverhead Rock** is now a state monument, 19 miles north of Dillon on Highway 41.

As the Sheep Creek Back Country Byway begins to stretch across the open plain, it passes beneath a power line and then makes a few twists and turns, swinging back to the power line near **Island Butte.** You'll know Island Butte when you see it; it's the large, grassy, round bump seemingly plopped down and forgotten in the valley. If you want to hike up to the top, the best place to access the butte is across BLM land on the south end. A sign near the south end of the butte will point you west to Morrison Lake. The road is a bumpy dirt track 2.5 to 3 miles long. **Morrison Lake** is small but with good fishing, and you can camp here on undeveloped sites. From the Morrison Lake turnoff, the byway swings around Island Butte and travels under the power line again.

Island Butte to Clark Canyon Reservoir

Once past Island Butte, take the road that follows the power line north. You pass a sign that marks the old Bannack Road, which used to connect the gold-mining town of Bannack with Corrine, Utah, in the 1860s and was used to move freight and possibly gold. Its two-wheeled tracks are still clearly visible. Just below the Bannack Road crossing, you will go over a small pass. Parts of it can be steep for short pitches, so go slowly. As the road draws closer to Hildreth Creek, it smoothes out and widens a bit. A few ranch homes appear on the range. The

The Medicine Lodge area in Big Sheep Creek. BRAD CHRISTENSEN

mountains are closer to the road, and the landscape is not as open. The scenic drive now follows Medicine Lodge Creek, which provides water here; the rangeland is noticeably lusher than the landscape you just came from. During drought years, however, the creek can disappear as quickly as it can pour from the volcano-like Medicine Lodge Peak to the west. Look for the bright mountain bluebirds here flitting low to the ground on a feeding frenzy of insects. American kestrels hover over the grasslands in their hunt for small rodents. As you near the end of the drive, you might see pronghorn in the hayfields along the road, especially late in the afternoon.

Soon you come to an intersection with an obvious main road, paved CR 324, where a right turn takes you to **Clark Canyon Reservoir** and back to I-15. Clark Canyon has plenty of camping, boating, and fishing opportunities. Cattail Marsh Nature Trail, along its edge, is a good place to see yellow-headed and red-winged blackbirds, snipes, and many waterfowl species. Interpretive signs describe the various birds and other wildlife.

A left turn at the paved road will take you to the 7,300-foot-high **Lemhi Pass**—Sacagawea Historical Area—where Lewis and Clark crossed the Continental Divide on August 12, 1805. Take the road about 20 miles to the junction with Trail Creek Road. From here the pass is another 12 miles along Trail Creek Road,

Lemhi Pass crosses the Continental Divide from Sheep Creek into Idaho. Tom Kilmer

a rough ride most of the way. Large RVs and trailers are not recommended, but it is a nice walk if you need a leg-stretcher. You can camp at Sacagawea Memorial Camp, just below the pass and on the Salmon-Challis National Forest in Idaho. At the top of the pass, Lewis and Clark got their first view of the headwaters of the Columbia River. Lewis wrote:

> At the distance of 4 miles further the road took us to the most distant fountain of the waters of the Mighty Missouri in surch of which we have spent so many toilsome days and wristless nights. thus far I had accomplished one of those great objects on which my mind has been unalterably fixed for many years, judge then of the pleasure I felt in allying my thirst with this pure and ice-cold water which issues from the base of a low mountain. . . . below McNeal had exultingly stood with a foot on each side of this little rivulet and thanked his god that he had lived to bestride the mighty & heretofore deemed endless Missouri.

From Clark Canyon Reservoir you can head north and pick up Scenic Route 6, just south of Dillon. Or you can head south on I-15 and pick up Scenic Route 8 in Monida.

The Centennial Valley

Henrys Lake, ID, to Monida, MT

General description: A 55-mile gravel road that skirts the Centennial Mountains, offering views across marshlands and a valley bounded by the Gravelly and Snowcrest Ranges.

Special attractions: Red Rock Lakes National Wildlife Refuge; backpacking, camping, fishing, floating, hiking, mountain biking, wildlife viewing.

Location: The extreme southwest of the state, from Montana/Idaho Highway 87 just south of the Montana border on Raynolds Pass to I-15 in Monida, Montana.

Drive route numbers: South Valley Road (CR 509), Red Rock Pass Road.

Travel season: South Valley Road from I-15 to refuge headquarters in Lakeview is periodically closed throughout the winter

and is closed in winter east of Lakeview. Elk Lake Road and North Valley Road are not plowed in winter, leaving it open to local snowmobile traffic only.

Camping: Henrys Lake (Idaho) has a few campgrounds. Two more are located at Red Rock Lakes National Wildlife Refuge, one at Upper Red Rock Lake, and one at River Marsh on Lower Red Rock Lake. Elk Lake has a commercial campground.

Services: Lodging and food are available at a few resorts near the wildlife refuge. There are also limited services at Henrys Lake in Idaho and in Lima. There are no services at Monida along I-15.

Nearby attractions: Cliff and Wade Lakes, Lima Reservoir, Nez Perce Trail, West Yellowstone.

The Route

The Centennial Valley has to be one of Montana's most alluring regions. Ripping through the high plains from east to west, the Centennial Mountains make **Red Rock Lakes National Wildlife Refuge** (www.fws.gov/redrocks) one of the prettiest wildlife viewing sites in the state. Groves of quaking aspen cloak the foothills. In spring their new leaves are a bright and tender green; in autumn the leaves shimmer like gold coins dangling from the branches. With plenty of opportunities to hike, bike, fish, and boat, you can experience a variety of wildlife any way you like it. Watch for moose trotting across the road, badgers snuffling about for grubs in the barrow pit, and soaring hawks and eagles above. Red Rock Lakes is a great place for bird watching, too, especially if you like trumpeter swans, for which the refuge was established. Be sure to stop by the refuge headquarters (weekdays only from 8 a.m. to 4:30 p.m.) and learn about these graceful birds.

The Centennial Valley

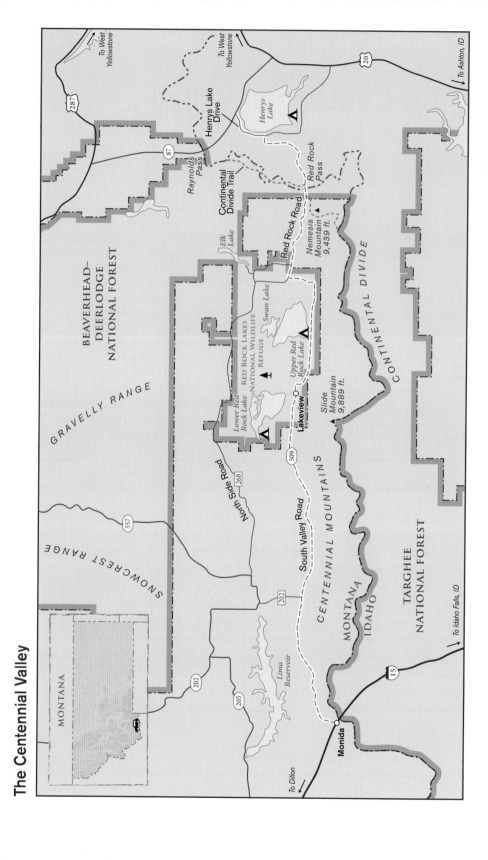

A curlew flies over the wetlands at Red Rock Lakes National Wildlife Refuge.
JAMES N. PERDUE, WILDANDSCENICPHOTOS.COM

Henrys Lake, Idaho, to Red Rock Lakes, Montana

You can approach this scenic drive from Raynolds Pass on Montana Highway 87 or from West Yellowstone on US 20. From either direction, head to **Henrys Lake, Idaho,** a popular fishing and boating site—check Idaho regulations if you intend to do either of these activities. Follow the paved road along the lakeshore then turn west where signs indicate the route to Red Rock Lakes. From the north, the first 3 miles of this road are paved before turning to gravel. The road is in good shape but narrow in spots, especially when approaching oncoming traffic.

As you follow the signs and head west, enjoy the scenic mountains to the south. These are the 10,000-foot Centennials, with aspen grove hemlines. Part of the road passes right through some of the aspen groves, which cast sparkling shadows across the road. Look for a safe place to pull over and walk among the trees. Many of the trees are genetically identical because aspens clone themselves by sending out tremendous root systems, called rhizomes, from which new trees grow.

Red Rock Pass Road rises over a small pass of the same name, at just above 7,000 feet elevation, after which the land before you opens with magnificent vistas.

You are now back in Montana. This is open range, so watch for cattle on the road. The Continental Divide National Scenic Trail winds its way along at the top of the pass, heading north for a short way before trailing east through Yellowstone National Park.

Drive on and you will soon reach the first of the Red Rock Lakes. For a pleasant side trip, take a right at Elk Lake Road and go for a walk around Widgeon Pond. Look for American white pelicans, trumpeter swans, great blue herons, and several species of duck. Farther up the road is **Elk Lake,** where you can camp in the low, grassy hills of the Gravelly Range, stay at a small lodge on Elk Lake, or camp at the lodge's private campground. If you continue up the road from here, you will have a very bumpy ride to Hidden Lake. Hikers and mountain bikers can take the trail beyond Hidden Lake to Cliff and Wade Lakes (see Scenic Route 9). Many other unimproved roads in the area are excellent for mountain biking, but be sure to stick to the roads because cycling on game trails is not permitted.

Just near MacDonald Pond (south of Elk Lake) a road to the left (west) takes you to North Side Road 268, which travels along the opposite side of Red Rock Lakes from the main route. If you choose to take this alternate route, you will meet up with the Centennial Valley Road just east of Lima Reservoir, about 30 miles west. You can also make a loop of this scenic drive, taking the North Side Road west (the view of the Centennial Mountains is much more panoramic) and returning by way of the main drive route, South Valley Road (CR 509).

Back on the main scenic drive, at the junction of Elk Lake Road, the refuge marshes and lakes come into view. Watch for moose in the willow thickets here, especially during autumn. Because they're so tall, you can see these gangly members of the deer family from a long way across the marsh. Moose are mostly solitary animals, unlike elk, bison, and deer, but it is not uncommon to see two bulls together during summer, a bull with a cow, or a cow and a calf. Females are very protective of their calves and can seriously injure people who venture too close, so please keep your distance. Moose are also excellent swimmers and are said to be able to swim as fast as two people can paddle a canoe.

The 32,350-acre Red Rock Lakes National Wildlife Refuge was established in 1935, originally to protect trumpeter swans—the largest of all North American waterfowl—which were nearing extinction from unregulated hunting. In 1939 only 69 swans existed in the Greater Yellowstone Ecosystem, of which Red Rock Lakes are a part. A year-round resident population of trumpeters now numbers more than 500; during winter another 4,000 swans arrive from Canada. Many of them settle at the refuge. Unfortunately, the Greater Yellowstone Ecosystem can support only about half of the swans that winter here. A severe winter or disease outbreak could kill hundreds of trumpeters. Biologists have tried to capture and relocate many of the birds to reduce their vulnerability to a catastrophic die-off.

The Centennial Mountains form a dramatic backdrop to South Valley Road in Red Rock Lakes National Wildlife Refuge. JAMES N. PERDUE, WILDANDSCENICPHOTOS.COM

But because swans tend to return to their same wintering habitat every year, getting them to winter elsewhere has proved difficult.

Other refuge residents and visitors include ferruginous hawks, red-tailed hawks, Swainson's hawks, and peregrine falcons. Shorebirds such as willets, avocets, long-billed curlews, in addition to terns, gulls, and sandhill cranes, wade in the shallows probing for insects and small shellfish in the mud. Look for cranes west of Upper Red Rock Lake and south of Lower Red Rock Lake. You can canoe from the upper lake to the lower lake and see wildlife that you might otherwise miss from the bank. Mink usually cavort along the water's edge, and if you're lucky, you may see a river otter. Red foxes also skulk around the marsh edges, especially at nesting time. Check at refuge headquarters for boating regulations and restrictions.

One of two campgrounds on the refuge lies just below the road at Upper Red Rock Lake, situated in a small grove of quaking aspen. This campground offers one of the best places to view trumpeter swans. Also, you have a good chance of seeing swans at both Shambow and Culver Ponds or from the Lower Red Rock Lake turnout.

Red Rock Lakes to Monida, MT

From the refuge on the main route, continue west on South Valley Road and look for pronghorn in the sagebrush north of the lakes in the Centennial Valley. Keep your eyes peeled for cerulean-colored mountain bluebirds perching on fence posts along the road. You'll probably see them hunting for flying insects close to the ground, sometimes hovering in midair before swooping down on their prey. Just east of Mud Lake, you can take CR 202 north to Lima Reservoir. This is where you would emerge if you take the North Side Road from Elk Lake. CR 202 will also take you to the Gravelly Range Road and into the town of Ennis, more than 70 miles north.

Just west of this turnoff, the main road begins to climb to a plateau before dropping into Monida, so named for its proximity to the Montana-Idaho border. Here the landscape is much drier than around the refuge. There is not a tree in sight—except at the horizon, where the Bitterroot, Beaverhead, and Lemhi ranges mingle along Montana's southern border. For the most part, Monida is a ghost town, with a row of boarded-up storefronts facing I-15. One or two families live here, but you won't find any services.

From **Monida** you can head north on I-15 and go 23 miles to Dell to check out Scenic Route 7. Scenic Route 6 begins about 13 miles beyond Dell and north of Dillon.

Madison River Country

Missouri Headwaters State Park to West Yellowstone

General description: A 119-mile drive that skirts the folds, crinkles, and arêtes of the high Madison Range and the sparkling waters of the Madison River and nearby lakes. Enjoy this fly fisher's paradise, or take a 28-mile side trip and relive Montana's gold rush days in Virginia City, a living ghost town.

Special attractions: Missouri Headwaters State Park, Lewis and Clark Caverns, Virginia City, Nevada City, Madison River, Quake Lake, Hebgen Lake; camping, boating, fishing, hiking, mountain biking, wildlife viewing.

Location: Southwestern Montana, from Three Forks to West Yellowstone.

Drive route numbers: Highway 2, US 287, Highway 287.

Travel season: Year-round. Snow and icy conditions can make winter travel hazardous.

Camping: Pitch your tent at Headwaters State Park, Lewis and Clark Caverns State Park, or one of several Bureau of Land Management and commercial campgrounds along the Madison River. You'll find commercial campgrounds at Virginia City and Cliff and Wade Lakes.

Services: Full services at Three Forks, Ennis, Virginia City, and West Yellowstone; limited services at Cardwell, Harrison, Norris, and Cameron.

Nearby attractions: Beaverhead-Deerlodge National Forest, Gallatin National Forest, Lee Metcalf Wilderness Area, Nez Perce Trail, Potosi Hot Springs, Red Rock Lakes National Wildlife Refuge, Yellowstone National Park.

The Route

A showcase of Montana history, this scenic drive not only includes one of the state's most attractive rivers, the Madison, it also offers you a chance to explore and learn about a few of the people and events that helped shape its reputation as a wild territory. The term *wild* might have been a pejorative in the late 19th century, but by the late 20th century, the wilds of Montana were synonymous with freedom from urban hassles. The Madison River Valley became one of many Big Sky destinations sought after by urban asylum seekers as a means to cure their social ills. As a result, much of the Madison valley sprouted ranchettes and boutique shops.

For some longtime residents the Madison was ruined under the weight of new arrivals, both permanent and seasonal. For others the influx brought opportunities to show off the region's natural merits to those willing to pay for it. *Kaching!* Dude ranches and recreational outfitters sprang up over night, catering to modern-day explorers and fun hogs who were quite willing to part with wads of cash. Chances are if you're holding this book, you already know that Montana is an oyster, and the Madison River Valley might just be your pearl.

Madison River Country

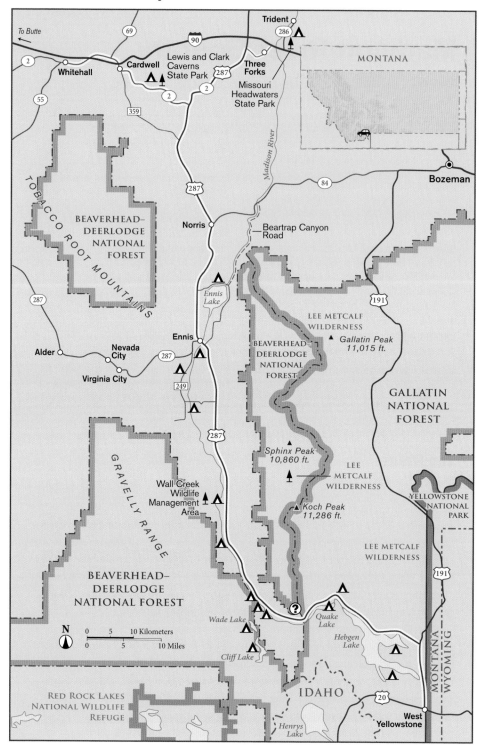

Missouri Headwaters State Park to Ennis

Begin this scenic drive at **Missouri Headwaters State Park** (http://fwp.mt.gov/parks/visit/missouriHeadwaters), where the Madison, Jefferson, and Gallatin Rivers join to form the mighty Missouri. You'll find it just off I-90, about 30 miles west of Bozeman. From the Three Forks exit, head 2 miles east on CR 205, then turn north and go 2 more miles on CR 286. The park is open year-round.

The three rivers were named by explorers Meriwether Lewis and William Clark for their president Thomas Jefferson ("that illustrious personage," according to Lewis), James Madison (then secretary of state), and Albert Gallatin (secretary of the treasury, who, incidentally, had refused financing for the expedition, believing it was a waste of money). The site is the place where the Shoshone woman Sacagawea was kidnapped before being sold to Hidatsa Indians in North Dakota, where she met her husband—a French trapper named Charbonneau—and later, Lewis and Clark (see Scenic Route 7).

The state park also marks the spot where, in 1863, Gallatin City was laid out near the Missouri headwaters. Its founders envisioned the area as the perfect location for a regional commercial center, given the dependence on travel by water at the time. The town founders' dreams never materialized, however. Gallatin City experienced brief prosperity in the 1870s when supplies were ferried up the Missouri River and taken overland to the mining boomtowns of Bannack and Virginia City, which at the time were several days' travel south. But Gallatin City breathed its last when the railroad bypassed it in 1883.

The headwaters area today is a fine place to camp or enjoy the riverine habitat. Rocky buttes and knobs punctuate the low cliffs along the river within Missouri Headwaters State Park. The campsites have few trees and the landscape is arid, but the picnic area is very pleasant—a big, grassy, shady place along the Jefferson River. Barrier-free trails with interpretive displays are an added feature. Boaters can launch their crafts on the Missouri here, and it's a quiet place to fish.

From the park head back to I-90, stopping in the town of Three Forks to take in the **Headwaters Heritage Museum** (www.tfhistory.org) on the corner of Main and Cedar in the old bank building (open June 1 through September 30; outside these times by appointment). The museum exhibits re-creations of late-19th-century life and an assortment of memorabilia, from a collection of barbed wire to mementos of war to a 29.5-pound brown trout, reported to be the largest ever caught in Montana. One weekend in July, Three Forks hosts a rodeo and parade. In addition, a local ranching family operates a horse round-up and drive, which up to 20 folks (that's you and me) can participate in. Expect to spend 3 days on the trail moving horses between their summer and winter ranges in the spring. Contact **Montana Horses** (www.montanahorses.com) for details.

To continue the main scenic drive from Three Forks, take Highway 2, south and west of town, about 16 miles to Montana's oldest state park—**Lewis and Clark Caverns.** If you're coming from the west on I-90, you may want to skip Missouri Headwaters State Park (although I would recommend seeing it anyway) and begin the drive at Cardwell instead, taking Highway 2 east to Lewis and Clark Caverns. The road to the caverns is quite narrow, with sharp curves, snaking along the Jefferson River. Look for raptors sailing above the rocky canyon.

These caverns, the largest in Montana, were once tilted layers of limestone filled with acidic water. As the water dissolved the limestone over thousands of years, the ceiling of the newly formed openings collapsed numerous times. Today stalactites and stalagmites still glisten and grow in the caves. The underground rooms also are home to a rare Montana mammal, the western big-eared bat. You are bound to see one or two streak by you on the 2-hour tour through the caverns. Tour guides discuss various limestone formations and cave history. The state park also has camping, rental cabins, nature trails, concessions, and picnicking year-round (water is turned off from October 1 to April 30). The caverns are open for tours from May 1 to September 30. Reservations are required for candlelight tours offered for just a few days each December.

From the caverns head back toward Three Forks on Highway 2 until you reach US 287. Turn south on US 287, following signs for Yellowstone National Park. The road crosses the Jefferson River then rolls over cattle and sheep pastures and grain fields dissected by shallow coulees. Surrounding hillsides sport scrubby lodgepole pines and junipers, with willow- and cottonwood-choked stream bottoms. The Tobacco Root Mountains, bored through by hundreds of old mine shafts and a few mining towns, rise to the west.

At Norris you'll find a small campground, hot springs (www.norrishotsprings .com), and a restaurant that serves food from ingredients sourced within 50 miles. On Friday, Saturday, and Sunday nights, you can listen to live music performed from a stage under a geodesic dome at the edge of the hot springs pool. Beyond Norris, US 287 takes on more hills and curves through the scrubby foothills of the northern Madison Range. The road climbs a pass known as Norris Hill. Look closely at the grass on top, since remnants of the Bozeman Trail still scar the hillside. A shortcut to Bannack and Virginia City, the trail was used to transport supplies to the gold-rush towns. Stop at the historical marker on the pass and look just beyond it. Take a moment to imagine what it was like to draw wagons over such brain-jarring terrain, then climb back into your SUV and enjoy your suspension, leather seats, CD player, and air-conditioning and continue on.

At the bottom of Norris Hill, **Ennis Lake,** also known as Meadow Lake, sits in a small basin below the impressive Madison Range. The lake has access for camping, boating, and fishing. White pelicans glide above its surface and bob along its

Gold fever drove many a Virginia City resident to his death by the old "California collar." Pam Arroues

marshy shoreline. You can also access several trails into the Madisons to the east of the lake or follow roads into the Tobacco Root Mountains to the west.

Ennis to Nevada City

Farther south the town of **Ennis** bustles with fly fishers in summer. A road sign near the town limits attests to the region's bread and butter: Ennis, 1,000 People and 11 Million Trout. Several fishing guides are available for trips on the blue-ribbon trout stream, the Madison River. Among river denizens are cutthroat trout, brown trout, brook trout, rainbow trout, mountain whitefish, and arctic grayling. Before wetting a line, check local regulations since the Madison River suffered from a severe outbreak of whirling disease in the 1990s. Please heed all recommendations for preventing the spread of this deadly fish disease.

The children of Irishman William Ennis, after whom the town is named, were supposedly the first white children to see Yellowstone National Park in 1873. Today Ennis has a collection of interesting of exhibits: a wildlife museum, an antler museum, and a rock hound museum among cafes, fly shops, art galleries, and real estate brokers. Check with the chamber of commerce (see For More

Information) for a list of several events throughout the year, including a rodeo, gallery walks, hunters' feed (featuring wild game dishes and a contest for the best), and fly-fishing festivals.

From Ennis take a side trip west on Highway 287, which snakes its way to the still lively ghost towns of Virginia City and Nevada City. On the way stop by the **Ennis Fish Hatchery** (www.fws.gov/ennis); go 2 miles west on Highway 287 and turn left onto Varney Road (near the Highway Department Quonset) and continue south for another 10 miles. Follow the signs.

Back on Highway 287, continue west to Virginia and Nevada cities. From the top of the pass between Ennis and the other two towns, an overlook provides a stunning 180-degree view of the Madison River valley below. As you descend the steep pass and enter Virginia City, you will see the remains of broken dreams in the form of tattered cabins scattered across the sagebrush hills. Newer homes among the century-old ruins are strangely conspicuous, as if some treasure hunters have not yet given up.

Virginia City sprang up in 1863 after the discovery of gold in Alder Gulch (named for the bushes that line it), another rich deposit like that found in Bannack a year earlier. The Alder and Grasshopper Creeks strikes were two of the richest ever discovered in Montana. Many prospectors left Bannack for the newer riches of Virginia City, and the latter town managed to wrest from the former the designation as territorial capital by 1865. The two boomtowns shared the notorious Road Agents, a gang of thieves and murderers who reportedly killed more than 100 people and robbed countless others before their glory days ended at the gallows (see Scenic Route 6).

In Virginia City take a historical bus tour through town and into the hills, where men dizzy with gold fever sweated to find the mother lode. This crash course in history is a delightful look into Montana's beginnings. View some of the former residents' artifacts at the Thompson-Hickman Museum. You can also relive the excitement while watching the Virginia City Players perform melodramas and variety shows nightly (Memorial Day through Labor Day). If you want something a little bawdier, check out the Follies at the Gilbert Brewery (www .breweryfollies.net). Shows run twice daily (reservations by telephone strongly advised; 800-829-2969) Memorial Day through Labor Day.

In its heyday Virginia City had the largest mercantile shop in all of Montana Territory. Many of its original buildings now house modern-day shops, while others have been left more or less in their original condition. The modern shops peddle everything from candy to trinkets to cappuccino. The old buildings are not open, but you can look through windows at displays of their 19th-century goods and services. Many of the buildings bulge with artifacts, including clothing, foodstuffs, tools, and dry goods.

Nevada City, 2 miles farther west along Highway 287, is a little less lively. You can also take the narrow-gauge railroad, the Alder Gulch Short Line, between the two towns. You'll find a steam railroad museum at the Nevada City end of the line.

The original Nevada City, a mining camp and trading post that thrived in the 1860s, is not really intact. Many of the buildings here now did not make up the original town but were brought in from other sites. Several are open, so you can wander around on a self-guided tour. The buildings have been restored or rebuilt to give visitors an idea of what a real Western mining town might have looked like. Check out the music hall, which purports to house the largest collection of automated music machines in North America. During summers, in-character locals from the 19th century engage visitors in conversation while going about old-timey business. On weekends, they stage entertaining living history events, like stagecoach robberies, trials and hangings (not real of course), and other colorful reenactments.

Nevada City to Cliff & Wade Lakes & West Yellowstone

Retrace your route back to the main scenic drive at Ennis and take US 287 south. The road narrows and straightens, with only a few dips in the pavement. To the east the Madison Range crowns the sprawling ranchland. **Sphinx Peak,** which is best seen from the overlook on the way to Virginia City, stands sentinel over the valley. Its 10,000-foot, red-rock cliffs cast a striking glow in the setting sun. The gravel conglomerate forming the Sphinx is unique to that mountain in all of the range.

As you follow the highway along the **Madison River,** you'll find many campgrounds; most have open, flat landscapes with wonderful views of the Madison Range and the river. The campgrounds tend to fill up quickly during the summer when fishing is good. During winter you can view a thousand or so elk on the sagebrush flats of **Wall Creek Wildlife Management Area** near the McAtee Bridge campground.

US 287 begins to curve a bit when it turns toward the mountains again near **Quake Lake.** Where it meets Montana Highway 87, the vista narrows as the road passes through a narrow canyon. Soon you'll see loads of rubble and rock bars providing a rapid course for the Madison River. Pull over into the interpretive center describing the origins of Quake Lake and look across the lake to the south, where a bare mountainside is visible. On August 17, 1959, an earthquake measuring 7.5 on the Richter scale shook loose 80 million tons of rock and sent it sliding 100 mph downhill toward the river. The road you just drove over now sits on top of this 300-foot-deep rubble pile, which forms a bench and dam across the

Quake Lake was created when debris from a 1959 earthquake dammed the Madison River. USDA FOREST SERVICE

Madison River. The visitor center overlooks the 37,800-acre slide area where 28 people were killed. Although the earthquake formed Quake Lake about half a century ago, the slide area is still sparsely vegetated.

Continuing southeast on US 287, wind around Quake Lake where you can see the tops of dead trees (called snags) sticking out of the water. When the earthquake struck, the Madison River dammed to form this body of water. Many summer cabins now lie beneath its waves. If you get out and walk around parts of the lake, you can see a rooftop or two protruding from the water. As you drive east toward Hebgen Lake, several numbered pullouts along the road tell stories about events that took place the night of the huge quake. At point 7, take a short walk to see where cabins had been submerged until the lake's shoreline dropped 19 feet.

Farther east at **Hebgen Lake,** you'll find several places to put in your boat, as well as fish and camp. The mountains on the other side of Hebgen form the Continental Divide. Lionhead Mountain thrusts its rocky nose southeast into Idaho. On the north side of the road, sage-covered hills are interrupted by groves of quaking aspen. As you near the east end of Hebgen Lake, deeper waters give way to shallow marshes choked with willow. US 287 bumps into the southern end of US 191 shortly after passing the lake. At the junction head south to the tourist town of West Yellowstone and Yellowstone National Park (see Scenic Route 10).

You can end your drive in West Yellowstone or take another side trip back to Cliff and Wade Lakes. To do the latter, head west from West Yellowstone on US 20, which dips into Idaho for about 12 miles, going over Targhee Pass (7,072 feet); pick up Highway 87 heading north toward Henrys Lake, Idaho. This short loop passes through sagebrush range rimmed by rolling hills. Henrys Lake sits below the road to the southwest. You then go over another pass, 6,800-foot Raynolds Pass, and head north back into Montana.

Two miles beyond the top of the pass, a gravel road to the west leads to **Cliff and Wade Lakes.** The blue-green lakes sit in deep basins surrounded by high pine ridges. Both have nice, lightly forested campgrounds. Drop a boat in the water and spend an hour or two fishing. If you are brave enough, or a little crazy, you can even go for a swim. Bald eagles and ospreys nest along the shores. In winter you stand a good chance of seeing moose, elk, and trumpeter swans; look for river otters in Wade Lake. You can cross-country ski at Wade Lake Cabins (http://wadelake.com) or above Cliff Lake at the Cliff Lake Natural Area. There are several hiking trails as well.

From Cliff and Wade you can pick up Scenic Route 8 to the south or Scenic Route 10 from West Yellowstone.

10

Gallatin Canyon

West Yellowstone to Bozeman

General description: A 90-mile trip from West Yellowstone to Bozeman through a narrow mountain canyon cut by the sometimes green, sometimes whitewater Gallatin River. The drive passes through a little-traveled and attractive portion of Yellowstone National Park.

Special attractions: Yellowstone National Park, Lee Metcalf Wilderness, Big Sky Resort, Montana State University, Museum of the Rockies, petrified forest, hot springs, concerts, festivals, art shows, county fairs; hiking, camping, fishing, whitewater rafting, floating, backpacking, skiing, snowmobiling, wildlife viewing, swimming, shopping.

Location: Southwestern Montana, from West Yellowstone to Bozeman.

Drive route number: US 191.

Travel season: Year-round. Heavy snowfall and slick ice conditions can make winter travel extremely treacherous along portions of US 191.

Camping: Campgrounds in Yellowstone National Park fill up quickly during summer and even after Labor Day. There are numerous Forest Service campgrounds along the Gallatin River and many undeveloped places to camp in Beaverhead-Deerlodge and Gallatin National Forests. There are KOAs and other commercial campgrounds in and around West Yellowstone and Bozeman.

Services: Full services in West Yellowstone, Big Sky, Gallatin Gateway, and Bozeman. There are a few gas stations, restaurants, and shops along the way.

Nearby attractions: Bear Creek Wildlife Management Area, Gallatin National Forest, Historic Crail Ranch, Karst's Camp ghost town, Red Rock Lakes National Wildlife Refuge.

The Route

Like Scenic Route 4, this route links two urban areas as it passes through a gorgeous river canyon heavily traveled by fun-seekers. And like Missoula, the Bozeman area has undergone tremendous changes through development, especially during the 1990s. One main difference about this drive, however, is that the main route cuts through national forest land rather than private land (like the Bitterroot Valley), so you don't have to go far off the main road to find trailheads into the forest and **Lee Metcalf Wilderness.** The road is narrow and heavily used, so please use caution when pulling over.

West Yellowstone

West Yellowstone, as the name suggests, is the western gateway to Yellowstone National Park and quite the tourist town year-round. In summer it welcomes campers, hikers, and vacationers coming to see our nation's first national park. In

Gallatin Canyon

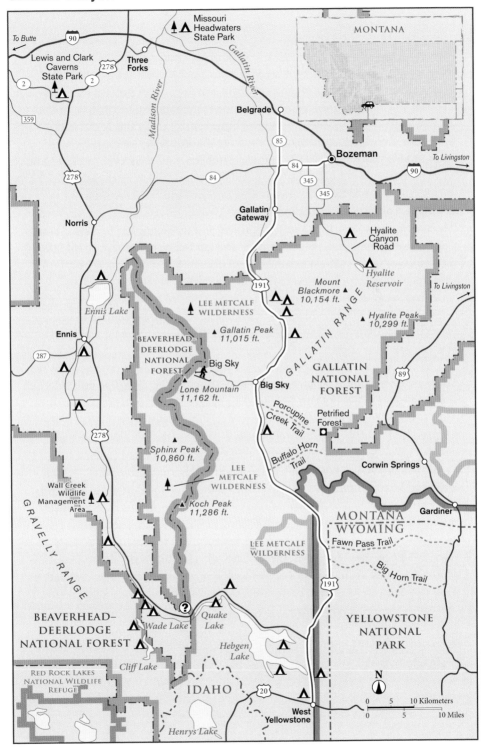

To Butte

90

Lewis and Clark
Caverns
State Park

278

Three
Forks

Missouri
Headwaters
State Park

MONTANA

Gallatin River

2

2

359

Madison River

278

84

Norris

Belgrade

85

Bozeman

To Livingston

84

345

90

345

Gallatin
Gateway

Hyalite
Canyon
Road

191

Hyalite
Reservoir

To Livingston

Ennis Lake

LEE METCALF
WILDERNESS

Mount
Blackmore ▲
10,154 ft.

GALLATIN RANGE

Hyalite Peak
10,299 ft.

Ennis

287

BEAVERHEAD-
DEERLODGE
NATIONAL
FOREST

▲ Gallatin Peak
11,015 ft.

Big Sky

Lone Mountain
11,162 ft.

Big Sky

GALLATIN
NATIONAL
FOREST

89

278

▲ Sphinx Peak
10,860 ft.

Porcupine
Creek Trail

Petrified
Forest

Buffalo Horn
Trail

Corwin Springs

LEE
METCALF
WILDERNESS

Wall Creek
Wildlife
Management
Area

▲ Koch Peak
11,286 ft.

MONTANA
WYOMING

Gardiner

GRAVELLY RANGE

LEE METCALF
WILDERNESS

Fawn Pass Trail

Big Horn Trail

191

BEAVERHEAD–
DEERLODGE
NATIONAL FOREST

?

Wade Lake

Quake
Lake

Hebgen
Lake

YELLOWSTONE
NATIONAL
PARK

RED ROCK LAKES
NATIONAL WILDLIFE
REFUGE

Cliff Lake

IDAHO

20

West
Yellowstone

N

0   5   10 Kilometers
0   5   10 Miles

Henrys Lake

winter it's a haven for snowmobilers and cross-country skiers. Proposed restrictions on snowmobile use in the park have gone back and forth between judges for more than a decade. As this book went to press, the issue was still being decided, so stay tuned. Whether you favor snowmobiles in the park or not, winter in Yellowstone is a must-see for everyone. Be warned that Yellowstone can be crowded well beyond Labor Day, after which most other tourist attractions in the state close down for winter. Although there are significantly fewer tourists, many of West Yellowstone's motels are full into September.

The town is composed mostly of gift shops, cafes, fly-fishing shops, and motels. You'll also find art galleries and an IMAX theater with the neighboring **Grizzly & Wolf Discovery Center** (www.grizzlydiscoveryctr.com). The latter has fenced enclosures for grizzly bears and wolves and is a refuge for "problem" bears that have gotten into trouble with people. Though I'm no fan of captive wildlife, the Discovery Center should be applauded for teaching people how to keep bears wild and free in their own habitat. Keep in mind these were once "good" bears gone "bad" as a result of human behavior, which has led bears to raid homes and tent camps—among other things—in search of improperly stored food or garbage. Please use common sense and never feed wildlife. Stop by the center and learn how you can keep wildlife wild.

At the old train depot, now the Yellowstone Historic Center (www.yellowstonehistoriccenter.org), exhibits of mountain men, Native American artifacts, wildlife dioramas, and the US Cavalry might interest you. The Rendezvous cross-country ski races pull in visitors in March. And, if snowmobiles are in favor, the third weekend in March is abuzz with folks coming for the annual World Snowmobile Expo, which holds races, music, entertainment, food, and exhibits.

Of course West Yellowstone's biggest attraction—and raison d'être—is **Yellowstone National Park** (www.nps.gov/yell/index.htm), established in 1872. It is interesting to note that Yellowstone's geyser activity takes place in a still-hot volcanic basin. In what is now the center portion of the park, a classic volcanic cone once loomed, having erupted in a big way several times in the last few million years. Following these eruptions, the volcano collapsed into itself, leaving a giant depression called a caldera. Most of Yellowstone's geysers, hot springs, and hot pools lie within the perimeter of this caldera. There is some evidence that these "hot spots" may be getting hotter. Geologists believe that the Yellowstone volcano has erupted with the force of a giant nuclear arsenal about every 600,000 years. Interestingly, the last time Yellowstone blew was about 600,000 years ago—give or take a few thousand years.

West Yellowstone to Gallatin Gateway

After you've exhausted all you want to see in West Yellowstone, head north on US 191. The road out of town is long, wide, and straight as a runway. Shortly after passing the turnoff for US 287 (and Scenic Route 9), the road begins to climb hills and wind a bit, tracing the path of Grayling Creek, which flows from Yellowstone's high peaks. After several miles, the road dips back into the very western edge of Yellowstone Park. There are places to pull over and fish the streams here, but you must have a Yellowstone National Park fishing permit. No permits are needed to hike the sage-covered hills. The surrounding dead trees you see were the cause of a double whammy—a mass tree disease and some spectacular fires that burned in 1988, in all charring 1.4 million acres of Yellowstone Park.

But the greenery has returned in this fire-prone and fire-dependent ecosystem. Fires can bring new life to forests by burning older trees, deadwood, and shrubs that are not as nutritious for wildlife as younger plants. Fires release nutrients back to the soil, which are stored in forest litter (dead branches, leaves, cones, conifer needles, and grasses). Some trees, such as older lodgepole pines, need fire to rid themselves of diseases and provide a seedbed for new and vigorous pines to grow. Lodgepole pine has serotinous cones, which means they need intense heat, either from hot sun or fire, to open the cones and release their seeds.

Cottonwoods and willows along the creek bottoms here are brilliant gold in autumn. The Madison Range and Taylor Peaks lie to the west of the highway. Due to moving faults along the edges of the mountains, the Madisons continue to rise. The same is true of the Gallatin Range on the east side of the highway.

Bighorn Pass and Fawn Pass Trails offer pleasant hiking in a mostly open landscape on the east (Yellowstone Park side) of the road. Keep your eyes open for hot springs along these trails if you feel like a soak. To the north you'll find Tepee Creek and Buffalo Horn Creek trailheads, which will take you into a section of the Gallatin's petrified forest. About 50 million years ago lava coated these mountains, along with ash and mudflows, to bury trees and other vegetation. Some of the trees were so well preserved that paleobotanists can identify the tropical and temperate species. The present-day cooler-weather species were carried down from higher elevations as the mudflows destroyed everything in their paths. If you hike in the area, please don't remove any petrified wood; leave it for others to enjoy. For trail information refer to a Gallatin National Forest map.

Following the main scenic drive, the road begins a winding route along the Gallatin River just before you leave this little piece of Yellowstone Park. Winter travel on this highway can be extremely hazardous, so please use caution. Even when the roads are dry, negotiating the tight curves is easily underestimated. Truck traffic can frighten the best of drivers here. Also, watch for wildlife,

especially bison, which occasionally wander to this part of the park during winter months.

As you leave the park boundaries and enter **Gallatin Canyon,** you'll find many wonderful hiking trails that take off from US 191. Look for turnoffs to Taylor Fork and Porcupine Wildlife Management Area. If you're in search of a wildlife experience, watch for the elk, deer, moose, and grizzly bears that frequent these areas. Please be mindful of wildlife by keeping your distance and minimizing any disturbance. You can fish just about anywhere along the Gallatin River, and numerous pullouts offer places to park. There are several designated camping sites as well. This is bear country, however, so be sure to store all food in airtight containers in your vehicle overnight. If you fancy a tumble in the river rapids, watch for signs directing you to rafting outfitters along the way.

Between Buffalo Horn Creek and Buck Creek, the canyon closes in to steep rocky cliffs on both sides of the road before opening up again north of Buck Creek all the way to **Big Sky,** a destination ski resort town that also offers plenty of summer sports like hiking, mountain biking, fishing, rafting, and golf. There are places to rent mountain bikes and other outdoor toys if you don't have your own. At the ski hill (www.bigskyresort.com) you can buy a ticket to ride the gondola up Lone Mountain for a head start on hikes along the ridge and scenic views of the Gallatin and Madison mountain ranges. Some of the several guest ranches at and around Big Sky allow drop-in visitors for trail rides, and their restaurants are open to the public.

North of Big Sky the narrow US 191 bends and turns recklessly until you get to Spanish Creek. Several more hiking trails cut through the steep ridges on both sides of the highway. Most of the trails on the east side in the Gallatin Range go up over the divide and into the Paradise Valley (see Scenic Route 11). From Spanish Creek the drive into Bozeman is mostly straight, and the road widens out to much safer dimensions. You will pass through flat, open range not far from urban sprawl. At Gallatin Gateway stop at the Gallatin Gateway Inn (www.gallatingatewayinn.com), along the highway. Once a stop on the Milwaukee Road (Chicago, Milwaukee, St. Paul and Pacific Railroad) train route, the inn has been refurbished. Its Spanish-style architecture and painted cathedral ceilings are impressive, and the food is also worth stopping for.

The Gallatin River was named for President Jefferson's Secretary of the Treasury, who had refused to finance the Lewis & Clark Expedition. ANDREA PIPP

Above, US 191 follows the sinuous course of the Gallatin River canyon. Andrea Pipp
Below, House Rock on the Gallatin River provides big rapids for boaters in spring.
Andrea Pipp

Gallatin Gateway to Norris

About 5 miles north of Gallatin Gateway, just before you reach Four Corners intersection, where US 191 crosses Highway 84, **Bozeman Hot Springs** is great for a pleasant soak—especially after a day of play at Big Sky or floating the Gallatin River. From Four Corners head east on Highway 84 into Bozeman or, alternately, take Highway 84 west, which is a cutoff to Norris (and Scenic Route 9), a nice little drive that winds over hills and along part of the Madison River. The Madison is a popular place on weekends during summer for floaters, swimmers, and fly fishers. You will reach the river at Black's Ford about 18 miles west of Four Corners. The Madison River here is gentle and warm enough to swim comfortably.

If you continue along the Madison, you will find another recreation area. At Bear Trap Road head south along a dirt track on the east side of the river. The large campground at the Bear Trap turnoff is on flat, arid ground and no longer maintains services. Bear Trap National Recreation Trail is 9 miles long into the canyon. Beyond Bear Trap, Highway 84 crosses the Madison River and snakes along the river's course for a few more miles before following a small creek cutting through low, red bluffs. At Norris you can pick up Scenic Route 9 or turn around and head back to Bozeman.

Gallatin Gateway to Bozeman

From US 191, if you turn east at Highway 84, you will follow a straight road right into Bozeman. Like Missoula, Bozeman is a college town with plenty to see and do. You can enjoy concerts, lectures, film festivals, art galleries, gift shops, and good food year-round. Visit the **Montana State University** campus, which houses the **Museum of the Rockies** (www.museumoftherockies.org). This is part of Montana's Dinosaur Trail (www.mtdinotrail.org). The museum is an affiliate of the Smithsonian Institution as well as a federal repository for one of the most spectacular paleontology collections in North America. This intriguing museum is the home of rare dinosaur eggs and a nest, part of the first North American discovery of such paleontological finds dug up near Choteau, Montana (see Scenic Route 22). The museum has a wonderful display of dinosaur bones and eggs, complete with fossilized embryos. The museum has additional exhibits, including bits and pieces of a *Tyrannosaurus rex,* pioneer and Native American artifacts, Western art, and photographs. The planetarium at the museum runs several different sky and laser shows throughout the year. In addition, there's a living history farm showcasing the homesteading era (Memorial Day to Labor Day). In a similar vein, the Gallatin Pioneer Museum (www.pioneermuseum.org) offers a glimpse into the lives of Montana's European settlers year-round.

Be sure to visit the **American Computer Museum** (www.compustory.com/index.html), a unique and impressive collection of those machines that make you wonder how you ever lived without them. They also display an interesting collection of machinery throughout the ages (computers of sorts in their day). During summer catch an outdoor performance of Shakespeare in the Park or attend the Sweet Pea Festival, which features music, dance, food, sports events, and artisans selling their beautiful craft work.

The mountains surrounding Bozeman offer great hiking to panoramic vistas, canyons, scenic lakes, and waterfalls. You might want to drive up to either Hyalite Reservoir south of town or Bridger Canyon north of town. Both offer hiking and recreation around high mountain lakes. You can get to Hyalite Canyon (named for a translucent mineral) via South 19th Street, heading about 7 miles out of town to Hyalite Canyon Road. Take this road for 10 miles to the reservoir. Check with the Gallatin National Forest for details about recreational activities.

Beyond Hyalite Reservoir, the East Fork of Hyalite Road will take you to the **Palisade Falls Trail.** This unique area is specially designed for people with disabilities. Scan the cliff walls and rocky slopes for nesting golden eagles, pikas, and marmots.

To access Bridger Canyon, head northeast from Bozeman on Bridger Drive. You'll find plenty of hiking along this road and downhill skiing at Bridger Bowl ski area (http://bridgerbowl.com/) from about November through April. Check a Gallatin National Forest map for directions to Fairy Lake and accompanying trailheads. Hardy hikers will enjoy climbing to the top of Sacagawea Peak. You may even run into some inquisitive mountain goats.

From Bozeman you can head west on I-90 to pick up Scenic Route 9 or go east toward Livingston to pick up Scenic Routes 11 and 23.

11

Paradise Valley

Livingston to Gardiner

General description: A 55-mile drive through the well-named Paradise Valley, coursing along the Yellowstone River from Livingston to Gardiner and featuring some of Montana's highest peaks.

Special attractions: Park County Rodeo, Chico Hot Springs, Yellowstone National Park; galleries, shopping, museums, county fairs, concerts, fishing, floating, hiking, backpacking, wildlife viewing.

Location: Southwest Montana from Livingston to Gardiner at the North Entrance to Yellowstone National Park.

Drive route number: US 89.

Travel season: Year-round. Snow, ice, and strong local winds can make winter driving hazardous.

Camping: Campgrounds in Yellowstone fill up quickly during summer and well into September. There are Forest Service campgrounds at Pine Creek and Mill Creek and undeveloped camping places elsewhere in Gallatin National Forest. Several RV parks and private guest ranches are found throughout the valley.

Services: Full services in Livingston and Gardiner. Emigrant has a store and gas station, and nearby Chico Hot Springs has camping, lodging, and food.

Nearby attractions: Bozeman, Gallatin National Forest, Dome Mountain Wildlife Management Area, Jardine ghost town, Montana Rockies Rail Tours.

The Route

Montana's Paradise Valley has long been a mecca for movie stars, rock stars, media stars, and other monied folk seeking a place to spend it. But don't let that put you off. You won't find many boutique strip malls á la Beverly Hills to satisfy the cravings of the rich and famous. Most who fit that category seem to come here to escape and would rather blend in with Ma and Pa at the county fair or just hide away on their ranches undisturbed. You'll know why when you drive down this front walkway to Yellowstone National Park. With Gallatin National Forest on both sides of the road, there are plenty of opportunities to explore on foot or mountain bike. I recommend some awesome side trips into Montana's highest mountain range, east of the highway. Take a Gallatin National Forest map along and discover some on your own.

Livingston

Begin your drive with a visit to **Livingston,** an attractive Old West town and one of the trendiest of the route, with many gift shops, art galleries, cafes, and

Paradise Valley

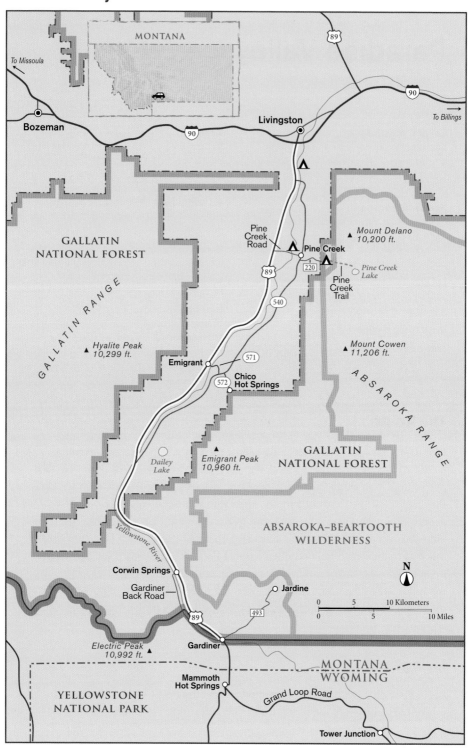

bookstores. The town grew up on both sides of the track in 1882 and was named for Crawford Livingston, once director of the Northern Pacific Railroad. During the neo-pioneer age of the 1990s, people streamed into Livingston, forcing long-time residents to grapple with growth issues affecting both social and environmental quality.

Nevertheless, Livingston is a fun place with many year-round events, including theater, art shows, and music festivals. The area's annual **Livingston Roundup Rodeo** July 2–4 draws top cowboys and cowgirls from all over the country to compete for cash prizes. If you prefer fish to horses, the town hosts the headquarters of the International Fly Fishing Center, offering lessons in fly tying and casting. It has exhibits of antique fishing paraphernalia and live coldwater stream aquariums.

The **Yellowstone Gateway Museum of Park County** (www.livingston museums.org/pcm/home.htm) is open year-round and features rocks and minerals, pioneer artifacts, archaeological finds, and displays of **Yellowstone National Park**'s early explorers. The museum has an original Yellowstone stagecoach, a caboose from the 1890s, and a railroad room. Museum staff have also re-created a Shoshone bison kill site from an actual one near here in use for 500 years until about 1700. The **Livingston Depot Center,** open Memorial Day to Labor Day (www.livingstonmuseums.org/depot), is a former passenger depot for the Northern Pacific Railroad and now a museum with changing exhibits. The building is on the National Register of Historic Places, as are 436 other structures in town, including private homes and downtown businesses. There's also the Natural History Exhibit Hall, featuring rotating exhibits of some incredible fossils and bones.

Calamity Jane first strolled into Livingston in the 1880s and from then on made the town her occasional watering hole. Her exploits were detailed in early newspaper accounts, and reporters must have had fun tracing her path through various saloons. In June 1901 the *Livingston Post* noted the following of the somewhat infamous woman:

> She reports having had great success in "hot airing" the tourists who are making park trips [Yellowstone], and says that if she could only hold onto the money she is making she would be a bloomin' millionaire in a short time. Unfortunately, however, she is unable to keep the proceeds of her work in this wet weather, when keeping the outside dry does no good unless the inside is kept in exactly a reverse condition.

Livingston to Emigrant

From Livingston take US 89 south, following the Yellowstone River toward its source. You can see the river as you drive for most of the way. Just south of town you enter the wide Paradise Valley, hemmed by the Absaroka (pronounced *ab-SOR-kee*) Range to the east and the Gallatin Range to the west. The Absaroka Mountains are high, steep, and sharply defined. Several trails head into the mountains and the **Absaroka-Beartooth Wilderness Area,** where hikers must be prepared for all kinds of weather conditions. Because of its easy access to a set of waterfalls, Pine Creek is the most popular trail. To get to the trailhead, turn east onto Pine Creek Road (CR 540) about 11 miles south of Livingston. When you reach the little community of Pine Creek, turn south onto East River Road and make a left onto FR 202, following signs east to the Pine Creek campground. The falls are only 1 mile from the parking lot. Mill Creek, 7.5 miles south of Pine Creek, has many additional trails that lead to several small lakes within the Absaroka-Beartooth.

Back on the main road, US 89 cuts through arid, scrubby plains to the west; beyond lie the Gallatin Mountains. On the east side of the valley, the Absarokas spring seemingly from the river's edge. As ancient volcanoes, these mountains have seen many eruptions and mudflows, which account for the tons of petrified trees in the southern portion of the range. Today the Paradise Valley supports ranches and ranchettes, including guest lodges that cater to anglers trying their hand at the meandering Yellowstone River. You can find several access points for fishing and floating, too, many of which are well marked. At Point of Rocks fishing access, look for rounded hills west of the highway. These hills were vents for volcanoes that erupted some 50 million years ago.

The valley was also a paradise for miners. Gold was discovered in Emigrant Gulch, east of the modern community of Emigrant, near **Chico Hot Springs.** Miners bathed in the natural hot springs, and soon a little town developed around them. The young town of Chico had a store, meat market, hotel, schoolhouse, five dozen cabins, and a blacksmith shop. Now Chico Hot Springs (www.chico hotsprings.com) serves a slightly different clientele, with clean, developed pools and quaint hotel rooms. Two small restaurants and a saloon serve the inn, and a few log cabins, cottages, and houses are for rent as well. The resort offers horseback riding in summer and dog sledding and cross-country skiing in winter. You can also rent mountain bikes and skis. And when you're done with all that recreating, lie back and get a massage at the spa.

The Absaroka Mountains flank the east side of Paradise Valley. Donnie Sexton

The Yellowstone River courses through the aptly named Paradise Valley. DONNIE SEXTON

Emigrant to Gardiner

South of Emigrant beyond Big Creek, US 89 makes a left-hand curve into Yankee Jim Canyon, named for James George, a gold prospector in the mid-1800s who built a toll road through here. Yankee Jim was renowned for his cantankerous nature and tall tales, as author Rudyard Kipling once noted: "Yankee Jim saw every one of my tales and went fifty better on the spot. He dealt in bears and Indians—never less than twenty of each." The canyon is narrow for just a few miles before the landscape reveals high plateaus to the west on the other side of the river. A stretch of challenging rapids through Yankee Jim Canyon makes a good run for experienced rafters.

On its way into Gardiner the road winds a little more, with spruce and Douglas fir scattered on the surrounding hillsides. Through this section of US 89, watch for wildlife crossing the road. The **Corwin Springs** area is winter range for the largest group of hoofed animals in the country. Antelope (October), bighorn sheep and mule deer (November and December), and elk (January) move through from the highlands of Yellowstone National Park. Thousands of elk from the northern herd winter in the area. From December through April you may see some of them along the base of Cinnabar Mountain. To view wildlife, cross the river on the bridge at Corwin Springs, turn left, and head south on the gravel Gardiner Back Road. During winter, watch for bald eagles along the river. It's about 8 miles to Gardiner.

You may also see some of the wintering animals from the main highway at a turnout near **Devil's Slide.** The "slide" is made of sedimentary deposits, about 200 million years old. Some geologists speculate from its red color that the Earth's atmosphere may have had more oxygen during the Triassic period, when the rocks were formed. Oxygen reacts with iron to create the red pigment and devilish color.

When you reach Gardiner by way of the main highway or the back road, take a side trip on the gravel road that leads northeast to Jardine. More wildlife winter range is scattered throughout the hills near what was once the **Jardine** mine and ghost town. Arsenic was mined here for the US government during World War II.

Gardiner was named for an early-day trapper, Johnston Gardiner, who spent much of his time along the upper tributaries of the Yellowstone River. Crow Indians hunted here, too, and conflicts with Gardiner's first settlers were frequent. The new town had no sawmill, and pioneers lived in tents or hand-hewn log shacks. By 1883 Gardiner bustled with a half dozen restaurants, 5 stores, a couple of fruit stands and barbershops, 21 saloons, and 4 brothels—all to serve its 200 residents.

Today Gardiner is surprisingly busy year-round, the main attraction being the northern entrance to Yellowstone National Park through Teddy Roosevelt Arch. The town's somewhat drab character makes it unique among the so-called gateway towns of national parks. Gift shops sell "genuine" Indian trinkets made in Taiwan. Floaters and anglers have found an outpost in Gardiner as well. It is the nearest town to Cooke City on the eastern border of the park, and teenagers endure long bus rides to go to high school in Gardiner during winter. Throughout the summer Gardiner hosts numerous events, including a music festival, triathlon, rodeo, and local celebrations. Check with the Gardiner Chamber of Commerce (see For More Information).

A few miles inside the Yellowstone National Park (www.nps.gov/yell/index .htm) boundary you'll find the town of **Mammoth Hot Springs,** park headquarters. The Horace Albright Visitor Center has information about park events and exhibits of natural and human history in the park, as well as photographs of Yellowstone taken during the 1850s Hayden Expedition by W. H. Jackson. These pictures are magnificent, and they were largely responsible for convincing the government to preserve Yellowstone as a park. From Mammoth and its giant hot springs terrace, you can take the Lamar Valley Road through the stunning Lamar Valley to pick up Scenic Route 13. Or during summer you can drive through the park to West Yellowstone and pick up Scenic Routes 9 and 10.

12

Boulder River Road

Big Timber to Box Canyon

General description: A 50-mile route (one way) tracing the Boulder River upstream from Big Timber toward the heart of the Absaroka-Beartooth Mountains.

Special attractions: Absaroka-Beartooth Wilderness; waterfalls; fishing, hiking, camping, backpacking, wildlife viewing.

Location: South-central Montana from Big Timber south to the Absaroka-Beartooth Mountains.

Drive route number: CR 298 (Boulder River Road).

Travel season: In winter the road is maintained to the national forest boundary; beyond that, it is open as weather permits. Weekday traffic can be heavy during hunting season.

Camping: There is one campground without water near McLeod. There are also several Forest Service campgrounds farther into the mountains.

Services: Full services in Big Timber; food in McLeod.

Nearby attractions: Big Timber Water Slide, Crazy Mountain Museum, Greycliff Prairie Dog Town, Lewis and Clark Native Plant Garden, Livingston.

The Route

This scenic drive winds its way up the Boulder River drainage through pastoral ranchland as it heads toward the looming wall of the Beartooth Mountains. It's a one-way-in, one-way-out drive and slow going and rough in some places the farther south you go from McLeod. Despite the bumps, the drive is worth your effort if your vehicle can handle it, taking you right to the edge of the Absaroka-Beartooth Wilderness. You'll find several wilderness access trails, campgrounds, and plenty of chances to fish. The end of the road, at Box Canyon, is a well-used trailhead for horse packers.

When this book went to press, the road was paved to Natural Bridge State Park (about 23 miles from Big Timber). Beyond that, extensive flood damage in 2011 has made for rough driving, though the road was passable. Because the road meanders between two counties, maintenance has been an issue, although this could be resolved in coming years. Until then officials recommend 4-wheel-drive vehicles only—and no trailers—beyond Natural Bridge to Box Canyon. Another road from Box Canyon continues for 7 more miles to the wilderness boundary, but only ORVs should attempt it. For up-to-date road information, contact Counties Park and Sweet Grass (see For More Information).

Boulder River Road

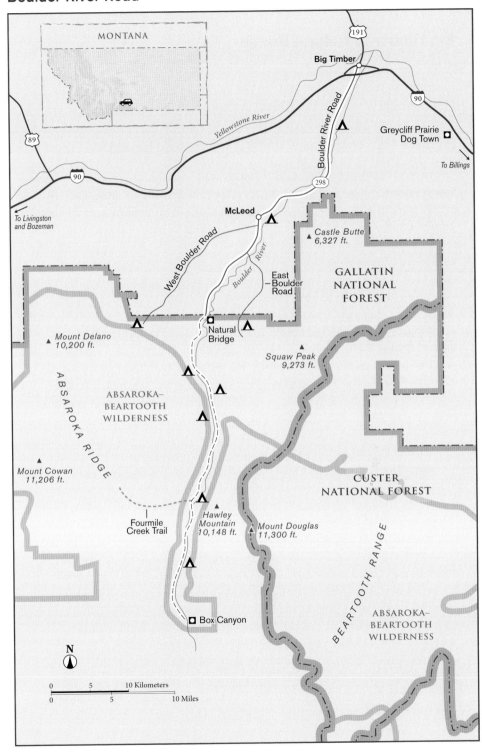

MONTANA

191

Big Timber

Yellowstone River

89

90

To Billings

Boulder River Road

298

To Livingston
and Bozeman

McLeod

Castle Butte
6,327 ft.

Greycliff Prairie
Dog Town

West Boulder Road

Boulder River

East
—Boulder
Road

GALLATIN
NATIONAL
FOREST

Mount Delano
10,200 ft.

Natural
Bridge

Squaw Peak
9,273 ft.

ABSAROKA–
BEARTOOTH
WILDERNESS

ABSAROKA RIDGE

Mount Cowan
11,206 ft.

CUSTER
NATIONAL FOREST

Fourmile
Creek Trail

Hawley
Mountain
10,148 ft.

Mount Douglas
11,300 ft.

BEARTOOTH RANGE

ABSAROKA–
BEARTOOTH
WILDERNESS

Box Canyon

N

0   5   10 Kilometers
0   5   10 Miles

Big Timber to Natural Bridge

Begin your drive in the small sheep and cattle town of Big Timber (see Scenic Route 24), west of Livingston on I-90. Follow the signs for CR 298 (Boulder River Road) through downtown Big Timber, heading south. The first 23 miles of the road are paved and pass through private and state range. There are several fishing access sites and one or two campgrounds between Big Timber and the small community of McLeod.

Near McLeod you can turn off the main road and take side trips up either the East Fork or the West Fork of the Boulder River. Both roads are gravel and cross private land, so heed all No Trespassing signs. The West Boulder road comes to a dead end after about 15 miles (or you can carry on Swingley Road to I-90). At the end of the West Boulder Road, you'll find a trailhead and a campground just outside the **Absaroka-Beartooth Wilderness** boundary. The East Boulder road travels upstream for about 4 miles before branching in a Y. Both options take you into the mountains and to hiking trails. Again, please respect private property rights.

If you decide to follow the main Boulder River Road instead, pull over at the **Natural Bridge Falls** interpretive site for a gander at what was once a natural arch over the river. Unfortunately, the bridge has collapsed, but the limestone formation under the narrow river canyon here is still cool to see. The roiling Boulder River flows over it during high water (usually in spring), tumbling over the rock and plunging 80 feet to a large pool and riverbed below. During drier periods, the river seems to disappear, since the water goes underneath the limestone and blows out a hole in the cliff as a waterfall. Signs along a short interpretive trail explain how this interesting gorge was formed; another, longer trail leads across the river. When the limestone riverbed is dry, you can look for fossils in the calcite. Paths along the river are paved. If you want to take off into the hills, follow Green Mountain Trail 94; it's only about 5.5 miles from Natural Bridge to Green Mountain, and the trail is moderately difficult.

Back on the main scenic drive, the Boulder River Road south of Natural Bridge Falls becomes rough and narrow in places. Having suffered from flood damage in 2011, local officials recommend 4-wheel-drive vehicles only beyond this point until the road can be fixed. Leaving the open range behind, you enter a narrower, almost pinched, canyon. Look to the west to see a band of rock called Coal Mine Rim, running across the bluff like a jeweled necklace.

There are a half dozen campgrounds along the route, some of which are in grizzly habitat. Please follow the food storage instructions posted at each campground to avoid a tragic bear encounter. The road also passes several trailheads, most marked with small signs depicting a hiker. This is steep country, so hiking here isn't for the faint of breath. At Fourmile Guard Station you can take a 15-mile loop trail up and around 9,000-foot-high Carbonate Mountain and come out near Hick's Park Campground, about 4 miles farther up the road.

Just beyond the Fourmile area, the road becomes particularly bumpy and tight. An early hunting season (late September) in the wilderness area brings out many horse-packing hunters, making some weekday travel busy—and dusty. If you plan to hike during the hunting season, be sure to stay on well-used trails, wear hunter-orange clothing of some type, and keep unleashed dogs within sight and under your voice command. It's not a bad idea to make your pets wear orange too.

Box Canyon, near the end of the road, has a large parking lot to accommodate the packhorse trains that use this area frequently. From here a main trail continues into the wilderness. You can choose from several trails, some of which lead into the northern reaches of Yellowstone National Park. About an hour of hiking from Box Canyon will take you to the ruins of an old mining camp, Independence. Refer to a Gallatin National Forest map for more information.

Retrace your route back to Big Timber, watching for whitetail deer in the lower meadows. On your way back, you may want to stop at the Road Kill Cafe just north of McLeod. The bar and restaurant's motto: "From your grille to ours."

About 7 miles east of Big Timber, along I-90, visit the **Greycliff Prairie Dog Town State Park** for an interesting side trip. You can take a quick drive or walk through the short-grass prairie where interpretive signs teach you all about black-tailed prairie dogs. You might even see a hawk or golden eagle swipe one of the furry creatures from its mound. If you're into birding, watch for western bluebirds, meadowlarks, and vesper sparrows flitting about the grassland.

From Big Timber you can take Scenic Route 24 north or head west to Livingston and pick up Scenic Routes 11 and 23.

13

Beartooth Highway

Silver Gate to Red Lodge

General description: A 70-mile drive that takes you near alpine meadows and glacial lakes at the top of the world, providing access to Montana's highest terrain.

Special attractions: Silver Gate, Cooke City, Red Lodge, Beartooth Nature Center, Carbon County Museum; alpine lakes and tundra; canoeing, fishing, camping, hiking, backpacking, wildlife viewing.

Location: South-central Montana at the northeast gate to Yellowstone National Park in Silver Gate, dipping into a portion of Wyoming, climbing a mountain plateau, and dropping into Red Lodge.

Drive route number: US 212 (Beartooth Highway).

Travel season: Late spring or early summer until snow season. The lower sections of road are well used by snowmobilers in winter. Extreme weather can strike any time of year, making travel hazardous. Check local forecasts before setting out.

Camping: There are 3 Forest Service campgrounds just east of Cooke City and 5 campgrounds in Shoshone National Forest in Wyoming. Seven more campgrounds can be found on the other side of the plateau at Rock Creek, just south of Red Lodge.

Services: Full services at Cooke City and Red Lodge. Most services in Silver Gate. Limited services at Top of the World Store.

Nearby attractions: Custer National Forest, Gallatin National Forest, Red Lodge Mountain Ski Area, Yellowstone National Park.

The Route

Like Going-to-the-Sun Highway in Glacier National Park (Scenic Route 2), this route is one of Montana's most dramatic for big mountain scenery and endless plateaus, the kind you see in SUV commercials. So, unless you are an avid backpacker, this is probably your best chance to experience Montana's most incredible alpine scenery. Alpine meadows, ice-cold glacial lakes, boulder-strewn plateaus, groves of shimmering aspen, and spruce and fir forests make up the Beartooth Plateau's habitat. It really is another world, and to truly experience it you must get out of the car as often as possible. *Be warned about the weather:* It can snow any time of year here, and during bad storms, portions of the road may be closed. Keep an eye on the skies and bring warm clothes and extra food and water just in case.

The Beartooth Highway was conceived in 1919 by J. F. Siegfriedt, a Red Lodge doctor, as a way to save the dying mining towns the route connects. He believed that if a road were built through some of the most amazing landscape of the Beartooth Plateau, the mining towns could survive on tourist dollars. Construction began in 1931, and the road was completed in 1936, costing $2.5 million. Dr. Siegfriedt's foresight has since proved correct.

Beartooth Highway

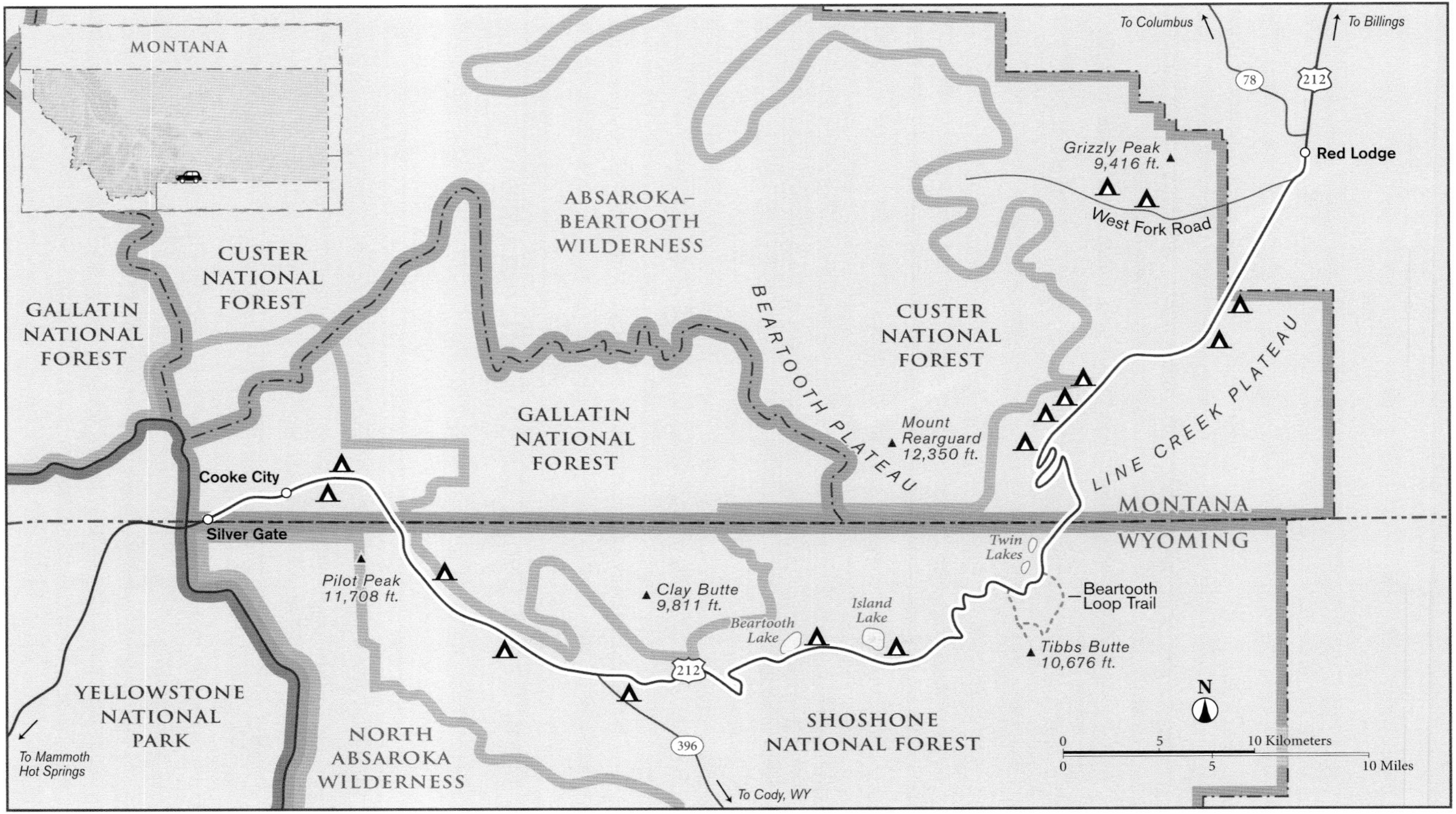

The Beartooth Scenic Byway is the highest drivable road in Montana. MICHAEL LYNCH

If you are coming from Scenic Routes 9, 10, or 11, the quickest way to get to the Beartooth Highway is to go through the Lamar Valley of Yellowstone Park, a wonderful scenic drive in itself.

Silver Gate & Cooke City to Beartooth Lake

Begin this scenic drive along the Beartooth Highway (US 212) from the northeast entrance of Yellowstone National Park in the tiny mining towns of Silver Gate and Cooke City. The smaller of the two, **Silver Gate** is less developed, but you will find food and lodging here. Both communities are sandwiched between narrow canyons whose rock walls stand guard. The only way through by wheeled vehicle is via Wyoming. Densely forested hills below the granite bluffs slope to the towns' borders. In the recent past, area forest fires have burned frighteningly close to homes and businesses here. You can see how near the fires raged from the standing dead trees that serve as an eerie reminder that fires are part of Montana's forest ecosystem.

Like so many western Montana towns, **Cooke City** was built to serve mining prospectors in the 1870s. Named for Jay Cooke, who had nearby claims, the little town is about 3 or 4 blocks long with a few cafes, motels, gift shops, and bars.

You'll also find an art gallery and bike shop, as well as several outfitters who can guide you on an outdoor sport of your choice. At its peak the town had 13 saloons and 135 log cabins. If you do decide to camp, you have a choice of 3 designated campgrounds just east of town. Be sure to have a warm sleeping bag, since the elevation here is close to 8,000 feet; temperatures plummet along with—and as quickly as—the sun.

From Cooke City head east on US 212, climbing and winding your way up to the **Beartooth Plateau.** Much of the drive passes through Wyoming, so remember, if you plan to wet a line, Wyoming fishing regulations differ from Montana. Note also that you are about to enter superb grizzly bear habitat. Please mind campground and trail signs regarding proper storage of food and use bear avoidance techniques if you plan to camp or hike anywhere along the way. Don't let careless behavior be your last act on Earth or cause the death of an awesome creature (both you and a bear).

Continue up US 212 through the spruce and fir forest and watch for wildlife on the road. Listen to the rustle of shimmering groves of quaking aspen along the roadside. In late summer they turn a brilliant gold, as enticing as the ore that drew early settlers to the area. A few ranches in the meadows below the road have open livestock range, so watch for cattle wandering across your path. As you drive atop this giant rock reef, pockmarked by hundreds of lakes and ripped through with shards of granite outcrops, you can't help but marvel at its flat-topped geology. The schist and gneiss that make up portions of the Beartooths are more than 3 billion years old—some of the world's oldest known formations. And supposedly the plateau is the largest single expanse of relatively flat land above 10,000 feet in the United States.

Imagine cutting a piece of cake in the center of a pan and lifting it out with a spatula. The cake has loads of frosting, and as you're lifting, the frosting slides off. The frosting, in this case, was several thousand feet of sedimentary rock. And when you consider that the piece of cake rose more than 11,000 feet into the sky, it's easy to see how some of the frosting could slide off—into Wyoming. That was 50 million years ago, when plenty of volcanoes and earthquakes rocked this continent.

During the ice ages snow piled up thousands of feet deep. Gargantuan sheets of ice slid down the plateau's sides, carving valleys and razor-sharp ridges. Although the last of the granddaddy glaciers melted yesterday, geologically speaking—10,000 years ago—only the top several inches of soil remain unfrozen today. The subsoil is frozen year-round, so water trying to pass through it either freezes or stays on the surface. The surface water flows down even the most trifling of slopes, since it has nowhere else to go. The water brings topsoil with it, filling up basins and over years creating a more level topography.

The Beartooth Plateau is pockmarked with thousands of lakes and ponds. MICHAEL LYNCH

Hugging the steep crests of Mount Wilse and Iceburg Peak is another ancient part of the terrain, **Grasshopper Glacier.** Millions of frozen grasshoppers (locusts, actually) are visible beneath the ice of this snowfield. That particular insect species is believed to have been extinct for more than 200 years. The theory goes that swarms of the locusts flew over the mountain, became chilled, and dropped, eventually freezing in the snow and ice. Sadly, climate change is causing the glacier to recede. In recent years, many of the little carcasses have been exposed and are now decayed. If you want to see it, hardy hikers can take a trail 4-plus miles from Goose Lake (longer depending on how far in you can drive). Check Gallatin or Custer National Forest maps for details.

Wyoming Highway 296, the Chief Joseph Scenic Byway, takes off from US 212 about 14 miles east of Cooke City. You can take this route, heading southeast through an area known as Sunlight Basin to Cody, Wyoming, which houses the splendid Buffalo Bill Museum. Near the WY 296 turnoff, the foreground opens up to sagebrush hills. The bottomlands here are grassy with forested pockets to break up the continuity. A rift of rock to the south of the road juts out from the block of mountain like a bulging vein.

Several scenic turnouts give you the chance to get out and look at the scene behind you. It's well worth the stop to view the spire-like point of 11,313-foot

Index Peak and its neighbor Pilot Peak, piercing 11,708 feet into the sky. **Pilot-Index Overlook** offers almost a 180-degree view of the plateau along its southern border. Just up the road is **Clay Butte Lookout,** where you can expand your view to 360 degrees. Turn off the main road to the north. The Clay Butte road is gated in autumn, but you can still walk up to the lookout if you need to stretch your legs. It's about 2 miles if you follow the road. Shortly after the turnoff to Clay Butte, the Beartooth Highway narrows, winding past massive walls to the north and high cliffs to the south. Use caution as you drive through here.

Beartooth Lake to Red Lodge

Beartooth Lake has a small, forested campground and is the perfect base from which to explore the plateau. If you're passing through, you can take a hiking trail leading northward from the parking lot to hundreds of other small lakes on the plateau. Farther up the road is **Island Lake,** also with a campground and access to the same trail system through the glacier-scoured plateau. The Top of the World Resort (www.topoftheworldresort.com) is on the main highway between the two lakes. Here you can buy food, fuel, and camping supplies and get tourist information. They also have some modest lodging (4 rooms only) and rent outdoor toys like bikes, snowmobiles, fishing equipment, and boats. A small network of gravel roads on the south side of the highway across from Island Lake will take you to other tiny lakes. If you choose to walk around up here, please stick to the trails and spare the alpine habitat. Most alpine plants take decades to develop, growing by the inch and dying by the foot—your foot.

East of Long Lake near the top of Beartooth Pass, look for signs marking the Beartooth Loop Trail. It will take you a few miles in to Losekamp Lake, where you can pick up the **Beartooth Loop National Recreation Trail,** skirting Tibbs Butte through the alpine plateau. The hike is about 10 miles, so plan on at least a half day if you're a moderately experienced hiker. You can access another trailhead for this loop near Gardiner Lake, farther up the road on the other side of the pass.

Continuing on beyond Long Lake, US 212 snakes its way to the top of the pass in loose hairpin loops. Use caution here, since your natural tendency is for your eyes to wander toward the beautiful world around you. At the top of the pass, you're 10,947 feet above sea level and just about to head back into Montana again. The view is unobstructed, and you get a feel for the wide, wild expanse in all directions. Get out and take a stroll through the boulder-strewn meadows, and don't be afraid to express your euphoria of being here; whoop out loud and tread lightly on the fragile ground. In the past, Red Lodge Chamber of Commerce hosted "Snow Bar Day," offering free (nonalcoholic) drinks at the summit on a random day. Unfortunately, they don't do this anymore but maybe someday they'll bring it back.

As you descend toward Red Lodge, the road becomes much steeper and twisty in places. Pull out at **Twin Lakes Overlook** just south of the Montana border. The view here is worth the short walk, and if you haven't already climbed out of your vehicle, this is one of your last opportunities to do so before descending into Rock Creek. Just north of the Montana state line, one last short trail to the east leads to a small lake that lies on the Montana-Wyoming border.

Watch for another big turnout (with restrooms) where you can take a short jaunt along a gravel path to an overlook of the Rock Creek valley. The road makes several hairpin turns from this point on as you near Red Lodge. You'll find a few hiking trails, Forest Service roads, and several campgrounds along the glacier-gouged drainage. The West Fork of Rock Creek Road just south of Red Lodge will take you to Red Lodge Mountain Ski Area and Silver Run Cross-Country Ski Area. In addition, there are a few campgrounds and hiking trails leading to cold, tiny lakes. For a detailed description of **Red Lodge,** refer to Scenic Route 14, which begins here.

14

Red Lodge & Rosebud Country

Red Lodge to Columbus

General description: A 49-mile drive that takes you from the sharp peaks of the Beartooth Mountains into coulees and grassy foothills that in summer smell of sweet, newly mown hay.

Special attractions: Red Lodge Mountain Ski Area, numerous festivals in Red Lodge, art shows, museums, alpine lakes; camping, hiking, skiing, backpacking, fishing, mountain biking.

Location: South-central Montana from Red Lodge to Columbus.

Drive route number: Highway 78.

Travel season: Year-round. Snow and ice conditions make winter travel hazardous.

Camping: There are several campgrounds south of Red Lodge along Rock Creek. You will also find campgrounds on the way to Mystic and East Rosebud Lakes and south of Columbus along the Stillwater River.

Services: Red Lodge, Absarokee, and Columbus have full services. Limited services are available in Fishtail and Dean.

Nearby attractions: Beartooth Scenic Byway, Billings, Cooney Reservoir State Park, Nez Perce Trail, Washoe Ghost town.

The Route

A short drive, this one is a continuation of Scenic Route 13, the Beartooth Highway. If you love small yet lively mountain towns, Red Lodge is your place. There's easily enough here to keep you busy for a few days, both in town and in the surrounding mountains. Side trips to East Rosebud or Mystic Lakes will give you a taste for the razor-like mountains, where civilization will feel like a million miles away. The Red Lodge area has also become popular for out-of-staters escaping their urban travails, so the place is a little more crowded now than in days past. Where once the biggest hangout was the local soda fountain—for the under-21 crowd that is—Red Lodge now boasts more restaurants and designer coffee joints than you can shake a soy latté at. If that's not your style, fear not; just see what you want to see in town and then head for the mountains. Be sure to bring a Custer National Forest map for more information about hiking trails.

Red Lodge

Sitting in a small hollow at 4,650 feet, **Red Lodge** is the quintessential mountain town, with its quaint storefronts, cool climate, and proximity to great hiking, fishing, and skiing. Borrowing from its immigrant heritage, it also has a tiny bit of European flavor. Several different stories relate how Red Lodge got its name. One attributes the name to the Crow Indians, who frequently set up camp here and

Red Lodge & Rosebud Country

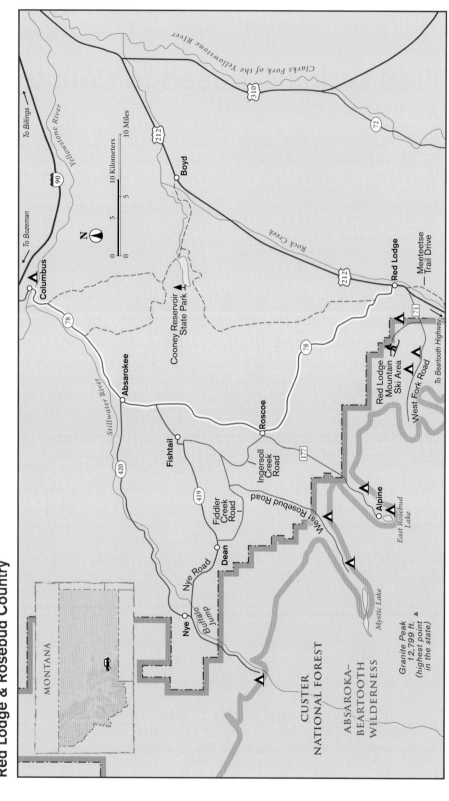

used the local red clay to color their tepees. Another—derogatory—tale says the name refers to the "red men" themselves rather than the color of their tepees. A third story points to a red rock outcrop west of town that, when viewed from several miles away, resembles a Native American-style lodge.

Whatever the name's origin, coal is what brought European immigrants to the valley. By 1911 Red Lodge's population numbered 5,000. A tragic mine disaster in 1943, however, trapped and killed 74 men, closing the coal mine permanently. That incident, coupled with the opening of giant coal mines near Colstrip, Montana, farther east eventually drew many settlers away from Red Lodge. The town's population now hovers around 2,500.

Spend a few hours in town before heading north on the scenic drive. Visit the **Carbon County Historical Society Museum** (www.carboncountyhistory .com), which houses small exhibits about mining, Native Americans, homesteading, and the rodeo. For years two local families, the Greenoughs and Lindermans, have taken top awards at rodeos across the country; the display features their memorabilia. The museum also owns the cabin of John Johnston, better known as "Liver-eatin' Johnston," a late-19th-century mountain man said to have sought vengeance on the men who killed his Native American wife. Once, after killing a man, he supposedly ate his victim's liver. Portrayed by the actor Robert Redford in the 1972 film *Jeremiah Johnson*, Johnston was the first constable of Red Lodge. Children and adults will enjoy **Beartooth Nature Center** in Coal Miner's Memorial Park, housing many wild animals that cannot be returned to the wild. Follow the signs on US 212 north of town toward Billings to find it.

If you're here during July, check out the **Mountain Man Rendezvous** (www .redlodge.com/rendezvous), a weeklong festival of mountain men, Native Americans, traders, bison hunters, whiskey runners, bullwhackers, horse traders, and other assorted characters. Participants dressed in period costume sell handcrafted jewelry, beadwork, knives, buckskin-and-fur costumes, and artwork. Games, music, and dance are also part of the rendezvous.

The **Festival of Nations** (http://redlodgefestivalofnations.com), held in August, celebrates the cultures and traditions of the many Europeans who immigrated to Red Lodge. The festival features food, exhibits, a parade, entertainment, crafts, and dancing of the countries represented—one massive European hoopla. If you happen to miss any of these summer events, Red Lodge Mountain Resort (www.redlodge mountain.com) hosts a winter carnival to help chase away cabin fever and usher in the coming spring. Other Red Lodge events include art and music festivals, rodeos and runs, as well as mountain bike races and competitions. Check the Red Lodge Chamber of Commerce for more details (see For More Information).

Wildlife watchers will want to experience the **Meeteetse Wildlife Trail** southeast of town. On this 19-mile nature drive (4-wheel recommended) through arid sagebrush plains, river bottoms, and rolling foothills, look for moose, deer, prong-horn, beavers, hawks, golden eagles, coyotes, and foxes. If you're really lucky, you may see a badger. You can get out and walk just about anywhere or go for a spin on your mountain bike. For more information ask at the nearby ranger station.

Those with disabilities will find a barrier-free day-use area with trails and fishing docks at **Wild Bill Lake** southwest of Red Lodge. Follow the paved FR 71 (West Fork Road) toward Red Lodge Mountain Ski Area, bypassing the road to the ski hill. Follow signs to Wild Bill Lake, about 3.5 miles farther. There's also good mountain biking up the West Fork Road. Ask at Wacky's Spoke and Hackle or Granite Cyclery about places to mountain bike.

Red Lodge to Columbus

When you've exhausted your options in Red Lodge, follow signs for Highway 78, leading northwest out of town. The sinuous road billows over hilly grain fields and rangeland. The Beartooth Mountains to the southwest seem to rise up out of the plateau as if they had been carelessly set down and forgotten in the middle of the flat farmland. A network of braided willows along the route laces the thousands of stream channels trickling their way from the mountains.

When you reach Roscoe, named for the favorite horse of the town's first postmaster, you can take a bumpy but spectacular side trip to **East Rosebud Lake.** It's easy to miss the turnoff from Roscoe to the west, so watch carefully for the signs. Go through the 1-street town of Roscoe and take the main gravel road south. After about 4 miles you'll come to a fishhook turn. Just after the hook, take a right and follow the gravel road through ranchland dotted with summer homes. The road (FR 177) is windy, bumpy, and rough for several miles, so take it slowly. After 5 or 6 miles from the second turnoff, the road becomes pavement for 6 miles then gravel again for the last leg into East Rosebud Lake. A 4-wheel-drive vehicle is not necessary but it does help.

The road takes you deeper into the Beartooth Mountains as you approach the lake. The surrounding spruce and fir forest makes excellent cover for all kinds of wildlife. Watch for mule deer that could bound in front of you. You'll find a couple of campgrounds along the paved stretch of road, if you'd like to spend more time here. At Jimmy Joe Campground, get out and look for butterflies. Some species seen here include anglewing, blue butterflies, lesser fritillaries, and Weide-meyer's admiral.

Continuing on FR 177, you finally reach East Rosebud Lake sitting in a deep chasm with a small, private community of summer cabins. There is also a public boat launch and campground. Many of the summer homes here were burned to the ground in a severe wildfire that ripped through in autumn 1996. So although the

A side trip up East Rosebud provides more scenic views. MICHAEL LYNCH

community of Aspen looks fairly new, it's been around since the early 1900s. Some cabins were burned to the ground while neighboring cabins weren't touched; such is the nature of fire.

Signs mark the few hiking trails, one of which takes you up and over the peaks to **Mystic Lake,** to the west. You can also drive to Mystic Lake from the West Rosebud Road; refer to a Custer National Forest map for directions. From Mystic Lake only the most experienced mountain hikers should attempt the 12,799-foot summit of Granite Peak, Montana's highest mountain. Moderately skilled hikers can take Trail 15 from East Rosebud Lake to Elk Lake. Along the 3-mile trail you will see a waterfall and awesome views of both lakes.

From East Rosebud Lake you can either retrace your route to Roscoe and take Highway 78 north to Absarokee (pronounced the same as the mountain range, *ab-SOR-kee,* but spelled differently), or take a cutoff gravel road just before you reach Roscoe on the way out. The latter is Ingersoll Creek Road, and it heads northwest through private ranchland. Take this road until you reach the dead end at West Rosebud Road, then turn left. After about 4 miles, the road turns into Fiddler Creek Road and dead-ends at Nye Road. Here you can turn left and head toward the community of Dean and on to **Buffalo Jump Campground** near Nye. It is a primitive campground administered by the state of Montana. There's no water but there are toilets, picnic tables, fire rings, and fishing access to the Stillwater River. You can follow Nye Road east through Fishtail and back to Highway 78 just south of Absarokee.

East Rosebud Lake is cradled in the Beartooth Mountains. AMY FALCIONE

Back on the main scenic drive between Roscoe and Columbus, Highway 78 passes through private ranchland bisected by coulees. If you want to fish, you'll find a few access points along the Stillwater River.

The town of **Columbus** was named for that illustrious explorer rumored to have discovered America. Past residents have changed its name as frequently as a couch potato changes channels—from Eagle's Nest to Sheep Dip (a type of whiskey sold here) to Stillwater, and finally to Columbus. Rocks from a nearby quarry were used to build the state capitol in Helena. Columbus is now a railroad shipping depot for the harvest that comes from ranches in the surrounding region. Stop by the **Museum of the Beartooths** (http://museumofthebeartooths.com) and check out its exhibits on military artifacts, vintage furniture, historic washing machines, and mining (Memorial Day through Labor Day).

From Columbus you can drive east on I-90 to Scenic Route 15, which begins 35 miles south of Billings, or west to Scenic Routes 11 and 12 near Big Timber and Livingston.

15

Crow Country

Pryor to Lodge Grass

General description: A little-traveled route taking you through 70 miles of the Crow Reservation, near Bighorn Canyon and Yellowtail Reservoir.

Special attractions: Chief Plenty Coups State Park, Bighorn Canyon National Recreation Area, Pryor Mountains National Wild Horse Range, Crow Fair; boating, fishing, mountain biking, camping, hiking, backpacking.

Location: Southeastern Montana on the Crow Reservation from Pryor east to I-90 and Lodge Grass.

Drive route numbers: Crow Reservation Road, Bureau of Indian Affairs (BIA) Roads 91, 193, and 73.

Travel season: Year-round. Snow and ice conditions make winter travel hazardous. During severe conditions the road is not maintained.

Camping: Find campgrounds at Bighorn Canyon and north along the Bighorn River. You can camp just south of the reservation boundary in Custer National Forest.

Services: Full services at Fort Smith and Hardin. Limited services at Pryor and at Ok-A-Beh boat ramp.

Nearby attractions: Billings, Little Bighorn Battlefield National Monument, Nez Perce Trail, Pictograph Cave National Historic Landmark, Reno-Benteen Battlefield Memorial.

The Route

Few people venture beyond the main scenic drives that Montana has to offer, unwittingly passing up some great opportunities to explore the state's more remote regions—places that have remained relatively unaltered since forever. This drive introduces you to one such corner of the state, which seems to roll on forever, where coulees run like veins through the pine-covered bumps in the landscape. Multicolored rock formations will catch your eye. Though you won't find a lot of museums, shops, and other entertainment venues to occupy yourself when not behind the wheel, this drive highlights plenty of Montana's natural wonders. So give your senses a break from boutiques and bistros and immerse them in a world where sight, sound, and smell are honed to pre-civilization standards. Your inner primate will love you for it.

As you travel through Crow country, remember that nontribal members must have a permit to hike on tribal lands. Restrictions and permits for fishing on reservation lands also apply. Contact the tribal office in Crow Agency for details.

Crow Country

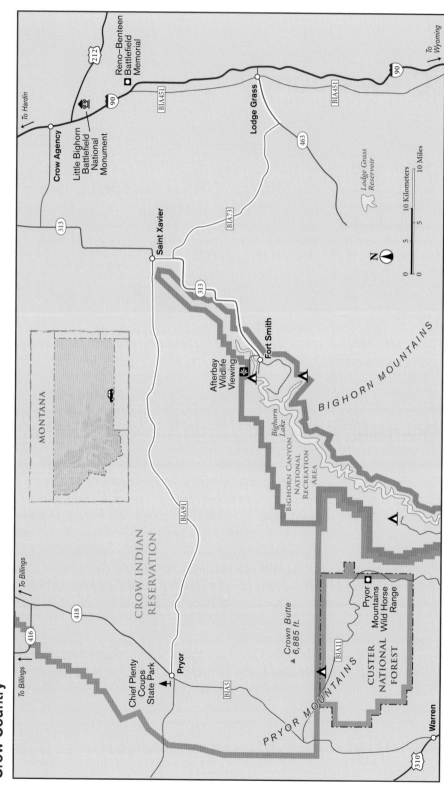

Pryor

Access the Crow Indian Reservation by driving south from Billings (CR 416 and 418) to **Chief Plenty Coups State Park** just west of Pryor. The Crow Indians honor Chief Plenty Coups as their greatest leader, so when he died in 1933 at the age of 84, they didn't elect a new chief. Chief Plenty Coups represented the Indian nations in Washington, DC, during the dedication of the Tomb of the Unknown Soldier, and a small visitor center at the eponymous park keeps his story alive. Take a short tour of Plenty Coups's house for a peek into his life. Enjoy a quiet picnic along nearby Pryor Creek. The park has vault toilets, grills and fire rings, picnic tables, trash cans, and drinking water. Camping isn't allowed.

The Crow people who settled this part of Montana likely originated in the Midwest, migrating here in the 1300s. These early Crow were related to members of the Hidatsa tribe, river agriculturists who lived along the Upper Missouri. They were so named by white explorers who interpreted from sign language in which the tribe was referred to by flapping one's arms like a bird. In Hidatsa the Crow are called *Apsalooke,* which means "children of the large-beaked bird." The Absaroka Mountains, a slight variation of the word, were named for the Crow.

In spite of westward settlement by Europeans on Indian lands, the Crow were mostly friendly to whites. They even acted as scouts for General Crook during the Battle of the Rosebud—and for General George Armstrong Custer. The Crow Nation has managed to maintain many of its traditions, including the clan system in which the family is the basic unit of society. Individual members consult with their clans before making important decisions. If you wish to learn more about the Crow, consider taking this scenic drive in August during **Crow Fair,** held in Crow Agency. Alternatively, come by in September to celebrate Chief Plenty Coups Day of Honor, held at the park bearing his name.

You may wish to take a side trip south before you begin the main part of this scenic drive. South of the reservation in Custer National Forest you'll find the **Pryor Mountains National Wild Horse Range.** Take the road that leads south out of Pryor (BIA 5) to Sage Creek Road (BIA 11 and FR 3085). The area is remote, and the road is impassable when wet. It's also quite rough in places, so high-clearance vehicles are recommended. You're not guaranteed wild horse sightings, but you have about a 50-50 chance, and it's a beautiful region besides. Another point of interest on this side trip is **Big Ice Cave.** Here, a thick layer of ice covers the cave floor year-round, even when outside summer temperatures reach the 90s. You might not think this hard to believe in a cave, but the mouth of the cavern is more or less open to the elements. It's cool—literally and figuratively. Bats roost in the limestone cliffs, while towhees, rock wrens, kinglets, hummingbirds, kestrels, and golden eagles haunt the stark hills. Set out on a mountain bike for a more intimate exploration. If you decide to check out this area, be sure to bring food, water, and a Custer National Forest map—and watch the weather.

Pryor to Saint Xavier

On the main scenic drive route from Pryor, take BIA 91 east and head toward Saint Xavier, a mission town founded by a Jesuit priest who sought to convert the Crows to Christianity. Directly to the south are the Pryor Mountains, named for Sergeant Nathaniel Pryor, a member of the Lewis and Clark Expedition. Castle Rocks, where medicine men once fasted, are also to the south but are now penetrated by a railroad tunnel.

BIA 91 dips in and out of shallow coulees. You'll drive through open range, so watch for cattle on the road. Despite the hazards of wandering livestock, it's nice not to see miles and miles of fencing blighting the prairie. To the north, the landscape is open and mostly flat with low buttes. The unobstructed views of expansive plains here make you feel alone in the world, or at least in this corner of it. But it's a good kind of aloneness. Western meadowlarks flit about or pose on mileposts. Their chortling song is one of the few birdcalls that truly announce spring's arrival when these black-and-yellow birds return to Montana around April.

Where it's safe to pull over, stop and look at the interesting geology along the road where it dips into one of the many coulees flowing like veins through the earth. This landscape, pejoratively referred to as "badlands," are not so aptly named. Whoever came up with the term obviously never appreciated the rich beauty of exposed black, red, and yellow gashes in the crumbly grassland soil. And although it may seem like no living creature would willingly plunk itself down in this open and harsh habitat, many of the coulees harbor mule deer, antelope, snakes, lizards, and birds. Then again, it's easy for us to appreciate this as long as we can get back into our air-conditioned luxury vehicles. Maybe I'd have a different opinion if I were bumping along in a Conestoga for endless weeks.

Saint Xavier & Big Horn Canyon to Lodge Grass

Carrying on the main scenic drive, you soon reach the town of **Saint Xavier,** a Jesuit mission founded by Father Prado in 1887. The church and the school (Pretty Eagle School) are still in use. From Saint Xavier turn south onto CR 313 and follow signs to Bighorn Canyon, about 20 miles. You will pass by fields of sugar beets, harvested in early October. **Bighorn Canyon National Recreation Area** (www.nps.gov/bica/index.htm) is a fine place for boating, fishing, and camping. There's a visitor center at Yellowtail Dam (Memorial Day to October 1) and a

Big Horn Canyon National Recreation Area along the Big Horn River. DONNIE SEXTON

smaller visitor center in Fort Smith, just below the dam, with a short nature trail. If you want to see the fort's remains, you must make prior arrangements at the Yellowtail Dam visitor center since the land is private.

Fort Smith was Montana's second US military post, established in 1866 to protect settlers traveling the Bozeman Trail, which crossed the river near the fort. Blackfeet, Sioux, and Cheyenne peoples attempting to keep possession of their favored hunting grounds often attacked the immigrants here. Native Americans won the battle for this far-flung piece of Montana (if not the war against settlement), and the fort was abandoned 2 years later when a treaty was signed ceding the land to them. The Bozeman Trail became too dangerous and was little used after Fort Smith shut down.

The 520-foot **Yellowtail Dam** is the highest in the Missouri River system. During winter you can view thousands of waterfowl in the afterbay below Yellowtail Dam. Canada geese, mallards, teals, goldeneyes, ring-necked ducks, mergansers, grebes, and cormorants ply the waters here. Bald eagles find the smorgasbord of birds delectable. During migration you can see tundra swans, white pelicans, common loons, and sandhill cranes.

The Bighorn River carved the 50-mile-long **Bighorn Canyon,** now mostly filled by water. The Bighorn Mountains to the south stretch for 150 miles from

Chief Plenty Coups State Park honors the Crow Indians' greatest leader. DONNIE SEXTON

Montana into Wyoming. Some of the peaks in Wyoming reach 13,000 feet. The mountains are largely composed of sedimentary rock, originating from a marine environment between 600 million and 65 million years ago. The river slowly sliced through the limestone deposits to create the canyon's high bluffs.

The only way to really see the red canyon cliffs of the 71-mile-long **Bighorn Lake** is by boat. Rentals are available at the lake. You can also see a portion of the bluffs from an overlook area near Ok-A-Beh boat ramp south of Yellowtail Dam. The 10-mile drive to Ok-A-Beh, complete with marina and store (mid-May to mid-September), is a wonderful little scenic drive in itself. From one point, you can look across the rangeland on top to the west and glimpse some of the cliffs that enclose Bighorn Lake.

To continue the main scenic drive, head back toward Saint Xavier and turn east to Lodge Grass. *You must watch carefully for the turn to Lodge Grass, since the road is not marked.* If you're heading north from Bighorn Canyon, turn east at mile marker 25 on BIA 73 just south of Saint Xavier. Again this is open range and cattle will wander into the road, so be alert.

From here the drive passes through more coulees and grass range, weaving along Rotten Grass Creek. Watch for kestrels perched on fence posts and telephone lines. Kestrels are the smallest and most common of Montana's falcons, and they like to hover low above the ground before dive-bombing their prey.

After 19 miles, you come to a stop sign. Turn left to go to **Lodge Grass,** a tiny village that was once a summer gathering place for the Crow. It was actually called "greasy grass" because the nutrient-rich grasses that grew here made the animals that ate them fat. The Crow words for *grease* and *lodge* are very similar, thus "greasy grass" was mistranslated. You won't find much entertainment in Lodge Grass, but Scenic Route 16, on the Northern Cheyenne Reservation, is not far to the east. Begin that drive at the Little Bighorn Battlefield, 20 miles north.

16

Tongue River Loop

Crow Agency to Decker to Ashland to Busby

General description: A 165-mile loop (portions are gravel road) that traverses badlands country with rock spires, arid plateaus, river bottoms, and rangeland. The northern part of the loop winds around knobby hills on the Northern Cheyenne and Crow Reservations, while the eastern part follows the Tongue River.

Special attractions: Little Bighorn Battlefield, Rosebud Battlefield, Tongue River Reservoir, Saint Labre Mission; fishing, boating, hiking, mountain biking, camping, wildlife viewing.

Location: Southeastern Montana, from Little Bighorn Battlefield toward Busby south to Tongue River Reservoir near the Wyoming border and returning north to US 212 and I-90.

Drive route numbers: US 212, Montana 314, Tongue River Road/Ashland–Birney Road (CR 566).

Travel season: Year-round. During severe winter weather conditions, portions of the gravel road may be closed.

Camping: Tongue River Reservoir has several campgrounds with many individual sites. You can camp in undeveloped sites on Custer National Forest land and at a developed site in Lame Deer. You can also camp in Hardin.

Services: Full services at Crow Agency, Lame Deer, Hardin, and Ashland. Limited services at Tongue River Reservoir. There is a small store in Decker but no gasoline.

Nearby attractions: Custer National Forest, Hardin, Reno-Benteen Battlefield Memorial.

The Route

This drive is a continuation of Scenic Route 15, in Crow Indian country. It's a wonderful and remote portion of Montana, seldom visited and therefore a personal favorite far from the crowds. If you live in Montana, take the time to explore these off-the-beaten-path drives and get to know the people whose families have lived in this region for centuries. You'll gain a much greater appreciation for those who came through this land before you. If you're not from Montana, well, explore this area all the same and tell the folks back home about the hardscrabble life Native Americans must have endured—and the settlers who passed through—in this harsh land compared with our cushy lives today.

Not much of anything has changed on the landscape in the last few hundred years, though perhaps the river bottoms are a little more trammeled from livestock. Though who's to say that the great herds of bison tromping through the West didn't do a fair bit of trammeling themselves. As for your own mark, get out of the car to explore but try not to leave any permanent signs that you've been here.

Tongue River Loop

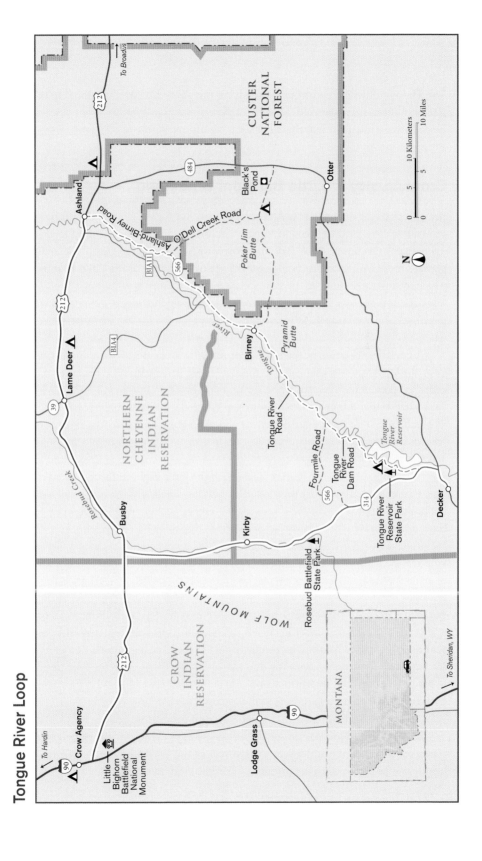

Though officials report that all roads on this route are passable, flooding in 2011 did cause some damage. As with all the remote drives in this book, especially those that are mostly unpaved, check local conditions before heading out. Use extra caution on CR 566.

Crow Agency to Little Big Horn Battlefield

Begin your scenic drive at **Crow Agency,** headquarters for the Crow Indian tribe and reservation. The third weekend in August, Crow Agency becomes one giant tepee town during the annual **Crow Fair and Powwow** (www.crow-fair.com). The town is perhaps more well-known as being near the site of the **Battle of the Little Bighorn,** which took place on June 25, 1876. The battlefield (www.nps.gov/libi/index.htm) is a must-see; it is not overdeveloped, and the car tour along the ridge is a short and wonderful scenic drive in itself. As you explore it, you get a feel for this sorrowful place where many US soldiers and Native American warriors died side by side.

A condensed version of the battle goes something like this: Following the Civil War, the US Army was charged with forcing Native Americans onto reservations in order to open up the West for white settlement. The Cheyenne and Sioux Nations were warned that if they didn't comply by a certain date, they would be rounded up like stubborn cattle and forced onto their allotted pieces of ground. The allied tribes resisted and troops were dispatched. But because of various twists of fate, the Sioux and Cheyenne forces managed to defeat General George Armstrong Custer and his accompanying cavalry. The bloody incident on the Little Bighorn River, however, was only a temporary victory for the Indian nations. Tragically, the battle marked the beginning of the end of their traditional lifestyles, sequestering Native Americans onto what were believed to be useless lands that no one else wanted.

In all about 270 US soldiers and about 100 Native American warriors were killed in the battle. Archaeological digs on the battlefield have yielded hundreds of artifacts, some of which are on display in the visitor center. A 1983 grass fire removed much of the vegetation on the battlefield, making investigations of the site easier. Many of the soldiers were buried where they fell, and although a stone marks the place where Custer likely fell, his remains were interred at West Point 1 year after the battle. Among the people buried in the Custer National Cemetery at the battlefield is a woman with the dubious honor of having been the first woman in Montana to be shot by her husband. Also interred here is the body of an army corporal whose wife—a laundress at the Yellowstone Depot—was discovered, upon her death, to be a man. That must have sent tongues wagging.

Incidentally, the visitor center, as well as the Stone Lodge by the cemetery, are reportedly haunted. Over the years, employees of the national monument have heard strange noises, seen apparitions, and could find no explanation for lights flickering on and off nor objects mysteriously moved from one place to another. Is it any wonder the spirits are restless? For more of these stories, check out the books for sale at the visitor center.

The battle is reenacted (in part) every year with a cast of 300 that includes descendants of both settlers and Native Americans who participated in the original battle. The hour-long affair ends in a skirmish near the battle site. Tickets and more information are available from the Hardin Chamber of Commerce (see For More Information).

Little Big Horn to Rosebud Battlefield

From the battlefield, head east on US 212 over rolling, grass-covered coulees for 23 miles before reaching the Tongue River Road turnoff, just west of Busby. The land probably looks much the same today as it did when the Crow and Northern Cheyenne hunted bison on these plains. Weather extremes are wicked, too; summer heat can sear your innards, and wintry blasts rival the Arctic.

Watch for signs for CR 314 directing you south to Decker, Montana, and Sheridan, Wyoming. The right-hand turnoff is just before the town of Busby, which you can see on the return trip. The road is a single lane with little or no shoulder and traverses the bottomlands along Rosebud Creek, rarely rising to the plateaus above. The stream bottoms turn brilliant gold and red in autumn before cottonwoods and dogwoods shed their leaves for winter. To the west are the low Wolf Mountains, ribbed with shallow coulees. Keep alert for cattle and pronghorn crossing.

About 23 miles south of the turnoff at US 212, look for signs to **Rosebud Battlefield State Park.** The Rosebud Battle was another significant event in US Army–Indian relations. The battle here, one of the largest Indian–white battles waged in the West, occurred just days before Custer and his troops fell at Little Bighorn. Had the Rosebud battle never happened, Custer's forces might have survived their battle.

In 1876 General George Crook led more than 1,000 men north from Wyoming to aid Colonel John Gibbon and General Alfred Terry in bringing the Sioux and Cheyenne "under control." Crook intended to meet up with the others to converge on the Indians, but he never made it. On June 17, 1876, fifteen hundred Sioux and Cheyenne warriors rode on horseback down the hill to ambush Crook and his company, which included Shoshone and Crow scouts. The battle lasted most of the day. Chief Crazy Horse was among the warriors. When the Sioux and Cheyenne finally withdrew, only nine of Crook's men were dead. Indian losses were unknown or not recorded, and both sides claimed victory. The conflict, however, turned Crook and his men away, so Custer (who split from Terry's group) never received his much-needed help just 12 days later on June 25.

The primitive 3,000-acre park has only a few interpretive signs, vault toilets, and a small homestead. Metal detectors and collecting and removal of artifacts are not allowed. Also, watch for rattlesnakes if you go walking through the grass.

Rosebud to Birney

From Rosebud Park, return to CR 314 and follow signs south to Decker. The turn-off to Tongue River Reservoir State Park is 12 miles south, and Decker is a few miles south of that on the Montana–Wyoming border. You're in coal country, and you'll see some processing plants near Decker and Tongue River Reservoir. If you go to **Decker,** you will also see signs of strip mining. The Decker mine is one of the state's largest producers of bituminous coal, a high-grade coal with low sulfur content for cleaner and hotter combustion. The coal seams here are from 12 to nearly 40 feet thick, and they are estimated to contain about 2 billion tons. Other than coal, Decker has a post office, store, a home or two, and small schoolhouse.

Tongue River Reservoir State Park is just north of Decker, and its "badlands" make for rich and interesting scenery. Red, brown, and yellow bluffs cut by the Tongue River and its tributaries are a wonderful contrast to Montana's mountains. The reservoir is a playground for boaters, anglers, and campers. You can ride mountain bikes here, too. The marina sells liquid propane gas, fishing supplies, and groceries. Plenty of picnic sites and campgrounds along the shore are more than adequate to accommodate visitors, and you can rent boats.

The road around the reservoir (Tongue River Dam Road) is very curvy, with some short, steep pitches as well. Rocky Mountain junipers, ponderosa pines, cottonwoods, sagebrush, and grasses blanket the shore and uplands. The road is in good shape when recently graded but can quickly become a potholed washboard with summer traffic. Heading north past the earthen dam, you enter Tongue River Canyon, full of old-growth cottonwoods along the river bottom. Most of the stretch along the river is private with open cattle range, so watch for cows on the road. The Tongue River has the only smallmouth bass population in the state able to support itself without restocking. The river is also home to the only rock bass population in Montana. Other fish that ripple and glide through the Tongue include walleye, channel catfish, shovelnose sturgeon, and northern pike.

The gravel Tongue River Dam Road follows the snakelike river, becoming narrow in spots with no guardrail. Slow travel is recommended. In other places the Tongue River Road is wide and flat. (***Note:*** Severe flooding in 2011 damaged

The Tongue River Road cuts through Montana's sagebrush lowlands. Tom Kilmer

some portions of the road, but officials report that it is passable. Regardless, the potential for subsequent flooding exists, so check local conditions before setting out.) Wherever you approach intersections in the road, keep following signs northward to Birney (when marked). Turn right at Fourmile Road. A couple of miles beyond that, bear left where the road splits again and becomes the Tongue River Road (CR 566). A few miles beyond Deadman Gulch, the road crosses the river and rises to a plateau from which you have a good view of the red bluffs to the north. You'll see Pyramid Butte's pointy top in front of you.

Birney to Ashland

The tiny burg of **Birney** is about a half mile or so long, but by now you've likely been choking on road dust, and Birney's short stretch of paved road is a nice little breather. In 1877 Oglala Sioux (led by Crazy Horse) and Cheyenne Indians (led by Two Moon) were attacked by General Nelson A. Miles here. Just north of town you should bear left up the hill at the fork in the road. Here the route name changes from the Tongue River Road to the Ashland-Birney Road, but it is still CR 566.

North of Birney the road rises above the river bottom and courses through expansive badlands. If you're eager to return to paved road, now is a good time to bail in favor of a shorter route. About 6.5 miles north of Birney you can take a cut-off to the left at the first major Y in the road, crossing the river and heading north to Lame Deer. This is BIA 4, which is paved. You can also take another paved road, BIA 11, which follows the Tongue River's west bank. To do so take the same left-hand turnoff as you would for BIA 4, then go right about 1 mile after crossing the river. This road meets up with US 212 about 1.5 miles west of Ashland.

If you're keen to carry on the main part of this scenic drive, continue along the gravel road (CR 566) along the east bank of the Tongue River from Birney. Watch for golden eagles soaring in the skies or perched on telephone poles. A section of the Custer National Forest is just to the east, so you are free to explore some of the side roads that slice through bluffs and buttes. O'Dell Creek Road, to the southeast, offers camping and wildlife viewing at **Black's Pond.** Look for bats in the evening and wild turkeys. **Poker Jim Butte** has a picnic area and a scenic overview.

North of O'Dell Creek, the Ashland-Birney Road (CR 566) passes through several dry washes reminiscent of a desert. Well, actually, this is desert, northern style. You may have been wondering what the white, frostlike patches along the road are. Resembling lingering snow, they are saline seeps, which occur where irrigated crops have replaced natural grasses. Since crops cannot always take up all the water that comes from irrigation, the excess water accumulates just below the surface, absorbing salts and minerals in the ground. As the water rises to the ground surface and evaporates, it leaves behind the crusty salts.

When you get to a high spot north of King Creek Road, stop and look behind you for some lovely sweeping views of the badlands. Farther north, the road dips down to the Otter Creek lowlands and arrives at US 212 in downtown Ashland.

Ashland is home to the **Saint Labre Mission,** an Indian school that has a small museum with some fascinating artifacts. You'll also find some beautiful Native American crafts for sale. Ask about a tour of the mission (Memorial Day through Labor Day). Its conical-shaped church—the cross on top falls to near a 45-degree angle—gives the intended appearance of a tepee.

Ashland to Lame Deer, Busby & Beyond

To finish the Tongue River loop, head west on US 212 from Ashland toward Lame Deer. The road is hilly and winds in spots as it passes through burned forest; black snags accentuate the green ground cover. **Lame Deer** was named for an Indian chief killed by US soldiers here. After a broiling battle that took place near the current town site, soldiers under the command of General Miles looted and burned Lame Deer's camp. Today it is a meeting place for the Northern Cheyenne people. The Tribal Museum depicts Northern Cheyenne culture. In the cemetery are buried Dull Knife and Little Wolf, two chiefs who fought in the Battle of the Little Bighorn and led their people out of exile in Oklahoma. Lame Deer's Fourth of July Powwow has dance contests, drumming, and a parade. If you've never been to a powwow, this is as good a place as any. For more information about the historical sites near here, contact the Northern Cheyenne Indian Reservation (For More Information). Another interesting stop is the **Jessi Mullin Picture Museum,** a fabulous home-grown collection of historic photographs of the Cheyenne people and places in the area. The museum is 2 blocks south of the intersection of Highways 212 and 39, behind the IGA store.

West of Lame Deer the little hamlet of **Busby** lies near the border of the Northern Cheyenne and Crow reservations. Custer supposedly made his last camp where Busby now sits. It is also the site of the 1993 reburial of 17 Native peoples who died more than a century ago in one of the many clashes with white settlers. The remains—once on display at the Smithsonian Institution, the National Museum of Health and Medicine, and Harvard University's Peabody Museum—were repatriated in a moving ceremony and buried near Chief Two Moon Monument.

From Busby you can head west on US 212 back to I-90 and pick up Scenic Route 15 to the south or return to Ashland and head northeast to Scenic Route 17, which begins in Miles City.

17

Powder River Country

Miles City to Baker to Ekalaka

General description: A 115-mile drive (one way) from Miles City to Ekalaka on the eastern fringe of Montana that begins and ends in Miles City and rolls through badlands and cultivated plains.

Special attractions: Range Riders Museum, Miles City Bucking Horse Sale, South Sandstone Recreation Area, Medicine Rocks State Park; museums; camping, fishing, boating, wildlife watching.

Location: East-central Montana from Miles City east to Baker, near the North Dakota border, and south to Ekalaka.

Drive route numbers: US 12, Highway 7.

Travel season: Year-round. Snow, ice, and wind can make winter travel hazardous.

Camping: There is some camping in and around Miles City, at Medicine Rocks State Park, and in Ekalaka. Baker has 2 campgrounds.

Services: Full services in Miles City, Baker, and Ekalaka. Limited services in Plevna.

Nearby attractions: Custer National Forest.

The Route

If you live in western Montana, you might not be likely to make the trip all the way out to Miles City just to do this drive. But if you're heading east anyway, it's a pleasant alternative to I-94. Yet, like other remote scenic drives in this book, this one was chosen precisely for those more adventurous types who can live without the crowds and the trendy place names on their summer vacation. If you've never been to Miles City, check it out. And Medicine Rocks State Park, with its bizarre sandstone features, is another outpost well worth a visit.

Miles City

The bustling town of **Miles City** was named for General Nelson A. Miles, whose army swept the West in a plan to rid the plains and mountains of "hostile Indians." He became a general at age 26 and was heralded by white men for defeating Crazy Horse, Sitting Bull, Chief Joseph, and Geronimo, all great leaders in their own right and well respected today not only among the Indian nations but also among descendants of white settlers.

Miles City was established as a military cantonment, Fort Keogh, at the confluence of the Tongue and Yellowstone Rivers. The fort was set up in 1877, a year after the Battle of the Little Bighorn, and named for an Irishman who is reported

Powder River Country

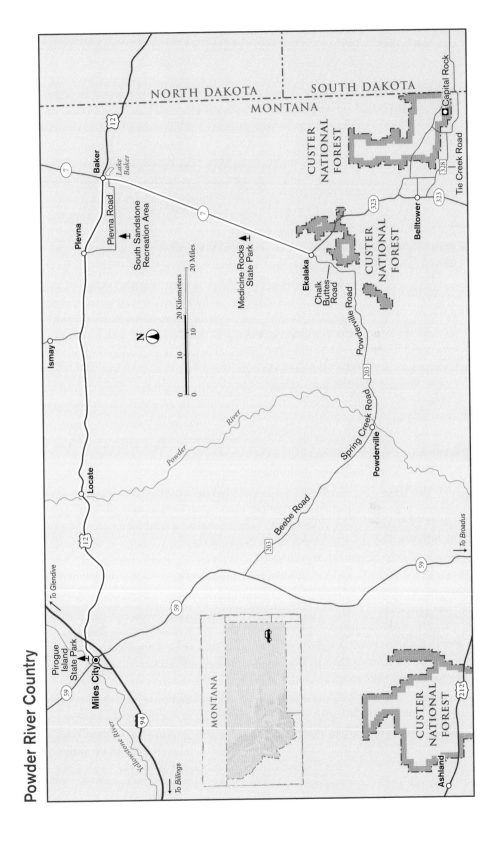

to have died alongside Custer. Many Northern Cheyenne surrendered to General Miles at Fort Keogh, joining the US Army as scouts. Today the 55,000-acre fort is an agricultural experiment station where research is conducted to "develop ecologically and economically sustainable range animal management systems."

The rich grasslands surrounding town were once the final destination for cattle drives from as far away as Texas. Here cattle were fattened before being sent by rail to slaughterhouses in Chicago. In eastern Montana today you may still get a chance to witness a cattle drive or overland travel by horse-drawn wagon. If you fancy rolling across the prairie yourself, contact Powder River Cattle Drives (http://powderrivercattledrive.com) for a multiday experience, albeit with a few more modern-day comforts than our ancestors had.

Be sure to check out the **Range Riders Museum** (www.rangeridersmuseum .org) on the eastern edge of town, a collector's paradise for every imaginable d'objet Western. Among some of the fanciful things you'll find are chaps, saddles, spurs, guns, plates, hats, waffle irons, knives, tools, seashells, Charles M. Russell prints, all varieties of barbed wire, broadaxes, telephone pole insulators, iron brands, dinosaur bones, rocks, and Native American artifacts (April 1 to October 31 and by appointment). You can also tour the original officers' quarters from Fort Keogh. Small-scale dioramas with audio narrations relate the history of the area, and life-size dioramas re-create 19th-century Main Street in Miles City. One room is dedicated to the riders of the range, with hundreds of pictures of weathered and rugged cowboys. Each photo sports the brand the cowboy rode for at the bottom.

The **Custer County Art & Heritage Center** (http://ccac.milescity.org) is off the beaten path but on the same side of town as the Range Riders Museum. It's housed in the old Miles City waterworks plant—you have to walk through a giant culvert to enter the gallery. In 1979 the center won an award for its adaptation of the facilities, and it is now listed on the National Register of Historic Places. A gift shop sells jewelry, pottery, woven items, and art by Montana and regional artists. Back in town, the Miles City Chamber of Commerce has a booklet if you're interested in a self-guided driving tour to view the city's historic buildings or a walking tour of the city.

One of Miles City's most renowned events is the world-famous **Bucking Horse Sale** (www.buckinghorsesale.com), an auction held annually on the weekend before Memorial Day. As many as 200 horses are auctioned, and some of the animals appear in top rodeos nationwide, including the Eastern Montana Fair and Rodeo here in August. The auction also features quarter horse and thoroughbred racing. Contact the Miles City Chamber of Commerce for details about events and attractions (see For More Information).

North of Miles City, on the other side of the Yellowstone River, **Pirogue Island State Park** is a pretty place with tall cottonwoods and grassy meadows.

Lewis and Clark's Corps of Discovery is believed to have camped here. To get to the island, head about 1 mile north of town on Highway 59 and turn east onto Kinsey Road. After another 1.5 miles, turn south at the signs marking Pirogue Island. Here you can look for birds and waterfowl, such as warblers, kingbirds, downy and hairy woodpeckers, flickers, American white pelicans, teals, wood ducks, and great blue herons. During winter bald eagles are more common. A few miles of rutted dirt roads through the park might best be traveled on foot or mountain bike. There are no designated trails, but walking is level and easy.

Miles City to Baker

Once you have exhausted Miles City and environs, head east on I-94 for 3 miles and exit at the signs for US 12 (exit 141). Just east of Miles City, US 12 slices through a landscape of buttes, coulees, and bluffs composed of crumbly black deposits laid down by an ancient inland sea. The sharply defined, pine-covered hills are unlike the rolling pine ridges in other parts of the state. Like massive piles of dirt dumped here by giants, their steeply sloping sides and knobbly tops give them an unpolished look. The road climbs up a plateau and dips every so often and the terrain begins to soften farther east.

At the small place called **Locate,** the road crosses the Powder River. This region was once favored hunting ground for Sioux and Cheyenne pursuing bison. More rough-cut hills and buttes rise above the plains for another 16 miles before flattening out to grass prairie.

Continuing on the main scenic drive, you reach the turnoff for Ismay, 13 miles west of Plevna and north of US 12. In 1993 the residents of Ismay—all 22 of them—renamed their town Joe in honor of the football player Joe Montana. To celebrate their new (unofficial) name, the residents hosted a rodeo and other activities to raise money for their volunteer fire department. The event drew more than 2,000 people and raised around $70,000!

Farther west is **Plevna,** a town that was named for the Bulgarian city where Russians and Turks clashed in a great battle; many Bulgarian immigrants built the railroad through here. You can take the Plevna Road to the **South Sandstone Recreation Area** for boating and fishing. It's roughly 7 miles south of town.

Baker to Ekalaka

The town of **Baker** is full of hardy souls who plunked themselves down on the great, windy plains of North America. Upon first sight, you might wonder who would want to put a town out here. Come to think of it, you might wonder that about a lot of towns in Montana. Back when pioneers were moving through, the

Stormy skies form near Baker. DONNIE SEXTON

area was a favorite stopover for wagon trains because of its abundant grasses for horses and other livestock and its many springs. You can still see their tracks north of the current town site; follow Highway 7 to mile marker 44. An interpretive sign will direct your gaze to ruts on the southwest ridge. Though the wagon trains have stopped passing through, today natural gas and oil discoveries keep the town alive.

So don't think Baker is boring; think of it as enterprising to have forged into the future quite well. At **Lake Baker** you can swim, boat, and fish. Or if you'd rather take your pleasures inside, check out the **Baker Recreation Center,** with an indoor pool, exercise classes, racquetball courts, and a weight room. The **O'Fallon Historical Museum** (www.falloncounty.net) exhibits Native American, pioneer, and explorer relics from Montana's early days. Check out the exhibit about Steer Montana, a roan polled shorthorn bovine bred here in 1923. Steer's claim to fame is that he was—and allegedly continues to be—the largest of his kind in the world at 5 feet 11 inches tall and just under 4,000 pounds. That's a lot of burger. During summer, Baker hosts the Fallon County Fair and a car show (http://falloncounty.net/).

If you've driven all this way, then another 25 miles south of Baker on Highway 7 isn't too far to go to see the fantastic **Medicine Rocks State Park.** The strange Swiss cheese-like monoliths and arches at Medicine Rocks may have been sand dunes millions of years ago. The holes were created by wind erosion over time. Sioux Indians called the place *inyan oka lo ka,* or "rock with hole in it." You can camp and picnic among the unique sandstone formations, where once Indian hunting parties gathered to pray to spirits. With its pockmarked sandstone buttes, the park is home to a variety of raptors. Drive around the park or go for a walk near Eagle and Castle Rocks, where you might see golden eagles, merlins, ferruginous hawks, prairie falcons, and kestrels, as well as sharp-tailed grouse, nuthatches, bluebirds, and meadowlarks. Mule deer, pronghorn, coyotes, and red foxes also live here. You can camp here, too.

About 10 miles south of Medicine Rocks lies the town of **Ekalaka.** In Sioux *Ijkalaka* means "swift one" and was the name given to a niece of Sitting Bull. The town was founded originally as a watering hole for thirsty cowboys. According to legend, a bison hunter named Claude Carter decided he could make more money mining "liquid gold." When his load of logs bogged down in mud at the current site of Ekalaka, he allegedly exclaimed, "Hell, any place in Montana is a good place to build a saloon!" Mr. Carter was not the only one to have subscribed to that philosophy.

In Ekalaka be sure to see the **Carter County Museum** (www.cartercounty museum-ekalaka.org), with its specimens of ancient marine life unearthed in the county. The museum is part of Montana's Dinosaur Trail (www.mtdinotrail .org). Most of southeastern Montana was a seabed more than 50 million years ago, and often marine fossils pop up in road cuts. The most complete skeleton at the museum is a duck-billed dinosaur called *Anatosaurus.* The building also houses remains of a giant lizard called a *Mosasaurus,* a triceratops skull, and a tiny tyran- nosaur. Former museum curator Marshall Lambert discovered the only Pachy- cephalosaurus remains in the world, which now reside in New York. You can see a plaster cast of the original here.

For a nice side trip, take CR 323 southeast of Ekalaka about 24 miles to the gravel CR 328 (Tie Creek Road); turn east and head toward the little section of Custer National Forest to view **Capitol Rock Natural National Monument,** a massive white limestone geological formation that looks like its namesake in Washington, DC. **Note:** Roads might not always be in good shape, so check local conditions before setting out.

If you want to head back to Miles City, you can either retrace your steps or take a back road through Powderville, west of Ekalaka. Much of this road is gravel, however, and should be traveled only in good weather. From Ekalaka take Chalk Buttes Road south about 9 miles to Powderville Road. Turn west and follow this road to Powderville. You can visit Boothill Cemetery in Powderville and view wagon ruts in the terrain where wagon trains once forded the river here. From

Hay bales dominate eastern Montana's landscape. Donnie Sexton

Powderville continue on Spring Creek Road (CR 203) northwest to Highway 59. About 6 miles beyond Powderville, the route is called Beebe Road. If you head north on Highway 59, it will bring you back to I-94 near Miles City. From there you can head south to Scenic Route 16.

Medicine Rocks State Park's unique sandstone formations were created by wind erosion over millions of years. Donnie Sexton

18

Fort Peck Dam

Junction Highways 24/200 to Malta

General description: A 155-mile drive that begins more or less in the middle of nowhere at the junction of Highways 24 and 200 and heads north along the eastern fringe of Fort Peck Lake, then crosses the Milk River a half-dozen times on the way to Malta.

Special attractions: Charles M. Russell National Wildlife Refuge, Fort Peck Dam and Lake, Pioneer Museum, Sleeping Buffalo Hot Springs, Bowdoin National Wildlife Refuge; summer theater; camping, fishing, boating, swimming, wildlife viewing, hot springs.

Location: Northeastern Montana, about 37 miles east of Jordan.

Drive route numbers: Highway 24, US 2.

Travel season: Year-round. Blowing and drifting snow can make winter travel hazardous.

Camping: You'll find dozens of campgrounds along Fort Peck Lake and commercial campsites at Sleeping Buffalo Hot Springs.

Services: Full services at Fort Peck, Glasgow, Saco, and Malta. Limited services at marinas around Fort Peck Lake.

Nearby attractions: Big Sky Back Country Byway, Fort Peck Indian Reservation, Montana Cowboy Hall of Fame.

The Route

Find your way to the junction of Highways 24 and 200, about 19 miles west of Brockway and 37 miles east of Jordan, and prepare to enjoy this scenic drive through the Missouri River Breaks near Fort Peck Lake. It's a shame that more people don't explore what eastern Montana has to offer. Then again, that makes it quieter for the rest of us. Though some prefer the mountains to the High Plains desert, you really can't compare the two. Each is a completely different ecosystem with unique and special characteristics. So if you're one of those Montanans who think life begins and ends in the mountains, take another look at what your eastern counterpart has to offer.

It's a wonder how pioneers ever managed to cross this part of the state, it is so deeply gouged with bluffs and coulees. It's a humbling experience to drive through this lonely country with nothing but sky between you and the road ahead. Miles of barbed-wire fencing seem out of place, almost intrusive, since you would expect pronghorn and bison herds to roam unhindered across the plains. There are no bison left here, though, and pronghorn and mule deer compete with cattle for grasses and forbs.

This drive, and indeed much of off-road Montana, warrants some caution. Eastern Montana's clayey soils—known as "gumbo"—become slick as ice with the

Fort Peck Dam

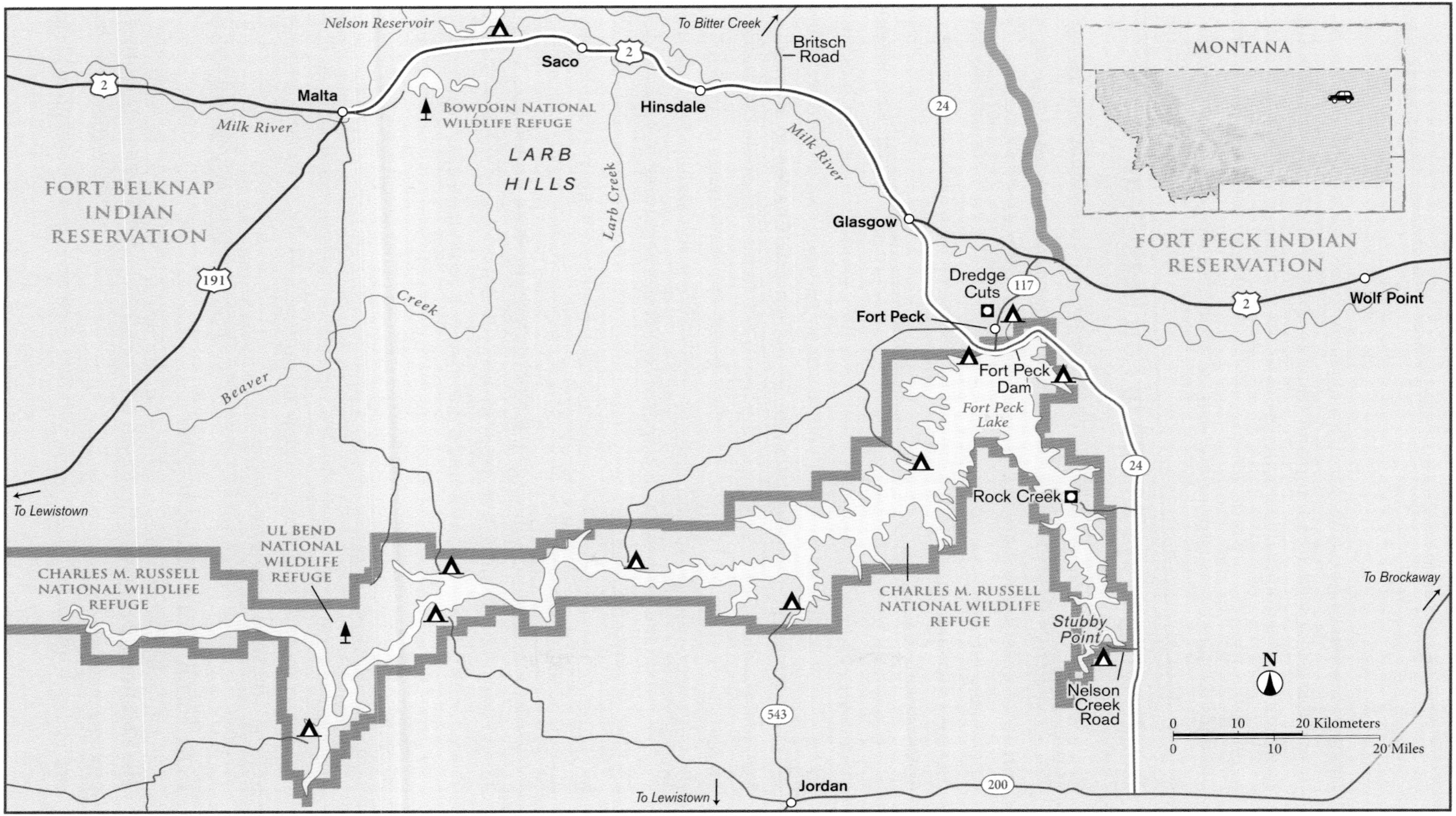

slightest amount of moisture. Most, if not all, unpaved roads in this region are impassable under wet conditions, and many roads bear signs indicating so. Take these warnings seriously. Don't attempt to drive on unpaved roads if rain is imminent. And if you get caught on the back roads in the rain, don't attempt to drive out until the rain clears and surface water evaporates enough to allow passage.

Junction Highways 24/200 to Fort Peck Dam

Begin the drive by heading north on Highway 24 from its junction with Highway 200. As you cross this section of road, among range scattered with sagebrush and cut by dry washes, you'll dip in and out of deeper coulees on a roller-coaster ride through the furrowed badlands and bluffs. Erosion is at work here, and the flat rocks perched atop giant mounds of dirt look like they're straight out of a Dr. Seuss book.

If you want to explore the funky landscape a little more closely, turn off the main route at Nelson Creek Road (road FWS 106), about 20 miles north of your starting point, and head west to Stubby Point at the south end of Fort Peck Lake. This detour takes you across part of the 1.2-million-acre **Charles M. Russell National Wildlife Refuge** that encompasses 1,600 miles of shoreline surrounding the lake (a reservoir really). The refuge began as a game range in 1936 for elk, mule deer, pronghorn, and sage grouse. In 1976 it was classified as a national wildlife refuge and now supports hundreds of species of mammals, birds, and reptiles. At **Nelson Creek** you can camp, launch a boat, or hike around the endless buttes of the refuge on this arm of the lake. Explore the many side roads on mountain bike.

Back on Highway 24, the south and north forks of **Rock Creek** (about 12 and 15 miles north of Nelson Creek, respectively) cut to the western shore of the lake. There are boat ramps, campgrounds, picnic sites, a restaurant, a bar, cabins, and fuel here. Driving through the Rock Creek area, you might think you've landed on the moon. This landscape is unapologetic, and you either love its labyrinthine-cut surface for its endless barrens, fickle weather patterns, and loneliness, or you hate it for the same reasons. And if you don't like these badlands, north of Rock Creek the scenery morphs into grass-covered hills and coulees. The town of Fort Peck and the dam site are another 29 miles north.

Fort Peck Dam to Glasgow

The **Fort Peck** area is well developed, with beautiful picnic grounds, beaches, campgrounds, and fishing access. Take some time to look at the spillway (3 miles east of the dam), an engineering marvel with 16 gates, each 25 feet high by 40 feet

Fort Peck Spillway, a Public Works Administration project under FDR's New Deal.
TOM KILMER

wide and weighing 80 tons. The entire structure is 100 feet high and 1,000 feet long. The **Fort Peck Dam** itself is 250 feet high, holding back a reservoir that is 220 feet deep and 130 miles long. Construction of the dam began in 1933 and took a decade to complete. Today it is one of the three largest earth-filled dams in the world.

Fort Peck Lake is a popular fishing destination. The 4-day Montana Governor's Cup Walleye Tournament (http://mtgovcup.com) each July awards $40,000 in cash and prizes. The lake is home to walleye, smallmouth bass, catfish, chinook salmon, northern pike, and the odd-looking—though weirdly charming—paddlefish. The latter is found only in Fort Peck, the Yellowstone River, and in China's Yangtze River. Paddlefish feed by filtering plankton from the water with their comblike "gill rakers." These behemoths can grow to 100 pounds or more and have shown up in fossils dated as old as 70 million years. The lake is also home to one of Montana's endangered species, the pallid sturgeon.

Once you've had a look at the earthen dam, take a drive across it. Notice how the view across the lake is so vast, it looks like an inland sea. Visit the museum at the powerhouse and learn about the history of Fort Peck Dam and its construction. You might want to read Ivan Doig's novel *Bucking the Sun* about the building of the dam. Doig's impeccable research opens a window on some real-life history of the dam. You'll also enjoy the museum's exhibit of prehistoric fossils and Native American artifacts. This is part of Montana's Dinosaur Trail (www.mtdino trail.org). In 1997 a T. rex skeleton was found in the area, a cast of which—plus a fleshed-out version—is on display. Follow the signs for the museum and for the Downstream Recreation Area, where you will find picnic grounds, beaches, and boat launches. The picnic grounds have horseshoe pits, playgrounds for the kids, and a nature trail.

Winter is the best time to see bald eagles at Fort Peck. During early spring you might see sharp-tailed grouse vying for mates near Flat Lake. For more information on wildlife-viewing sites in the vicinity, stop at the information kiosk on Highway 24 near Wheeler, a few miles west of Fort Peck.

The town of Fort Peck has a summer theater; show information is available from the Glasgow Chamber of Commerce (see For More Information). Performances run from June through August. Before the show you can view artworks by regional and local artists in the gallery.

Old Fort Peck was established in 1867 by Campbell Peck and E. H. Durfee as a trading post for Indians, trappers, and river traders. When Fort Peck Lake was created, the old town's 300-square-foot stockade with 12-foot-high walls was flooded, taking all its secrets down under. But that was not the first time the fort was flooded. In 1877 a wall of ice formed about where the dam now stands. In 20 minutes the Missouri River rose 20 feet, flooding the grounds with about 10 feet of water. By 1887 most of the fort buildings were dismantled for firewood to fuel riverboats.

To continue this scenic drive, head north from Fort Peck on Highway 24 toward Glasgow, through gently rolling hills and grain fields. About 3 miles southeast of Glasgow you will come to a junction where Highway 24 heads north to meet up with US 2. Bypass this turnoff and stay on the main road, which is now Highway 24W, and head into Glasgow.

Glasgow to Malta

Named by Scots for their home city, **Glasgow** is one of the oldest eastern Montana settlements, having sprouted from the railroad. Among some its first establishments were—you guessed it—saloons. Glaswegians, however, at least had the decency to hold their first Sunday school in a boxcar, not in a saloon.

If you want a little side trip (south of Glasgow), take the 65-mile auto tour through the coulees on the north shore of Fort Peck Lake. Called the South Valley Route, it includes reservoirs where you can fish and view wildlife. Take Highway 24 south from Glasgow 9 miles to Willow Creek Road and continue south for 3 more miles before turning west. It's another 31 miles to South Ranch entrance.

You can learn more about the Glasgow's history at the **Pioneer Museum** (www.valleycountymuseum.com/Home.html), which has exhibits of Western artifacts, wildlife mounts, and information on historic events (Memorial Day to Labor Day). Dioramas of the Lewis and Clark Expedition, fossils and dinosaur bones, and Indian and pioneer stories will interest and entertain you. Wild West fans might like the Buffalo Bill Cody bar, complete with bullet and lead slug. For details about events in Glasgow, contact the chamber of commerce (see For More Information).

From Glasgow take US 2 west to Malta. The surrounding gentle hills once supported short-grass prairie, which bison devoured on their great movements across the plains. The grasslands now support cattle, as well as crops such as wheat, alfalfa, and barley. Across these plains is one of the best places to see storms as they move over the land. With no mountains to stop a front, thunderheads roll in and quickly disappear again, leaving the air full of the scent of wet grasses. West of Vandalia the Larb Hills break up the flat terrain south of the highway, giving those storms something to mull over.

About 20 miles west of Glasgow, explore what has been called a "pint-sized Grand Canyon with an Old West atmosphere," more of Montana's badlands at the **Bitter Creek Wildlife Viewing Area.** Follow Britsch Road north about 9.6 miles until it becomes a dirt track. Continue for another 5 miles or so, staying to the right. Veer left and look for signs for Bitter Creek study area. Four-wheel-drive is recommended, but if you have any doubts about your vehicle or weather conditions, call the Bureau of Land Management in Glasgow (406-228-3750). You can hike or mountain bike just about anywhere as long as you stick to the roads, but keep in mind that these roads are impassable when wet. Keep your eyes toward the ground for sharp-tailed and sage grouse. Mule deer, white-tailed deer, and pronghorn hang out in the coulees and uplands, while ferruginous hawks and prairie falcons catch the thermals above.

If you're a fan of the cowboy artist Charles M. Russell, stop by the tiny town of **Saco**, farther along US 2, and look for a rock in a small grassy spot by the railroad tracks. The names of several area ranchers, indebted to Russell for his contributions to their profession, are engraved on a plaque. Russell is not the only famous person honored in Saco. Television commentator Chet Huntley attended school here, and the one-room schoolhouse where he studied is now a little museum.

Just west of Saco you'll see signs for **Sleeping Buffalo Hot Springs** (http://sleepingbuffalo.blogspot.com) to the north. This little oasis, which you can see from the highway before you get to it, looks a bit odd in the middle of the dry plains. It's a great place to stop if you feel like a soak and can tolerate the somewhat murky pools. The resort has a campground, motel, bar, store, cafe, and 2 indoor pools. In addition they have 4 new hotel rooms plus "vintage" hotel rooms and cabins with kitchens. Right across from the hot springs is Nelson Reservoir, where you can boat or fish.

An interpretive sign at the Sleeping Buffalo turnoff will tell you about the boulder, now under shelter here, where many people leave offerings of tobacco. The boulder was moved from a place near where the Cree Indians regularly crossed the Milk River. From a distance it's said to resemble a sleeping bison, but you may have to use your imagination.

Bowdoin National Wildlife Refuge (www.fws.gov/bowdoin) is just west of Sleeping Buffalo. This 15,551-acre refuge, established in 1936 along the central migratory flyway, teems with eared grebes, American white pelicans, cormorants, pintails, teals, gulls, sandpipers, godwits, pheasants, and grouse during the migration seasons. Pronghorn like the lavish short-grass prairie surrounding the lakes. If you're lucky, you may catch a glimpse of rare peregrine falcons hunting from the skies.

Lake Bowdoin was formed before glacial times, when it was part of the Missouri River. You can take a self-guided auto tour—a 15-mile loop—beginning and ending at the refuge headquarters. The auto tour is on a well-maintained gravel road that circles Lake Bowdoin; get a pamphlet that describes the numbered stops along the way. You can hike on parts of the refuge or boat on the lake. Ask at headquarters for information. To get to the refuge, turn south off US 2 at the signs just west of Sleeping Buffalo and make a right at the first big intersection you come to. Signs will guide you to the refuge headquarters, about 9 miles down the road. Watch for deer and pronghorn crossings.

When you leave the refuge headquarters, continue on the same road to Malta 7 miles west or backtrack to US 2. From **Malta** you can pick up Scenic Route 19 or Scenic Route 21.

Lewistown & the Little Rockies

Lewistown to Malta

General description: A 134-mile excursion beginning in Lewistown, the geographic center of Montana, and heading north to Malta on the windy High-Line.

Special attractions: Charles M. Russell National Wildlife Refuge, Mission Canyon, the Missouri River Breaks; boating, fishing, wildlife viewing, camping, hiking, mountain biking.

Location: Central Montana from Lewistown to Malta.

Drive route number: US 191.

Travel season: Year-round. Blowing and drifting snow can make winter travel hazardous.

Camping: There are a few developed campgrounds along the Missouri River and in the Little Rockies just south of the Fort Belknap Reservation.

Services: Lewistown and Malta have full services. Limited services in Hays, Zortman, and other small towns along the route.

Nearby attractions: Charlie Russell Chew-Choo, Fort Belknap Indian Reservation, Kendall ghost town, Lewis and Clark National Forest, Nez Perce Trail, Sand Creek Wildlife Station, War Horse National Wildlife Refuge.

The Route

This scenic drive is one of the more diverse in terms of scenery covered in this book. The changing landscape of mountains, river breaks, and flat prairies nourishes your soul, while the mix of history in Lewistown and Malta, and a little Native American culture, feeds your brain. Plenty of side trips offer ample opportunities to get out of your car and explore the not-so-ghostly towns of Zortman and Landusky and the Charles M. Russell National Wildlife Refuge. It's a great break-in drive for those who fear heading too far out into eastern Montana's wilds. In other words, you can have your fix of civilization at beginning and end. And if you prefer the wilds, then take off overland to the Charles M. Russell National Wildlife Refuge or connect up with Scenic Route 20 about halfway along this drive.

Lewistown

Lewistown, the seat of Fergus County, is a pretty place despite its rough beginning. Originally a trading post for trappers and hunters, Lewistown later became an agricultural center where cattle rustlers wrought havoc on local ranchers in the

Lewistown & the Little Rockies

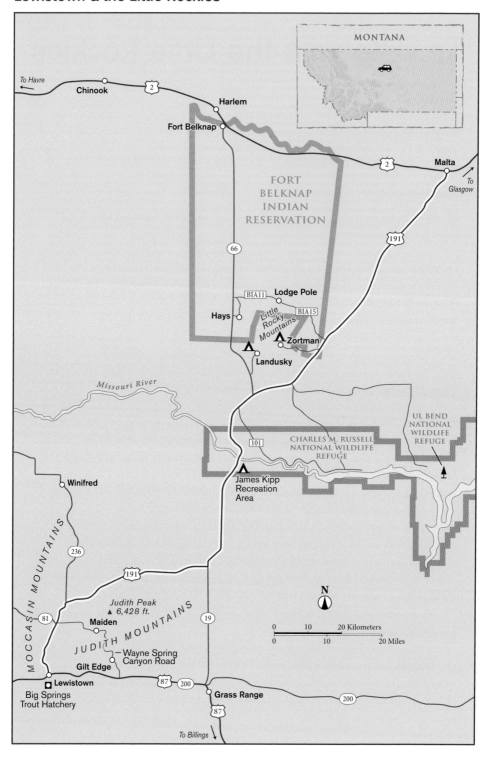

MONTANA

To Havre ←

Chinook

2

Harlem

Fort Belknap

2   Malta

To Glasgow →

191

FORT
BELKNAP
INDIAN
RESERVATION

66

BIA11   Lodge Pole

BIA15

Hays

Little
Rocky
Mountains

Zortman

Landusky

Missouri River

101

CHARLES M. RUSSELL
NATIONAL WILDLIFE
REFUGE

UL BEND
NATIONAL
WILDLIFE
REFUGE

James Kipp
Recreation
Area

Winifred

N

0   10   20 Kilometers
0   10   20 Miles

236

191

Judith Peak
▲ 6,428 ft.

JUDITH MOUNTAINS

19

Maiden

Wayne Spring
Canyon Road

81

MOCCASIN MOUNTAINS

Gilt Edge

Lewistown

Big Springs
Trout Hatchery

87   200

Grass Range   200

87

To Billings ↓

1880s. The rustler problem was eventually resolved by retaliating ranchers who quickly "dispatched" two suspected villains: Rattlesnake Jake and Longhair Owen. A photographer sold pictures of the men's dead bodies for profit . . . sort of like hanging dead crows from fence posts as a warning to other crows. The region was also the site of many battles between Indians and settlers over bison. Reed's Fort, a trading post east of town, was a stopping point for the Nez Perce shortly before their surrender in the Bears Paw Mountains to the north. Although Lewistown has quieted down a bit since the 19th century, there's still plenty to do here, and you might want to stay a day or two.

Many of Lewistown's buildings are listed on the National Register of Historic Places—Croatian and Norwegian immigrants handcrafted many of the buildings—and the chamber of commerce has a pamphlet of self-guided walks through town. The **Central Montana Museum** (Memorial Day to mid-September; winter by appointment) shows off Montana's past with a full-scale replica of a *Torosaurus* skull found in the area. You can also watch a DVD of area residents discuss Lewistown's history. The **Art Center** (http://lewistownartcenter.org/site) features the work of local artists as well as a nice gift shop.

If you're here in summer, check out the Central Montana Fair in July and the Cowboy Poetry Gathering (www.montanacowboypoetrygathering.com) along with the Western Arts & Gear Show in August. In September the 1-day **Chokecherry Festival** draws crowds from all over the state to sample fare from various Lewistown restaurants and buy or eat anything that has to do with chokecherries, which grow wild throughout Montana along river banks and stream banks. The festival also highlights a parade, a fun run, a children's bike rodeo, and a cherry pit spitting contest. Speaking of contests, Lewistown hosts a hay bale sculpture contest in September (http://montanabaletrail.com). Contact the Lewiston Chamber of Commerce (see For More Information) for details about other attractions and events throughout the year.

The **Big Springs Trout Hatchery** southeast of town is open to visitors year-round. Brown, rainbow, and cutthroat trout, as well as kokanee salmon, spend their formative years here before being introduced to rivers, lakes, and streams all over the state. To get to the hatchery, head south on 1st Avenue for about 4 miles and turn left onto CR 466 for another 2 miles; follow the hatchery signs. Lewistown's water supply comes from Spring Creek, one of the purest municipal water supplies in the country; the water is so clean, it needs no treatment. If you go to the fish hatchery, be sure to pick up the *Upper Spring Creek Day Trip Guide* from the Lewiston Chamber of Commerce. The pamphlet has a map listing points of interest along the way, including a short scenic drive along Castle Butte Road.

Lewistown to Charles M. Russell Wildlife Refuge

From Lewistown continue the scenic drive by heading north on US 191. The road skirts the Judith Mountains, named by Meriwether Lewis for his cousin. Some contend her name was really Julia and that the explorer got it wrong. Whatever her name, the Judith moniker also adorns a river, a town, and a county. The Judith Mountains first rose as magma oozing through sedimentary lake bed deposits about 50 million years ago. The crystallized rock yielded placer gold discovered by prospectors in the 1880s. Maiden and Gilt Edge, now ghost towns, were born from the boom. To explore them—and the Judith Mountains—turn east onto Warm Spring Canyon Road. You will pass the now closed Lewistown Air Force Base, built on the former townsite of Andersonville. Maiden is just under 9 miles up the road. Its peak population of 1,200 had no problem keeping 7 saloons alive.

If you carry on up Warm Spring Canyon Road, turn north at a fork 1 mile past Maiden to access **Judith Peak,** a recreation area managed by the Bureau of Land Management (BLM). In winter telemark skiers practice their skills on the south face of the peak, also called Big Grassy. From the top you get spectacular views of central Montana.

Back on the main gravel road, southeast of Judith Peak, lies the ghost town of **Gilt Edge.** Not much remains of this town, whose claim to fame is that Calamity Jane called it home from time to time. From Gilt Edge you can either head back the same way or continue on the road heading east, bearing right at the fork, then make your way south to Highway 200 (US 87), where you emerge about 12 miles east of Lewistown.

Back on the main scenic drive, head north on US 191. At Hilger you can take CR 236 north to Scenic Route 20. To complete this drive to Malta, stay on US 191 north as it flows around the base of the Judith Mountains, which now lie to the south.

When you reach the junction with Highway 19, east of Roy, turn north to continue on US 191. As you approach the Missouri River, you'll notice that the terrain quickly "breaks." That is, there's an abrupt change in landscape from grassland plateaus to high cliffs and bluffs, which have been cut by the river over millennia. This region of Montana is known, therefore, as the **Missouri River Breaks,** and it's one of the most spectacular sights.

Soon you reach the **Charles M. Russell (CMR) National Wildlife Refuge,** which encompasses the entire shoreline of Fort Peck Lake as well as this section of the Missouri River. Before you cross the river (on the south side), stop by the small information center to learn about the refuge; it's on the east side of US 191. Also on the river's south bank is the **James Kipp Recreation Area,** with a boat ramp and campground nestled among a grove of large cottonwood trees. Kipp

The Missouri River flows past James Kipp Recreation Area. DONNIE SEXTON

and a party of 44 men traveled up the Missouri River in 1831 and opened a fort at the mouth of the Marias River, where they traded furs with the Blackfeet Indians.

Just after you cross the bridge on US 191, you'll see a sign for an auto tour of the refuge, heading to the east. This 20-mile, well-maintained gravel road will take you along the river and through coulees covered with sagebrush, ponderosa pines, and grasses, then bring you back out to US 191 about 10.5 miles north of where you started. I recommend this side trip as a shorter alternative to Scenic Route 20 if you are uncertain about rough roads but still want to experience some of the Missouri River Breaks country. You can hike anywhere along the way except for a section along the river where a remnant population of prairie elk thrives, as indicated on the refuge map. The CMR refuge drive is about 2 hours long, unless you get out and explore on foot. Follow Refuge Road 101. When you come to the intersection at White Bottoms, you can continue straight along the river for about 6 miles but will have to turn around again and head north at the intersection to get to US 191. Just before you reach the main road, you'll find a campground and fishing access at Bell Ridge Recreation Site.

The area to the east of US 191 and north of the Missouri River is loaded with back roads, many very primitive and not maintained, also impassable when wet. Explore this area with a detailed BLM map or the *Montana Atlas and Gazetteer*.

Also, check local road conditions since severe weather can quickly turn passable roads into nightmares.

CMR National Wildlife Refuge to Landusky

If you continue north on US 191 (regardless if you take the side loop through the refuge), you will come to a junction with Highway 66. You can take this road north to the Fort Belknap Indian Reservation and the little towns of Landusky and Hays. This area has undergone extensive mining operations off and on from 1890 to 1998, and at one time a mill near here was the second largest cyanide mill in the world. (Cyanide is used to extract gold from ore—about an ounce of gold was obtained per 60 tons of rock!) There's a wooded campground near Landusky, but sadly, cyanide has poisoned the water and you are warned not to drink it.

The **Fort Belknap Reservation** is home to the Assiniboine people—who tend to live in the north—and Gros Ventre people who live in the Hays and Lodge Pole areas. *Gros ventre* is French for "big belly," and this particular nation of American Indians is believed to be the northernmost group of Arapaho.

If you look at your Montana highway map and locate the Fort Belknap Reservation, you'll notice a small notch (7 miles by 4 miles) at the southern tip. Zortman and Landusky are located in this notch, negotiated for by white representatives of the US government in 1895. The government had known about the gold deposits here and sent three delegates to bargain with the Indians for cash in exchange for the gold-rich land that they claimed the Indians were not using anyway. One of the delegates, Audubon Society founder George Bird Grinnell, summed up the anti-Indian sentiment of the day with suspect concern: "The only thing you have to sell is this little piece of land that you do not use. I should like to see you sell that, because if you don't, I cannot tell how after 2 years have gone by you are going to live."

The little speck of **Landusky** was named for Pike Landusky, who was the first to discover the gold here in the early 1890s. The town became a favorite hangout for gunmen, claim jumpers, murderers, robbers, rustlers, and other unsavory characters. Landusky himself was a cantankerous sort said to have single-handedly fought off a small war party of Native Americans (who had kidnapped him) with a frying pan. He also regularly hit people with a gold-headed, weighted cane, whether they deserved it or not. He was beaten and shot to death by the outlaw Kid Curry (Harvey Logan) in his own bar. This must be what they mean by the term "gold fever." It does funny things to people who get their hands on it.

Kid Curry was another lively character, ranking up there with Billy the Kid and Jesse James. Curry and his brothers were local ranch cowboys, and after Landusky was murdered, the Kid fled for a better life as thief, cattle rustler, and train

The town of Zortman once bustled with gold prospectors but experiences quieter times these days. DONNIE SEXTON

robber. Curry even kept company with Butch Cassidy, killing a few more people along the way until he was caught and jailed in Knoxville, Tennessee. By that time he had become a folk hero, and people were allowed to chat with him while he was incarcerated. He eventually escaped from Knoxville, and no one knows what became of him. One story places him in Alaska, where he supposedly died a poor prospector. Another story says he ended up in South America. You can see **Kid Curry's hideout** on Bull Creek Road, which is about 2 miles north of the junction of US 191 and Highway 66. Turn west on Bull Creek Road and drive for about 11.5 miles until you come to a pair of dirt tracks heading south. Take the second track. The hideout is about 1 mile south.

Hays & Fort Belknap Reservation to Malta

If you continue on Highway 66 north to Hays (check out the powwow in August), you can visit **Saint Paul's Mission,** established by Jesuits in 1886 and also used as a school. Gold prospectors volunteered to build the stone mission, maybe to atone for their sins committed under the influence of gold fever. Father Eberschweiler, the serving Prussian Jesuit priest, was loved and respected by the Assiniboine because he translated sermons into their own language. Nearby a tiny shrine built in 1931 to the Virgin Mary houses a replica of a carved wooden statue of the Mother of God. Mass is offered here some Saturdays.

Farther up the road is **Mission Canyon,** with several tiny picnic areas with interesting names; you'll find Bad Road, Lame Bull, the Boy, Lone Fly, and Isa Hoo along Peoples Creek. At the head of the canyon is a natural stone bridge. A gravel road cuts through the narrow 50- to 60-foot-high bluffs and leads toward Mission Peak, near the mine site. *Exploration of the mine site is forbidden.*

From Hays you can either retrace your route to US 191 or continue north on Highway 66 and turn east onto BIA 11 toward Lodge Pole. BIA 11 will take you through rolling hills and buttes, around the Little Rockies, and back to US 191, 17 miles northeast of Highway 66. About 2 or 3 miles past Lodge Pole, take a right at the first paved road, BIA 15, and follow it back to US 191. You don't need a permit to hike on the Fort Belknap Reservation, but you must have one to hunt or fish. Permits can be purchased at just about any store in Hays or Lodge Pole.

If you skip the side trip to Hays, or if you backtrack to US 191, you will pass through some interesting forested knobs, buttes, and plateaus along the southern fringe of the Little Rockies. The trees look out of place among the high desert plains, but they do provide more varied habitat for wildlife.

Eight miles east of the Highway 66/US 191 junction, you can take the Dry Fork Road to UL Bend National Wildlife Refuge within the CMR National Wildlife Refuge complex. (If you took BIA 11, you'll have to turn south on US 191 and backtrack 8 miles to Dry Fork.) Dozens of endangered black-footed ferrets (captive-bred) have been released here and also on the Fort Belknap Reservation in past years. The UL Bend area provides the ferrets with ample amounts of their favored prey: prairie dogs, whose active burrows number more than 10,000. The ferrets, which were thought to be extinct in the 1960s, are monitored with radio collars to determine their success. Since then scores of kits have been born in the wild in Montana!

Also at the Dry Fork Junction you can follow signs north to Zortman (the twin of Landusky and worth a leg stretch), where you'll find lodging, camping, and a small store. Look for bighorn sheep on the south side of Saddle Butte during winter. There are also several places to hike in the area.

Back on the main scenic drive, head north on US 191 toward Malta. Keep your eyes open for pronghorn in the draws and crossing the road. For a description of **Malta,** see Scenic Route 21, which you can pick up from there. Alternately, you can head west toward Glasgow on Scenic Route 18.

20

Missouri Breaks

Missouri Breaks National Back Country Byway

General description: A spectacular but rough 63 miles or so for 4-wheel-drive or high-clearance vehicles only, traveling through one of Montana's most geologically unique and historically significant regions.

Special attractions: Missouri River; wildlife viewing, hiking, mountain biking.

Location: North-central Montana beginning and ending in Winifred.

Drive route number: Missouri Breaks National Back Country Byway.

Travel season: Late spring until snow season. Wet conditions prohibit travel.

Camping: There is 1 campground with toilets at Woodhawk Creek Bottom, near the Missouri River. Primitive camping is allowed on public land anywhere along the route. Find the James Kipp Recreation Area campground where US 191 crosses the Missouri.

Services: Limited services (gas and a small store) in Winifred. Full services in Lewistown and Malta.

Nearby attractions: Charles M. Russell National Wildlife Refuge, Fort Belknap Indian Reservation.

The Route

Since this book was first written, portions of this drive have changed. Severe flooding in 2011 has rendered some sections impassable to vehicles, specifically the crossing at Lower Two Calf Creek. This part of the drive is actually part of the Charles M. Russell National Wildlife Refuge, and the crossing may one day be repaired, so check with either CMR Refuge or BLM's Lewistown Field Office for updates (see For More Information). In addition, a side trip to Sunshine and Deweese Ridges is not recommended for vehicles because of flood damage to the Woodhawk Creek crossing.

Despite these current conditions, this drive is still worth it and my personal favorite. As you bump and scrape through the arid outback, bordering wheat fields and high bluffs, this scenic drive will leave you exhilarated or cursing—or both. You may not see another vehicle the entire route, or you could run into several on the most well-kept section of the dusty Knox Ridge Road. If you're the adventurous type, or a Lewis and Clark fan, you'll love this journey. You can stand on 1,000-foot-high cliffs overlooking the wild and scenic Missouri River, but you'll have to hike or bike to them.

A few words of warning before you begin: Use caution at all times since road conditions can change from one storm to the next, and they certainly can change from season to season and year to year. So stay on established designated routes only. Some of the roads have a gravel surface; others do not. All traverse what are

Missouri Breaks

Get a feel for the Big Sky along the Missouri Breaks National Back Country Byway.
PHOTO COURTESY OF THE BLM

called "gumbo soils," which can become unbelievably slick with just the slightest amount of rain. Please take all warning signs and precautions seriously. If you get caught in wet weather while on this drive, make sure your legs are in good shape; it's a long walk out. Better yet, leave it for a sunny day or at least be prepared to spend a few hours, or the night, hunkered down. That means bring adequate food and water.

Large RVs, motor homes, and vehicles longer than 20 feet should not attempt the side roads. Regardless of what you're driving, you can always go as far as your vehicle will take you, or as far as you dare, then backtrack. Four-wheel-drive is best suited for this trip, although 2-wheel drives will do on the main route (even better if you have high clearance). Parts of the road are rough and sometimes washed out. Also, there are spots with quite steep grades into and out of deep coulees. So remember, it's easier to go down a steep hill than to drive back up it. If you're not an experienced driver, you may want to do only the Knox Ridge Road part of this loop, which takes you through rolling wheat fields. It's in good shape and mostly flat until you near the east end at US 191 across from James Kipp Recreation Area.

In addition, have good maps because byway signs are missing at some intersections. I highly recommend the Bureau of Land Management's handout on the

Missouri Breaks National Back Country Byway, with a map and historical anecdotes of the area. You can also use BLM maps of the Zortman/Winnett and Winifred/Lewistown quadrangles. And finally, throughout this route, private land is mixed with public land and you must have permission to access private lands.

I hope the precautions haven't put you off. If you heed them, you should enjoy this adventurous journey.

Winifred to Sunshine Ridge

The scenic drive begins in **Winifred,** one of Montana's many little backwaters plunked in the middle of the range. To get to Winifred, take US 191 north from Lewistown 14 miles to Hilger. At Hilger take CR 236 for 23 miles to Winifred. As you approach Winifred, keep your eyes open for a sign indicating Knox Ridge Road. Turn right onto this gravel road, near the gas station, just before you head down the main drag through town. You'll pass some grain elevators just after you turn; bear right beyond there and go over a little bridge. For the next 12 miles or so you'll be traveling mostly east through wheat fields and open cattle pastures. You'll begin seeing Back Country Byway signs as you follow Knox Ridge Road and the Missouri Breaks Back Country Byway. When you arrive at the intersection of Knox Ridge Road and Two Calf Road, turn north, following the signs to Lower/Middle Two Calf Road.

You'll still be traveling through wheat fields and open range; watch for cattle. A few buttes and ranch homes lay scattered across the plateau, and you may notice missile silos tucked away in the grain fields. The silos are the strange, square, fenced-in areas. As you come up over the first ridge, you can see the Little Rocky Mountains on the northeast horizon. Meriwether Lewis stood on high bluffs near here and took in the same view a couple hundred years ago. Thinking they were part of the Rocky Mountain chain, he wrote in his journal: "These points of the Rocky Mountains were covered with snow and the sun shone on it in such manner as to give me the most plain and satisfactory view. while I viewed these mountains I felt a secret pleasure in finding myself so near the head of the heretofore conceived boundless Missouri."

This region was covered with an inland sea between 135 and 65 million years ago, as evidenced by shale deposits exposed by downcutting streams that flow through here. Where you see darker deposits in the bluffs, deep waters once flowed. You may find fossils and dinosaur bones while exploring parts of this Back Country Byway. You are allowed to keep plant and shellfish fossils, but you must leave dinosaur bones in place and report your findings to the BLM. Who knows, maybe you'll come across a never-before-discovered species and have it named for you!

The Missouri Breaks Back Country Byway rolls along Middle Two Calf Road.
Photo courtesy of the BLM

After about 7 miles, the road makes a major curve to the right and continues due east for about 5.5 miles. It will begin heading slightly north for 1 mile or so before curving right again. From here east, all gravel roads now become graded dirt roads and trails. Just after the second bend, you will see a sign at an intersection with a dirt track heading north. This side road leads to **Sunshine and Deweese Ridges.** The Woodhawk Creek crossing, about 2 miles down this road, was heavily damaged from floods in 2011. The BLM recommends you do not drive a vehicle across it. So if you want to see the spectacular views of the **Missouri River** from the bluffs about 7 miles farther along, you'll have to hoof it or mountain bike from here. Biking is a slog, though, because of the soft soils. If you choose to drive, you've been warned. The Nee-Me-Poo Trail (Nez Perce Trail), which follows the 1,170-mile journey of Chief Joseph and the Nez Perce Indians from Idaho to the Bears Paw Mountains, runs across Sunshine Ridge.

If you do make it to Sunshine Ridge, you might be surprised to know that where the river now flows is a relatively new channel, about 12,000 years old. Before glacial times, the Missouri flowed much farther north in what is now the Milk River drainage. Southward-advancing glaciers pushed the river south with them to where it now cuts through millions of years of marine deposits.

MISSOURI BREAKS   **169**

The glaciers must have been as thick as 1,500 or 2,000 feet to move the mighty Missouri.

Lower & Middle Two Calf Roads

Back on the main route, Lower Two Calf Road, the road passes through more grain fields and hayfields, the foreground of an expansive vista. As the road nears the edge of a plateau, which drops down to the river channel, there are more opportunities to take short side trips to the river. If you don't want to drive out on the steep side roads, you can always try it on a bike or walk.

About 2 miles east of the turnoff to Sunshine Ridge, you'll come to a side road that leads north (about 5 miles) to **Woodhawk Bottom.** This primitive camp site provides toilets but no potable water. From here you can walk along the southwest bank of the Missouri and explore a small homestead built by a man called Gus Nelson. Lewis and Clark camped near here on May 25, 1805. You can also hike along the bank to **Cow Island,** the big island north (upstream) of Woodhawk. Steamboats began making journeys to this part of the Missouri River in 1859 and often stopped at Cow Island to refuel. On their flight north in 1877, the Nez Perce demanded supplies from soldiers guarding steamboat freight on Cow Island. A small skirmish ensued, and the Nez Perce continued up Cow Creek to the west of the river.

Not quite 2 miles east of the Woodhawk Bottom turnoff, there's a fork in the road where you can continue driving mostly east on the Lower Two Calf Road (which gets narrower, rougher, and becomes more of a trail than a road). If you do choose this route, you'll have to turn around when you reach the bottom (in about 10 miles) because the Lower Two Crossing is no longer passable by vehicle. Alternatively, you can turn south on Middle Two Calf Road, which takes you about 9 miles to Knox Ridge Road. From here head west back to Winifred or east to US 191.

If your adventurous soul urges you to take Lower Two Calf Road (dry weather only!), be warned: it's a brain-rattler, eventually narrowing to single dirt track with cobbles and a washboard surface. There are a few steep descents and ascents among the coulees before you dip down toward Two Calf Creek. Another side road to the river, Powerplant Ferry Road, takes you to the historic docking point of the Powerplant Ferry. But don't let the name fool you: the ferry has long since disappeared. Regardless of how far you make it along Lower Two Calf Road, you'll have to turn around and retrace your steps at some point. At the intersection with Middle Two Calf Road, turn south toward Knox Ridge Road.

The Little Rockies rise in the distance along the Missouri Breaks Back Country Byway.
PHOTO COURTESY OF THE BLM

Knox Ridge Road

If you head west on Knox Ridge Road from Middle Two Calf Road, you'll be heading back to Winifred on a nice gravel, if not dusty, surface. You'll wind and dip through sagebrush and grain fields scattered with a few buttes. If you head east on Knox Ridge Road, you'll come out on US 191 across from **James Kipp Recreation Area,** where the highway crosses the Missouri River. When you approach US 191 from Knox Ridge Road, the latter becomes steep and narrow—and maybe just a little too anxiety inducing for some travelers. Along it you can take another short side road to Knox Bottoms, where Lewis and Clark camped on May 24, 1805.

At US 191 you can pick up Scenic Route 19 in its middle and head north to Malta to connect with Scenic Routes 18 and 21. Or you can go back to Lewistown and take Scenic Route 19 from its starting point.

21

High-Line

Malta to Havre

General description: An 85-mile drive following Montana's High-Line, named for the railroad and US 2 along which Montana's northern residents live.

Special attractions: Black Coulee National Wildlife Refuge, Bear Paw Battlefield, Fort Assiniboine, Wahkpa Chu'qn Archaeological Site, Havre Beneath the Streets; hiking, mountain biking, fishing, camping.

Location: North-central Montana from Malta to Havre on US 2.

Drive route number: US 2.

Travel season: Year-round. Blowing and drifting snow can make winter travel hazardous.

Camping: There are a limited number of commercial campgrounds in and around Havre.

Services: Full services in Malta, Chinook, and Havre. Limited services in Fort Belknap Agency, Zurich, Harlem, and Dodson.

Nearby attractions: Lake Thibadeau National Wildlife Refuge, Nez Perce Trail, Rocky Boy's Indian Reservation.

The Route

Along this High-Line drive, you're likely to see more trains on the old Great Northern Railway tracks than cars on the road. The line later became Burlington Northern. The upland prairie and fields of grain, stretching for miles into Canada, are potholed with hundreds of small lakes that attract migrating waterfowl and shorebirds by the millions. With no landscape features to stop it, the wind can be ferocious here, especially in winter, moving like the freight trains that connect East and West. And as you pass through the small communities the rails connect, you might wonder about the foreign place-names. From Glasgow to Shelby, several little towns were named for European cities. Some believe that immigrant railroad workers chose the names after their hometowns. Others believe the names were chosen with the spin of a globe; the railroad owner, perhaps, stopping the spin with his finger, picking the name it landed on and thus making his way along the tracks, bringing the world to his world.

Whatever the case, you won't find much European flavor, as any similarity begins and ends in name only. What you will discover is how Montana got its nickname, the Big Sky State, along with friendly and hardworking people.

Malta to Fort Belknap Agency

From the 1870s to the turn of the 20th century, **Malta** was the center of a great cattle empire that stretched from Canada to the Missouri River and from Glasgow

High-Line

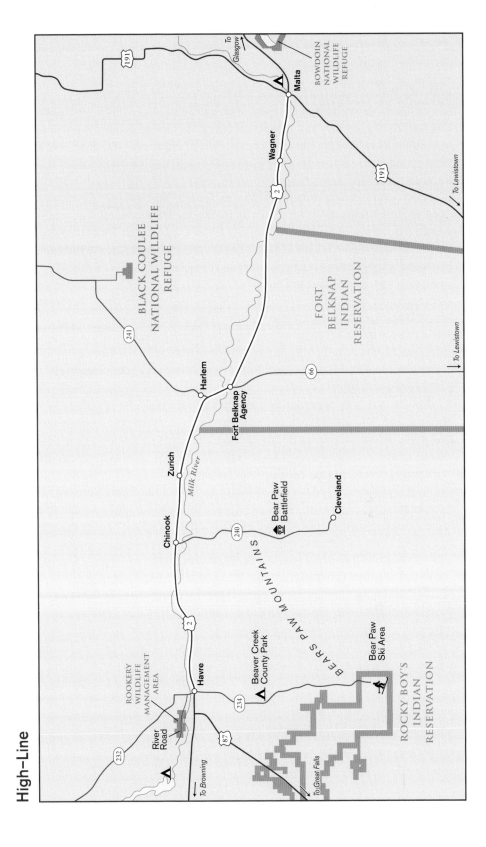

to Havre. The town also served as the entertainment capital for cowboys coming in from the range and looking to spend their hard-earned two bits. Every Labor Day weekend the cowboy and pioneer spirit lives on during the annual gathering of the **Milk River Wagon Train.** In a funny twist of evolution, you can now follow them on Facebook. Horse-drawn wagons and buggies tumble and bounce across the plains on a 60-mile journey, ending their 5-day trek in Malta. Their arrival is celebrated with a parade and other festivities. Contact the chamber of commerce (see For More Information) for details on joining the wagons and for more information about other Malta events.

You'll find the full range of Malta's history at the **Phillips County Museum** (www.phillipscountymuseum.org), with everything from dinosaurs to homesteaders, Native Americans, and outlaws. Check out the restored 1910 house and garden near the museum. For more dino displays, you shouldn't miss the **Great Plains Dinosaur Museum & Field Station** (www.greatplainsdinosaurs.org), where you can watch scientists as they work on recently discovered bones. "Leonardo" lives here, too; he's a rare dinosaur mummy claimed to be the best preserved dinosaur ever discovered. This is part of Montana's **Dinosaur Trail** (www.mtdinotrail.org).

You must stop by **Bowdoin National Wildlife Refuge,** east of Malta, a beautiful spot complete with its own scenic drive (see Scenic Route 18). Much of the land north of Malta is saturated with potholes and marshes, the perfect place for a wildlife refuge.

To begin the main scenic drive, head west from Malta on US 2, following the course of the Milk River all the way to Havre. Lewis and Clark gave the river its name because its color resembled a cup of tea with a splash of milk. Assiniboine Indians called it *wahkpa chu'qn,* "the river that scolds all others." Today the Milk River flows in the old channel left by the Missouri River after glaciers pushed the Missouri south to its current spot (see Scenic Route 20).

Nine miles west of Malta you reach the town of **Wagner,** where once Kid Curry and his gang of infamous Montana outlaws robbed a train in 1901 (see Scenic Route 19). Some say the hoodlums made off with a satchel full of worthless papers; others say they snagged $80,000 in cash.

Carrying on, US 2 flows over flat prairies and around minor hills and coulees across Montana's High-Line. Most of eastern Montana was short-grass prairie before European settlement, and much of it now supports cattle and a smattering of crops, although premier growing for dryland wheat is west of Havre. The wind is a constant, and coupled with the absence of mountains, it might make people who aren't used to it feel lonely and vulnerable. Sometimes you have to dig deep, but the High-Line country has true beauty all its own.

Even though it's mostly flat, the country you're driving through is dissected by a network of shallow coulees and scattered with low buttes. Northeast of Harlem you'll find **Black Coulee National Wildlife Refuge.** If you need more birds to check off your life list, stop by. To get there take CR 241 northeast from Harlem for 24 miles. Ignore the major left-hand bend in the road. Instead, continue on the gravel spur road due east. Turn right and head south on CR 128 for about 3 miles. Turn east and go for 1 mile, then south for 0.5 mile until you reach the gate. From here you can walk into the marshy area, where you might also find mule deer, pronghorn, and golden eagles. Tundra swans pass through in October.

Fort Belknap Agency to Havre

Back on US 2, pop in at **Fort Belknap Agency** on the south side of US 2 opposite Harlem. Fort Belknap sits on the northern border of the Fort Belknap Indian Reservation, home to both the Assiniboine and Gros Ventre Nations. The Assiniboine came from a division of Yanktonai Sioux who originally lived near Lake Superior. They eventually split to form their own nation and moved westward, settling in eastern Montana around the early 1800s. The name Assiniboine, or *assnipwan,* is of Sioux origin, meaning "stone Sioux," and probably refers to a traditional cooking method that employed hot stones.

If you're here in late July, you can take in **Milk River Indian Days,** featuring dances and games. The information center in Harlem exhibits Native American arts and crafts, and the staff provides tours of ancient tepee ring sites, Snake Butte (a sacred area), tribal bison pasture, and the Old Mission. You don't need a permit to hike on the reservation, but you must buy a permit to hunt or fish. You can get one from just about any store on the reservation.

West of Fort Belknap is the larger town of Chinook. Be sure to visit the **Blaine County Museum** for more local fossils and dinosaur bones, homestead-era mock-ups and displays, and Native American cultural objects. You can also learn about the Battle and Siege of the Bear Paw (see below). The name "Chinook" was adopted from a Indian word meaning "warm wind." Thus the word has been borrowed by meteorologists to describe the warm winds that blow through the High-Line country in late winter. Many livestock owners, past and present, have been grateful for these winds, which can quickly melt snow and uncover grass for their grazing herds. Chinooks have even caused ambient temperatures to rise as much as 50 degrees in just minutes. Charles M. Russell's drawing of a lone, skeletal cow bracing against the hard winter wind is titled *Waiting for a Chinook, or The Last of the Five Thousand.* This small sketch won Russell fame as an artist after he sent it to the cow's owner in response to an inquiry about his herd's condition.

South of Chinook lie the **Bears Paw Mountains,** onetime volcanoes that last erupted about 50 million years ago. The Bears Paws are where Nez Perce Chief Joseph (aka Thunder-Rolling-in-the-Mountains) laid down his weapons and surrendered to General Nelson A. Miles. On October 5, 1877, Chief Joseph—with 87 warriors and 147 women and children—gave up trying to reach Canada while fleeing the US Army. After leading his people 1,170 miles, the weary leader delivered his moving speech:

> Tell General Howard I know his heart. What he told me before I have in my heart. I am tired of fighting. Our chiefs are killed. Looking Glass is dead. The old men are all killed. It is the young men who say yes or no. He who led the young men is dead. It is cold and we have no blankets. The little children are freezing to death. My people, some of them, have run away to the hills and have no blankets, no food; no one knows where they are, perhaps freezing to death. I want time to look for my children and see how many of them I can find. Maybe I shall find them among the dead. Hear me, my chiefs, I am tired; my heart is sick and sad. From where the sun now stands, I will fight no more forever.

To get to **Bear Paw Battlefield** (www.nps.gov/nepe/planyourvisit/bear-paw-battlefield.htm), head south from Chinook on CR 240 for about 16 miles. The battlefield is on the east side of the road. If you're here during the first week of October, many Native Americans from Montana and Idaho journey here to remember the plight of their ancestors against the streaming tide of white settlement. The gathering usually falls on the weekend closest to October 5, the anniversary of the surrender.

On October 7, 1877, more than 400 Nez Perce were led by US soldiers away from the battlefield and out of Montana. They would cross North Dakota, South Dakota, and Kansas, eventually arriving at Indian Territory in Oklahoma. Generals Miles and Howard promised the Nez Perce they could return to their homeland, but they were overruled by senior officers. Chief Joseph and Yellow Bull continued to work for their peoples' return to their homelands. In 1885, with the help of General Miles, about 100 Nez Perce were allowed to go back to Idaho. The remaining 150, including Chief Joseph, were sent to the Colville Reservation in what is now the state of Washington. Chief Joseph continued to lobby for the freedom of his people until his death—of a broken heart—in 1904. After becoming familiar with the workings of the US government, he once remarked, "White men have too many chiefs." Who could argue with this great and wise man?

Chief Joseph of the Nez Perce surrendered to US Army General Nelson A. Miles.
Donnie Sexton

Havre & Surrounding Area

Return to US 2 and continue the main scenic drive west, following the Milk River and the railroad line until you reach the town of **Havre.** One of eastern Montana's larger towns, Havre is home to the Montana State University–Northern Campus (previously Northern Montana College), and its campus atmosphere provides much to see and do. In its early days the town was a trading center and refuge for range riders. In the recent past cowboys fought for the right to tie their horses to parking meters downtown. It's not clear who won the skirmish, but don't be surprised if you find yourself parking next to a bay mare. In July take in the Great Northern Fair. In September celebrate Havre Festival Days.

Discover a much earlier part of this region's history, behind the Holiday Village Mall, at the **Wahkpa Chu'qn Archaeological Site** (www.havremt.com/attractions/wahkpa_chu.htm). For about 2,000 years, until about the year 1400, Native Americans used a buffalo jump located behind what is now the mall. In addition to a jump—where bison were chased over a bluff—there was a corral site, where bison were rounded up and killed with spears, rocks, and arrows. Guided walks at the site are available from June 1 to Labor Day and last about 1 hour.

One of the many archaelogical finds at Wahkpa Chu'qn. DONNIE SEXTON

The **H. Earl Clack Museum** (May 15 to Labor Day) exhibits artifacts from Wahkpa Chu'qn, as well as pioneer exhibits and horse-drawn farm equipment. Tour information is available at the museum. This is part of Montana's Dinosaur Trail (www.mtdinotrail.org).

Fort Assiniboine, south of town, was once a US military post, established in 1879 to protect settlers from possible Indian attacks. Following Custer's defeat by the Sioux and Cheyenne at the Battle of the Little Bighorn, settlers were a little uneasy, and the US government was afraid that Sitting Bull (one of the strongest chiefs who led the charge against Custer) would return from exile in Canada, causing more trouble for white settlers. The fears never materialized. General John Pershing of World War I fame (then a lieutenant) served at the fort under General Miles. "Black Jack" Pershing was head of the Tenth Cavalry here in 1896, an African-American unit called the Buffalo Soldiers. For a guided tour of Fort Assiniboine (www.havremt.com/attractions/fort_assinniboine.htm), June 1 to Labor Day, contact the H. Earl Clack Museum.

One highly recommended tour is **Havre Beneath the Streets** (www.havre mt.com/attractions/beneath_the_streets.htm), a unique guided walk under Havre's main streets. The subterranean city was once a commercial strip full of thriving businesses, including a bordello, opium den, speakeasy, pharmacy, barbershop, meat market, and saloons, among others. The tour guides like to say that the opium dens in Havre weren't illegal, but the Chinese who ran them were. When the railroad was completed, the Asian workers who had labored on it weren't allowed to remain in this country legally. And with little incentive or means to return to their homelands, where else to go but underground? Literally.

Many of the underground passages and businesses that make up Havre Beneath the Streets are original; others have been re-created. Several of the original businesses eventually moved to street level, and some were restored at the original underground location. No one is sure why some legitimate businesses chose to go below ground, but it could be that a 1904 fire, which destroyed much of downtown Havre, forced people to set up temporary shops beneath the burned-out areas. Others theorize that cold winters and hot summers may have been more tolerable underground.

North of Havre you'll find the **Rookery,** a wildlife management area with tremendous birdlife. The old-growth cottonwoods and Milk River bottomlands, combined with surrounding uplands and coulees, provide outstanding habitat for golden eagles, great-horned owls, American kestrels, hawks, great blue herons, American avocets, and several species of duck and goose. On foot explore several river trails; or canoe a 4- or 5-mile stretch of river. There are boat launches at the upper and lower ends of the wildlife area. To get to the Rookery, take 7th Avenue north out of town. Cross the tracks and the river, then turn west on River Road. The Rookery is about 5 miles farther.

South of Havre, **Beaver Creek County Park** (www.havremt.com/attractions/beaver_creek_park.htm) is another outstanding natural area. At 17 miles long by 1 mile wide, it is one of the largest county parks in the United States. It rests comfortably between slopes of the Bears Paw Mountains and is dotted with small lakes and ponds. Rolling, grassy hills give way to pine forests and aspen groves above. As the name suggests, this is a good place to see beavers, as well as to add birds to your life list. Deer, elk, coyotes, and raccoons also frequent the park. To get to Beaver Creek, take 5th Avenue to Beaver Creek Road and head south for 9 miles. There is a minimal user fee.

From Havre you can continue west on US 2 about 160 miles to Browning, where Scenic Route 22 begins. Or you can head back to Malta and pick up Scenic Route 18 or 19.

22

Rocky Mountain Front

Browning to Wolf Creek

General description: A 137-mile drive along the Rocky Mountain Front that is a tremendous way to view the gigantic spine of the continental mountain mass.

Special attractions: Museum of the Plains Indian, North American Indian Days, Heart Butte, Freezeout Lake Wildlife Refuge, Sun River Game Range, Holter Lake Recreation Area; dinosaur digs, museums; hiking, backpacking, mountain biking, fishing, boating, camping, wildlife viewing.

Location: Northwest Montana from Browning south to Wolf Creek.

Drive route numbers: US 89, US 287.

Travel season: Year-round. Extreme winter weather can make travel hazardous and sometimes prohibitive.

Camping: There are several Forest Service campgrounds in Lewis and Clark National Forest. Holter Lake also has campgrounds.

Services: Full services in Browning, Choteau, Augusta, and Wolf Creek. Limited services in other small towns along the way.

Nearby attractions: Crown Butte Preserve, Glacier National Park, Helena National Forest, Lewis and Clark National Forest, Meriwether Lewis Fight Site.

The Route

Imagine a 200-mile-long wall of mountains butted up against river-cut plains rich in wildlife and history. Actually, you don't have to imagine it, because this drive will take you there. Plan to start in the morning when the sun is shining on the mountain crests. Like many of the other scenic drives in this book, there are so many places to stop and explore, you might want to take this trip over the course of a few days.

If you're not a member of the Blackfeet Nation, you can still explore some parts of the reservation, but be sure to get permit information before hiking, hunting, or fishing. Permits are available from most shops in Browning.

Browning & the Blackfeet Reservation

Begin on the **Blackfeet Indian Reservation** in the town of **Browning,** east of Glacier National Park. Your first stop must be the **Museum of the Plains Indian** (www.browningmontana.com/museum.html) on the west edge of town. The small museum is expertly conceived and exhibits Native American clothing, toys, weapons, jewelry, arts, and crafts all wonderfully laid out in glass cases with great interpretation. Hanging maps illustrate other American Indian nations and their homelands.

Rocky Mountain Front

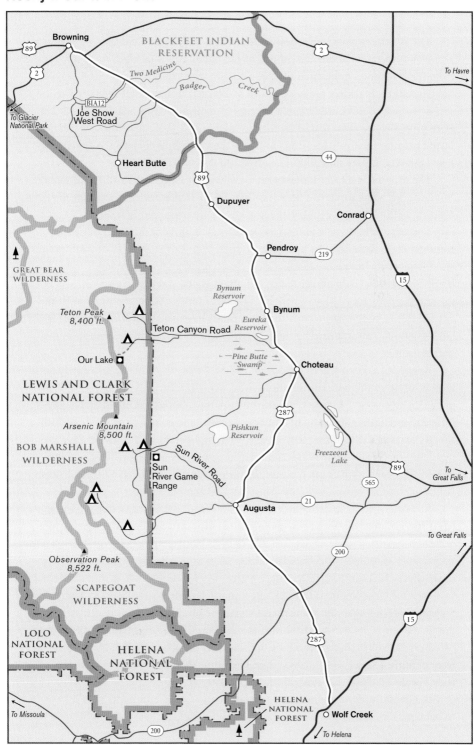

The Blackfeet have the largest membership of all Indian nations in Montana. There is uncertainty about the origins of the name, but "blackfeet" may have come from the blackened moccasins the people wore when they first met white explorers. Montana's Blackfeet are also known as Piegans, a name that refers to the southernmost of three tribes spread across Canada and Montana. The Blackfeet were probably the most feared by white settlers of all Montana tribes, as well as feared by other Native Americans for their ferocious bravery and the aggressiveness with which they raided other camps and defended their own.

The original Blackfeet Reservation encompassed roughly two-thirds of western Montana but had shrunk to a little less than 1.5 million acres by the turn of the 20th century. In the late 19th century, the Blackfeet were pressured into selling a significant portion of their scenic and sacred lands, much of them now part of Glacier National Park. Because of its proximity to the Front Range of the Rocky Mountains and the diversity of habitat, the Blackfeet Reservation and adjacent lands today are home to grizzlies, elk, bighorn sheep, mountain goats, and pronghorn.

Accompany a Blackfeet native on a cultural tour of **Glacier National Park** (www.blackfeetnationstore.com/suntours.html) to learn about the neighboring park's natural, cultural, and historical features as viewed from the standpoint of native peoples.

Be sure to take in **North American Indian Days** (www.blackfeetcountry.com/naid.html) if you're here during the second week in July. This Native American gathering is one of the largest, pulling visitors from both the United States and Canada, and highlights some incredibly beautiful and colorful costumes at traditional dance and drumming ceremonies. Overnight stays in traditional Blackfeet tipi camps are available through the Lodgepole Gallery and Tipi Village (www .blackfeetculturecamp.com). Cultural history tours of some of its historical sites, including buffalo jumps and tepee rings, can be arranged.

To begin the scenic drive, take US 89 south from Browning, following the signs to Great Falls. Just south of Browning the road dips into the Two Medicine River bottom then into Badger Creek. Just east of here Meriwether Lewis had the first and only deadly encounter with Indians during his entire 2-year expedition. The Corps of Discovery had camped for the night with 8 or 9 Blackfeet men, whom Lewis had mistaken for Gros Ventres. The next morning, 2 Blackfeet were killed by the explorers when, according to the white man's story, the Blackfeet men were caught stealing horses and guns. In fear of retribution, the exploring party made quick tracks for the Missouri River. The Blackfeet have a different story and believe that their ancestors were unfairly accused of thievery. Given white man's historical and unfavorable attitude toward Native Americans, it's quite possible.

Incidentally, if you're interested in Lewis and Clark landmarks, you'll have to backtrack a little to US 2, east of Browning to mile marker 233. You'll see a historical marker indicating Camp Disappointment (www.nps.gov/nr/travel/lewis andclark/dis.htm), so named by Lewis when he discovered that the Marias River did not flow as far north as 50 degrees latitude, which would have extended the boundary of the Louisiana Territory. Lewis's party camped 4 miles north of the marker, and you can view this state historical site from CR 444 heading north.

Back on the main scenic drive route, southwest of Badger Creek lies **Ghost Ridge,** where during the winter of 1883–84, more than 600 Blackfeet starved to death following the extermination of bison by commercial hunters. The dead were buried on Ghost Ridge, and you can tour the site as part of the package tour from Browning mentioned above.

The Badger–Two Medicine region, from which the Badger Creek waters flow, is forested land held sacred by the Blackfeet people. Along with the Blackfeet Nation, conservationists are trying to get the Badger–Two Medicine area federally designated as wilderness to protect wildlife habitat here. In 2002 nearly 90,000 acres of the Badger–Two Medicine were declared eligible for listing as a Traditional Cultural District in the National Register of Historic Places.

The wild lands of the Rocky Mountain Front are vital to wildlife with large habitat needs, such as grizzly bears, that roam between Glacier National Park and the Bob Marshall Wilderness. Preserving the Badger–Two Medicine lands would connect these two important habitats and provide wildlife more room to migrate and disperse.

If you want to get a little closer to the Badger–Two Medicine area and hike some trails in **Lewis and Clark National Forest,** you can do so. About 11 miles south of Browning and just after you cross the Two Medicine River, you'll find BIA 12, also called Joe Show West Road. Turn west and follow it until it dead-ends at Heart Butte Road. If you turn north here, you will end up in Browning again. If you turn south, you will follow the foothills of the mountains. You can access some trails from the Heart Butte Road. The roads end at the reservation boundary, where the public trails begin. Please respect treaty rights and do your exploring on public lands only. Refer to a Lewis and Clark National Forest map for details.

If you continue on the main Heart Butte Road, it will take you to Badger Creek Road and back out to US 89. Or you can continue south on Heart Butte Road to the small Blackfeet community called Heart Butte. From here you can continue on to Birch Creek Road, also called Arrowhead Road, back to US 89 at the southern boundary of the Blackfeet Reservation.

You have probably noticed by now how the rolling, grassy hills and plateaus are the perfect medium for drawing your eyes to the western wall of mountains. Montanans call this the **Rocky Mountain Front,** or East Front, referring to the east side of the Continental Divide. The section known as the Front Range

The Rocky Mountain Front on the way to Pishkun Reservoir. Tom Kilmer

stretches all the way down to I-15. This drive is so stellar mostly because of the stark contrast of the relatively flat plains smacking into the spine of mountains.

The hummocky land around you was formed by glacial moraine—gravel and debris dumped by piedmont glaciers, which were fairly stagnant blocks of ice. Larger glaciers moved south from Canada and east from Glacier National Park, leaving the remnant ice blocks and a boulder-strewn trail across what eventually became the upland prairie.

Dupuyer to Choteau

Dupuyer is about 11 miles south of the junction of US 89 and Highway 44. Called after the French word *depouilles*, the name refers to bison back fat, a delicacy for both Native Americans and white explorers. The writer Ivan Doig, whose novels about early settlers in Montana have made him a favorite of new and old Westerners alike, based his novel *English Creek* on old-timers' stories and the landscape surrounding Dupuyer. The town itself was settled in 1874 as cattle began replacing bison. Cowboy artist Charles M. Russell hung out near here at the Home Ranch.

South of Dupuyer, US 89 curves through hilly country until you reach Pendroy. The road is narrow so use caution here at all times of year but particularly in winter. At the small community of Bynum, be sure to visit the Two Medicine Dinosaur Center (www.tmdinosaur.org) housed in an old church building with dinosaurs painted on the sides. This is part of Montana's Dinosaur Trail (www .mtdinotrail.org). The center houses the skeletal remains of what they allege to be the world's longest dinosaur: the *Seismosaurus*. If you dig dinosaurs, you can really dig them in this region. The center offers full-day, half-day, and multiday tours of the Choteau area. Contact them for details. On the north end of town, Blackleaf Road will take you west to **Bynum Reservoir** for fishing and to Blackleaf Wildlife Management Area below Volcano Reef. Both grizzlies and black bears frequent the marshes and the limber pine habitat of these ridges. You might see one of these magnificent bears, so please keep your distance.

South of Bynum, and just before you reach Choteau, Teton Canyon Road heads west to **Eureka Reservoir,** the Pine Butte Swamp Preserve, and numerous trails into the **Bob Marshall Wilderness** complex. Some of the trails you might want to explore include Mill Falls, Green Gulch, and Our Lake, where you can take a 3.5-mile hike to look for mountain goats and view the Chinese Wall, an eponymous rock formation in the Bob Marshall Wilderness. Refer to the Lewis and Clark National Forest map for details on roads and trails.

The 18,000-acre wetlands of **Pine Butte Swamp Preserve,** owned by the Nature Conservancy, was established in 1978 primarily as a preserve for grizzly bears. The flatlands along the East Front are the only place where grizzlies still roam the prairies, once traditional habitat for these awesome creatures. The preserve also supports more than 150 bird species, deer, elk, beavers, and muskrats. Most of Pine Butte Swamp is off-limits to people, but you can use some areas with permission from the preserve manager. You don't need permission to hike along the ridge across from the information signs at the "swamp." Contact the manager for information on guided nature walks and other events throughout spring and summer.

In the 1970s paleontologist Jack Horner discovered the first duck-billed dinosaur nesting colony in North America near **Choteau,** complete with fossilized eggs and embryos. The site is called Egg Mountain. The eggs belonged to a species of dinosaurs called *Maiasaura peeblesorum*, which is now Montana's state dinosaur. Ash from volcanoes in the Elkhorn Mountains to the south had buried the dinosaurs, preserving their nests and eggs so well that the find at the **Willow Creek Anticline** is considered among the most incredible dinosaur discoveries in the world. Horner further rocked the world of paleontology with his theory, now widely accepted, that some dinosaurs were caring beasts, raising and nurturing their babies much as birds do today. Other dinosaur finds along the East Front include a troödon, which is a smaller version of the vicious velociraptor that made

Signs of early European settlers can still be seen along the Rocky Mountain Front.
Tom Kilmer

its infamous appearance in the book (and movie) *Jurassic Park.* The Willow Creek site has also yielded dozens of other types of dinosaurs.

In Choteau stop at the **Old Trail Museum** (also part of Montana's Dinosaur Trail; www.mtdinotrail.org) to learn a bit about local history and more about dinosaurs. Be sure to check out a unique "fossilized" creature at the museum—*Trapper canadensis*—who suffered extinction from a combination of lead poisoning to the brain and arrowhead in the spine. In September Choteau holds a **Threshing Bee,** where you can see old-time methods of threshing wheat, milling timber, making shingles, and blacksmithing, among other things. There's a fiddle contest and street dance in July.

Choteau to Wolf Creek

South of Choteau the main scenic drive road forks; US 89 heads to Great Falls, while US 287 takes you to Wolf Creek and is the main part of this scenic drive. For a side trip take US 89 about 10 miles southeast of Choteau to **Freezeout Lake Wildlife Management Area.** During peak times (spring and fall) the refuge supports up to 1 million birds on their migration stopover. Here you can see tundra swans and snow geese, sandhill cranes, curlews, stilts, and black-crowned night herons. Upland game birds, raptors, and mammals are also abundant. You can also hike, boat, and hunt here.

Back on the main scenic drive, take US 287 south from Choteau for about 26 miles to the Old West town of **Augusta,** a picture-perfect place of the quintessential old cowboy town of Western imagination. Augusta has some wonderful characters. It was named for Augusta Hogan, the daughter of rancher J. D. Hogan, who managed extensive land holdings here for Conrad Kohrs, a Helena businessman. Augusta prides itself as the home of the "wildest show on Earth"—its annual rodeo during the last weekend in June. It's also a gateway to the incredible Bob Marshall Wilderness complex to the west. Be sure to stop by the century-old general store, a charming real West mercantile with a few nice things to spend your money on.

Northwest of town lies the **Sun River Game Range** situated in the foothills of the Rockies. From Augusta follow Willow Creek Road for about 4 miles over glacial moraine and bear right at Sun River Road. You'll pass **Willow Creek Reservoir,** where you can drop a fishing line if you wish. The Sun River, called the Medicine River by the Blackfeet, has food-rich bottomlands that provide winter range for Montana's largest elk herd. When Captain Meriwether Lewis passed through here on July 10, 1806, he noted in his journal about the vast herds of bison here: "we hered them bellowing about us all night." Lewis also observed "vast assemblages of wolves" and "saw a large herd of Elk making down the river."

If you follow the road into Sun River Canyon about 15 miles, you may see bighorn sheep, especially near Home Gulch Campground or in Hannan Gulch across the way. Winter is the best time to see both sheep and elk from selected vantage points, since the game range itself is off-limits to hikers during winter. The road up Hannan Gulch can be rough, so you may want to walk or ride your mountain bike.

To continue this scenic drive, head south on US 287 from Augusta. After you cross Bowman's Corner, at an almost hidden intersection with Highway 200, you leave the expansive plains and enter a landscape of more rugged, grass-covered hills, forested buttes, and rocky ridges. The hills on the east side of the road are the **Adel Mountains,** the highest of which is Birdtail Rock. These ancient volcanoes erupted 50 million years ago. To the southeast the peaks of the **Gates of the Mountains Wilderness** pop over the horizon and are part of the Big Belt Mountains east of Helena.

At the end of this drive, you reach I-15 just north of **Wolf Creek.** You can head into Wolf Creek proper and follow signs to **Holter Lake,** a dammed portion of the Missouri River, for camping, fishing, and boating. You might also see pelicans, loons, and a variety of ducks and geese paddling around the lake. Keep

US 287 rolls through the upland prairies and foothills of north-central Montana.
Tom Kilmer

your eyes peeled for peregrine falcons. These once-rare birds of prey have made a comeback in Montana after DDT almost wiped them out.

The **Beartooth Wildlife Management Area** is just south of Departure Point on the southeast end of Holter Lake. It's a good place to see elk and bighorn sheep, as well as a prairie dog town. You can hike or mountain bike on the dirt roads that cut through the wildlife area, which is open from May 15 until November 30. You can also take a scenic wildlife viewing tour just south of here at Gates of the Mountains. Look for the Gates of the Mountains exit off I-15. From here you can take a boat tour on a portion of the Missouri River through which the Lewis and Clark Expedition passed, or you can launch your own boat. A Lewis and Clark journal entry dated July 19, 1805, tells how the place got its name: "This evening we entered much the most remarkable clifts that we have yet seen. These clifts rise from the waters edge on either side perpendicularly to the hight of 1,200 ft. . . . I called it the gates of the rocky mountains."

The 2-hour boat tour winds through bighorn sheep, mountain goat, and mule-deer country. It also passes **Mann Gulch,** where in 1949 thirteen smoke-jumpers were killed trying to fight a blaze that exploded up the mountainside.

You can read about that incident in the book *Young Men and Fire*, by Norman Maclean.

From Gates of the Mountains, the closest scenic route is number 23 (about 70 miles northeast of here). You can also drive southwest about 120 miles through Helena to Anaconda and pick up Scenic Route 5.

23

Crazy & Little Belt Mountains

Livingston to Sluice Boxes State Park

General description: A 133-mile drive that takes you through the wide valley between the Bridger Mountains and the Crazy Mountains, winding through the south end of Smith River country before climbing to the top of the Little Belt Mountains.

Special attractions: Museums, hot springs, a ghost town, skiing, hiking, camping, fishing, swimming, floating.

Location: Central Montana, from Livingston north to Sluice Boxes State Park.

Drive route number: US 89.

Travel season: Year-round. Blowing and drifting snow can make winter travel hazardous.

Camping: You'll find many Forest Service campgrounds in the Little Belts, Bridger, and Crazy Mountains. You can also camp just about anywhere in the national forests.

Services: Full services are available in Livingston and White Sulphur Springs. Limited services are available in Clyde Park, Wilsall, Neihart, and Monarch.

Nearby attractions: Canyon Ferry Lake, Crimson Bluffs landmark; Gallatin, Lewis & Clark, and Helena National Forests, Livingston.

The Route

One of my favorites, if for no other reason than few people travel through here, this scenic drive traverses both open country and mountains. Some of the areas were heavily mined at the turn of the 20th century, but mostly it's quiet now. The rounded, forested knolls that characterize the Little Belt Mountains are a nice contrast to the sheerness of other Montana ranges, like the Bridgers and Crazies.

Livingston to White Sulphur Springs

Begin your drive just northeast of **Livingston** (see Scenic Route 11 for a description of the town) at the junction of I-90 and US 89. This is the Shields River Valley: open, dry, and scrubby ranchland lolling between the Crazy Mountains on the east and the Bridgers on the west. The river was named by Captain William Clark in honor of John Shields, a member of the Lewis and Clark Expedition. The Corps of Discovery camped at the mouth of the river on July 15, 1806, while exploring the Yellowstone River region. Jim Bridger—for whom the western mountains were named—was a trapper, trader, and scout who guided wagon trains from Fort Laramie to Virginia City in the 1860s. He used this valley on treks from the

Crazy & Little Belt Mountains

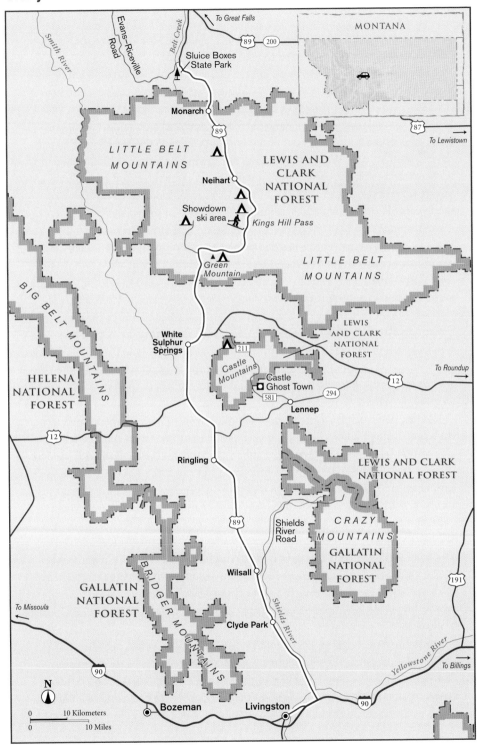

To Great Falls

89 200

MONTANA

Smith River

Evans-Riceville Road

Belt Creek

Sluice Boxes State Park

Monarch

89

87

To Lewistown

LITTLE BELT MOUNTAINS

LEWIS AND CLARK NATIONAL FOREST

Neihart

Showdown ski area

Kings Hill Pass

LITTLE BELT MOUNTAINS

Green Mountain

BIG BELT MOUNTAINS

White Sulphur Springs

LEWIS AND CLARK NATIONAL FOREST

211

Castle Mountains

Castle Ghost Town

581

294

Lennep

HELENA NATIONAL FOREST

12

To Roundup

12

Ringling

LEWIS AND CLARK NATIONAL FOREST

89

Shields River Road

CRAZY MOUNTAINS

GALLATIN NATIONAL FOREST

191

Wilsall

GALLATIN NATIONAL FOREST

BRIDGER MOUNTAINS

Shields River

To Missoula

Clyde Park

Yellowstone River

To Billings

N

90

0   10 Kilometers

0   10 Miles

Bozeman

Livingston

90

Yellowstone River to what is now Bozeman. The Crazy Mountains to the east, isolated and mysterious, were sacred to the Crow Indians.

Driving north on US 89, you soon reach the little town of **Clyde Park,** named for the Clydesdale horses that were bred on a nearby ranch in the late 19th century. If you're passing through in late August or early September, stop by Old Settlers Days, featuring games, dancing, a barbecue, and parade. Just 6 miles up the road is **Wilsall,** a contraction of the names Will and Sally, the son and daughter-in-law of an early settler who laid out the town. The annual Wilsall rodeo takes place in June. In recent years human bone fragments and stone tools were unearthed on a private ranch near the town and were found to be several thousand years old, indicators of early human inhabitants in the valley.

North of Wilsall, US 89 is mostly straight and flat as it courses through hayfields and cattle range. To the east loom the Crazy Mountains, little used by recreationists because of limited access but nevertheless both eerie and spectacular. Geologists remain perplexed by the odd mix of igneous rocks that form the mountains. The higher southern end of the range was heavily glaciated, although glaciers left the lower northern end unscathed. A small piece of one of these glaciers remains as a snowfield, which entombs insects frozen during the last ice age. You can backpack to the glacier from Cottonwood Creek near Clyde Park. The Shields River Road just north of Wilsall provides one of the few access points for the Crazies' limited trails. Refer to the Gallatin and Lewis and Clark (Jefferson Division) National Forest maps for details.

When you reach the little town of **Ringling,** you will see an abandoned church on a small hill above the highway, a clue that times were once better here. The Milwaukee Road (Chicago, Milwaukee, St. Paul and Pacific Railroad) used to snake its way all through this part of the state, but now the tracks are abandoned, and many of the whistle stops—like Ringling—are quiet and lonely, if they have survived at all. Ringling got its name from John Ringling of circus fame who also built another railroad through here (the Yellowstone Park and White Sulphur Springs Railroad) when this town was a big shipping depot for wheat and cattle. The latter was eventually incorporated into the Milwaukee Road. Contemporary singer Jimmy Buffett once described Ringling in song: "The streets are dusty and the bank has been torn down / It's a dying little town / The church windows are broken, the place ain't been used in years / Jail don't have a sheriff or a cell." A bar is about all that remains.

Just north of Ringling, US 89 intersects with CR 294, which heads east. If you want to take a side trip to explore a ghost town (read below for permission details), take CR 294 about 16 miles to the town of Lennep, then head northwest on FR 581 for about 7 miles to **Castle Town,** so named for the castle-like granitic spires in the Castle Mountains of the Lewis and Clark National Forest. At one

The Crazy Mountains are one of Montana's island mountain ranges. CHRIS MCGOWAN

time Castle was one of the richest mining camps in the state, with about 80 homes, 14 saloons, and 7 brothels. It also had its own brass band. Smelters were built here between 1889 and 1891, and the Cumberland Mine was once the biggest producer of lead ore in Montana. Fifteen hundred mining claims were heavily worked for 4 years, but by 1893 the town had begun to die. The last reported residents to live in Castle were two elderly gentlemen in the 1930s.

For liability reasons, the current owners of Castle Town request that you ask permission before exploring. For details, call the White Sulphur Springs Ranger District of the Lewis and Clark National Forest (see For More Information).

Back on the main scenic drive, US 89 continues north toward White Sulphur Springs, passing through high desert plains, with rolling hills, glacial moraine, and rangeland. Look for pronghorn on the range and great blue herons in the warm creek along the road, which is the South Fork of the Smith River.

White Sulphur Springs to Neihart

In **White Sulphur Springs** you can take a soak in the mineral baths at the **Spa Hot Springs Motel & Clinic** (www.spahotsprings.com) at US 89 and US 12. The

Small churches like this one near Ringling were among some of the first to be built by European settlers. KATHIE DeWITT & PAUL DUMOND

pools are drained and cleaned every day, and no chemicals are used to treat the water. Visit the **Castle Museum** (you can't miss it; it looks just like a small castle) built by B. R. Sherman in 1892. Sherman's wealth came from the livestock and mining industries, both booming businesses here at the turn of the 20th century. The house is full of antiques, most of which were donated by locals in memory of their pioneer ancestors. The cherrywood used for the staircase and entryway was imported from Europe. The stone used to build the castle was hauled by oxen from about a dozen miles south of White Sulphur Springs. There's also a small room full of artifacts and newspaper clippings about Castle Town.

If you're a boater, several miles northwest of town you'll find access to the gorgeous **Smith River.** Because of its popularity, though, in order to float the Smith you must apply for a permit in January. There are only a few fishing accesses. Much of the floatable portion of the river spirals through cliff-enclosed canyons and is not to be missed if you ever get the chance to experience it.

To continue this scenic drive, head north of White Sulphur Springs on US 89 toward the **Little Belt Mountains,** where the landscape changes dramatically. The main road through here is the Kings Hill National Scenic Byway. You enter the Little Belt foothills from the south, where your view of the surrounding country narrows a bit. The curvy road traverses hilly rangeland scattered with homes, and the hills are covered with Douglas fir and pine. The road climbs a low pass, then heads down again before reaching Newlan Creek Reservoir, where you can fish. Newlan Creek, flowing along the west side of the road, is flanked with lush willow thickets.

The Little Belt Mountains are composed largely of sedimentary deposits laid down by a giant inland sea. Evidence of its marine past is found in fossils embedded in the mountain range and dating from more than 200 million years ago. The Belts also contain igneous rocks, which form the round buttes you see. The buttes began as bubbles of magma punching their way through the sedimentary deposits. The rounded terrain here indicates that the Belts escaped the ice age's carving tool: glaciers.

US 89 climbs north through open, rolling hills that gently rise to rounded hilltops. As the road makes a sharp east turn around the base of Green Mountain, 7,047 feet high, the rangeland opens up even more. There are a handful of Forest Service campgrounds along the way, all of which are wooded and near the main road. The first one is a few miles east of the Green Mountain bend. The elevation at this point is about 6,000 feet.

Temperatures are cool here as evidenced by the surrounding spruce-fir forest. The road begins to ascend Kings Hill Pass, elevation 7,393 feet. **Showdown Ski Area** (http://showdownmontana.com) is at the top, where you can go downhill skiing or rent snowmobiles if you're visiting during winter. A fire tower near the top of the ski area on Porphyry Peak is occupied during summer. The road to it is narrow and rocky but passable. From the lookout you get a fantastic view of the Little Belt Mountains and valley below.

Descending Kings Hill Pass, the road winds through a somewhat narrow canyon with rocky slopes on both sides. You can see the bald knob of Long Mountain ahead. Just past Many Pines Campground you might notice a large area of trees blown over and strewn about the hill. A tornado of sorts blew through here on the heels of a severe thunderstorm in spring 1994. Winds damaged trees in about a 50- to 60-acre swath, but a solid 10 acres of trees were completely knocked down. No one was hurt in this "microburst," although some people were trapped at the campground and had to be rescued.

A little more than 1 mile past Many Pines Campground, where the road crosses Belt Creek, is a short trail to **Memorial Falls,** about 0.5 mile. Watch your footing carefully because the trail is rocky and ribbed with tree roots. During high water it may not be possible to cross the creek, which you must do to reach the falls. It's a nice little hike for stretching your legs, and the falls, only about 10 to 15 feet high, are pretty.

Eking out a living on Montana's windswept plains. Chris McGowan

Neihart to Sluice Boxes State Park

North of Memorial Falls on US 89, you reach the tiny community of **Neihart,** with a small grocery store, bar and restaurant, and motel. The hills northeast of the townsite are loaded with private mining claims dating back to the 1880s. Silver and lead were mined here until the silver crash of 1893 put most mines out of business. Some mining was revived in the earlier 20th century, but nothing significant was found. Neihart is now a winter recreation hub for snowmobilers and skiers. Just north of town is the cemetery, spread out at the foot of a forested hillside. Many of the headstones are so old, they're unreadable, and some were cut from wood instead of granite. Many markers were once circled by picket and iron fencing—to keep livestock out—now rotted and collapsed. Some of the iron grates have ornate designs. Continuing north, you reach the community of **Monarch,** which served as the processing center for silver ore mined from around Neihart. The Great Northern Railroad was built here in 1890, making the town a commercial center for the region's mines until the silver crash 3 years later.

Beyond Monarch, US 89 traverses more open rangeland, with coulees and foothills adding to the relief. As you near **Sluice Boxes State Park** (http://fwp

.mt.gov/parks/visit/sluiceBoxes), some of the country resembles eastern Montana's badlands. There's a scenic turnout above the park, from which you can look down into the deeply carved bottomland cut by Belt Creek. Access to the park is by Evans-Riceville Road, just beyond the scenic turnout. Sluice Boxes is considered a "primitive" state park, which means there is neither camping nor developed picnic areas with potable water. There is a wheelchair-accessible vault toilet at the parking lot, however.

The 8-mile trail that begins here is also not maintained, and the brush can grow high. The trail follows Belt Creek, then an abandoned railroad berm in a canyon with bluffs as high as 500 feet. The privately owned Montana Central Railroad (later part of the Great Northern Railway) laid the tracks in the 1880s to serve local mining communities. The rail bed was blasted into the cliff in places and needed 40 trestles to cross Belt Creek and tributaries on its sinuous route. It was also considered a scenic route, and people from Great Falls often hopped the train to get to fishing and picnicking sites along Belt Creek. The tracks were abandoned in the late 1940s when the mines finally closed.

There is little shade at Sluice Boxes State Park, and walking the trails on hot summer days can be unpleasant. If you're brave enough, though, you can go for a dip in Belt Creek. You'll find some great swimming holes, but the water is heart-stoppingly cold; trust me. One of those swimming holes is about 0.25 mile up the main trail. Take any one of the little paths through the brush to the creek.

Carrying on the trail in about another mile or so you will have to cross Belt Creek, which is about 50 feet wide here. During low water it's only a few inches deep and slow moving. On the other side you can continue up the trail past the former site of the Don Bosco Camp, last operated in the 1970s by the Boy Scouts and Lions Club. From here the trail crosses Belt Creek several more times, impassable during high water. If you want to wet a line, rainbow, brook, cutthroat, and brown trout are your main catch. You might even spot a mink hopping along the bank.

Just north of Sluice Boxes, US 89 ends at the intersection with Highway 200. From here you can head east about 65 miles on Highway 200 to Scenic Route 24, which starts on US 191 near Moore. Scenic Route 19 begins in Lewistown just east of Moore.

24

Judith Basin

Eddie's Corner to Big Timber

General description: An 88-mile scenic drive coursing through the heart of Montana's wheat-growing region and rangeland scattered with buttes and coulees.

Special attractions: Crazy Mountains, Crystal Lake, Judith River wildlife area, Ackley Lake State Park; camping, hiking, mountain biking.

Location: Central Montana, from Eddie's Corner south to Big Timber.

Drive route number: US 191.

Travel season: Year-round. Blowing and drifting snow can make winter travel hazardous.

Camping: There is limited camping in the Little Belt, Snowy, and Crazy Mountains and at Ackley Lake State Park.

Services: Full services are available in Big Timber, Harlowton, and nearby Lewistown. Melville, Judith Gap, and Moore have limited services.

Nearby attractions: Deadman's Basin Reservoir, Lewis and Clark National Forest, Nez Perce (Nee-Me-Poo) Trail.

The Route

Even the most urban of urbanites cannot help but love the thousands of acres of prairie and range this scenic drive takes in. Like much of the state, the land here looks much the way it did more than a century ago. There are one or two side trips to keep you occupied, but try to enjoy this drive for what it is—a drive. Every once in a while get out and take a few deep breaths of the prairie air and imagine what it must have been like to cross this country by covered wagon. If it's a hot summer day, I hope your car has air-conditioning. If you're here during winter, keep both hands on the wheel for the gusty wind, and thank your Maker you don't live in a one-room sod hut on the Great Plains.

Eddie's Corner & the Judith River WMA

Begin the drive at Eddie's Corner at the junction of US 87/Highway 200 and US 191 just west of Moore. If you want to do a little exploring in the low, mountainous bumps that rim the prairie to east and west near the drive's starting point, you can do so despite the paucity of access roads. To the west are the Little Belt Mountains, sedimentary deposits left by a giant inland sea with igneous intrusions. The Little Belts were never glaciated because they were too low to accumulate the tremendous amounts of snow needed to feed glaciers. The **Judith River**

Judith Basin

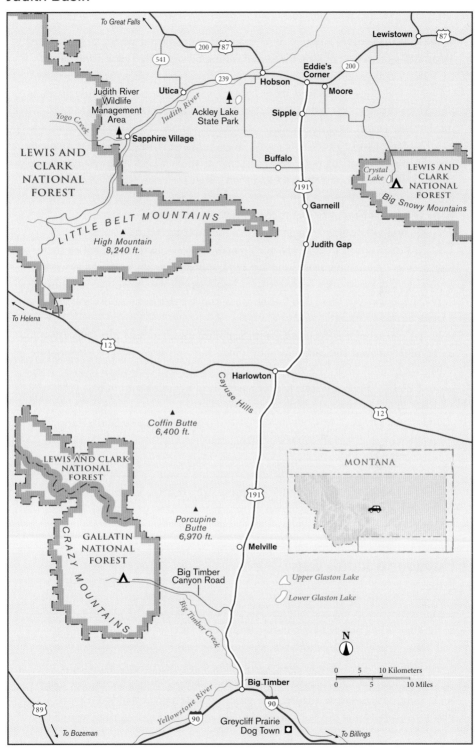

To Great Falls

Lewistown

87

200 87

541

239

Eddie's
Corner

Judith River
Wildlife
Management
Area

Utica

Hobson

Moore

200

Judith River

Ackley Lake
State Park

Sipple

Yogo Creek

Sapphire Village

LEWIS AND
CLARK
NATIONAL
FOREST

Buffalo

Crystal
Lake

LEWIS AND
CLARK
NATIONAL
FOREST

Big Snowy Mountains

LITTLE BELT MOUNTAINS

191

High Mountain
8,240 ft.

Garneill

Judith Gap

To Helena

12

Harlowton

Cayuse Hills

12

Coffin Butte
6,400 ft.

MONTANA

LEWIS AND CLARK
NATIONAL
FOREST

CRAZY

GALLATIN
NATIONAL
FOREST

Porcupine
Butte
6,970 ft.

191

Melville

MOUNTAINS

Big Timber
Canyon Road

Upper Glaston Lake

Lower Glaston Lake

Big Timber Creek

N

0   5   10 Kilometers

0   5   10 Miles

To Bozeman

89

Big Timber

90

90

Yellowstone River

Greycliff Prairie
Dog Town

To Billings

Wildlife Management Area (WMA) is on the mideastern flank of the Little Belts. This 5,000-acre refuge of pine forest and rolling hills supports elk during winter. There's also great birding here. The magnificent northern goshawk has been known to visit the area, as have other large raptors. Numerous songbirds flit about the shrubs that trim the Judith River. You can hike on the refuge from May 15 through November 30.

The easiest way to get to the Judith River WMA is via the town of **Hobson,** 6 miles west of the starting point for this scenic drive on US 87/Highway 200. From Hobson take CR 239 west to Utica and then follow the gravel road for about 12 miles toward the Little Belt Mountains. Just past Sapphire Village turn west onto Yogo Creek Road and take that to the wildlife area about 1 mile farther. Incidentally, brilliant deep blue sapphires were mined from Yogo Creek in the late 19th century. Rumors of gold sent men scurrying to the Little Belts, but all they found were the tiny blue stones that, in 1894, someone finally bothered to have appraised. The stones were identified as unique sapphires—most blue sapphires have a green tint, but these don't—and were mined extensively until about 1929. A few are picked sporadically today. Even the crown jewels of England are believed to have Yogo sapphires. At one time the sapphire mines in the Little Belts raked in more money than many Montana gold mines. Lots in the community of Sapphire Village were sold along with the partial claims to the sapphire mines. Buyers complained that the mining claims they received were worthless and in past years won a lawsuit that gave them rights to productive claims.

On your way back to Hobson, you can stop at **Ackley Lake State Park** (http://fwp.mt.gov/parks/visit/ackleyLake), southwest of town, for boating, fishing, and camping. From Ackley Lake you can weave through farm country east to US 191, picking up the main scenic drive from the hamlet of Buffalo. Without a detailed National Forest map or the *Montana Atlas and Gazetteer,* the roads will seem labyrinthine. The easiest way is to return to US 87/Highway 200 at Hobson and pick up the drive from Eddie's Corner.

Hobson to Judith Gap

Back on the main US 191 route, you'll see the Big Snowy Mountains to the east, a compact range of peaks and one of several "island," or isolated, mountain ranges in the state. The Snowys have a designated Forest Service campground and several hiking trails near **Crystal Lake,** a popular recreation site and easily accessed. You'll find trails to Crystal Cascades and some caves. The lake itself, set in a glacier-carved basin, bubbles from natural springs beneath its surface. The ridges, rocky outcrops, and cone-shaped hills above provide a great setting for picnics. Pick up a pamphlet at the campground for a self-guided walking tour around the

A resident of Greycliff Prairie Dog Town State Park. Donnie Sexton

lake. The lake is only about 13 feet deep in spring after runoff, and by autumn it's only about knee or waist deep. The national recreation trail here passes through subalpine forest and meadow ecosystems. Look to the cliffs above to spot foot-sure mountain goats introduced here in 1954. If you don't see them hopping about the cliffs, take a hike up Grandview Trail northwest of the campground.

To get to the Snowys from US 191, you have to follow a maze of roads. The easiest route might be to head east from Sipple, 4 miles south of Eddie's Corner. Take the gravel road east, following the signs for Crystal Lake Road, for just more than 6 miles and turn south. Go 1 mile more and turn east again for 2.25 miles. Turn south and follow the winding road along Rock Creek to Crystal Lake. The Snowys, which cradle the lake, are shaped nearly like a dome. Most of the range was deposited from an inland sea that covered this region about 300 million years ago. Like the Big Belts, the Snowys escaped scouring glaciers.

Retrace your path to return to the main scenic drive on US 191. Soon you come to the town of **Garneill.** Check out the interesting 2.5-ton "sculpture" here, made of granite rock on a concrete base into which several objects are imbedded. Known as the **Ubet and Central Montana Pioneers Monument,** it honors early pioneers and Native Americans with pieces of embedded ore, petrified wood, and

Once roaming much of the state, bison are now raised by ranchers in some places.
TOM KILMER

other relics. **Judith Gap** is the next town south. It sits in the "gap" between the Little Belts and Snowy Mountains. The surrounding area was a prime hunting ground for Native Americans, until pioneers arrived and turned Judith Gap into a bustling shipping depot for wheat.

The country all around you, and those covered in many of the eastern scenic drives in this book, is short-grass prairie, the most northwesterly of the Great Plains. You've probably noticed that standing water here is scarce, rainfall even more so, and the growing season is short. In the rain shadow of the mountains to the west, grasses here must be adept at sending out roots to capture the sparse soil moisture. To thrive, plants must be able to survive sometimes months without rain and take advantage of rain when it does fall. It's hard to imagine how beasts as large as bison survived, scattered across these plains with no shade from the fierce sun and nothing to block the wind, except other bison, during arctic-like winters.

Harlowton to Big Timber

Eighteen miles south of Judith Gap, you reach **Harlowton,** the only major urban area on this scenic drive, which makes it an oasis on the arid range. In the center of town is a railcar from the last electric railroad, the Milwaukee Road, which ended its run in Harlowton in 1974. The town was named for Richard Harlow, who built a branch line to Lewistown called the Jaw Bone. This part of the track was the longest stretch of electrified railroad in the country at one time. Much earlier in the region's history, dinosaurs roamed the once-tropical landscape. They left their legacy in bone fragments found throughout the area. Along with pioneer exhibits, the **Upper Musselshell Museum** (www.harlowtonmuseum.org) displays some of these finds (say "hey" to Ava for me). This is part of Montana's Dinosaur Trail (www.mtdinotrail.org). In July check out Harlowton's rodeo.

US 191 continues south of Harlowton, whisking you through sweeping country. The **Crazy Mountains** are visible in the southwest. Chief Plenty Coups (see Scenic Route 15) was said to have had a vision in the Crazies following several days of fasting and praying. The vision revealed to him that in his lifetime bison would vanish and be replaced by "the bulls and the calves of the white men"—a prophecy that sadly proved true.

As you enter Sweet Grass County, another oasis of sorts rises on both sides of the road. These are the **Cayuse Hills,** their coulees scattered with pine trees. It may seem strange to see the pines, relatively lush growth on these desert-like plains. The ground here is mostly sandstone, and its porous structure holds water well enough to support the pines. The road dips into some more lush lowlands with benches and mesa-like formations above. Several creeks meander through this land, all private, from the Crazy Mountains to the west and Glaston Lakes to the east. Big Timber Canyon Road turns off toward the Crazy Mountains 9 miles south of Melville and leads to a campground with hiking trails to several small lakes. It's a popular spot during summer.

Beyond the turnoff US 191 winds down through river-cut badlands into the town of Big Timber. The stream bottom is lush along Big Timber Creek, and you can fish at marked access sites. Big Timber Creek flows into the Yellowstone River just north of town. The Yellowstone, the longest undammed river in the Lower 48 States, is a popular fishing and floating river, meeting up with the great Missouri River near the Montana–North Dakota border. The Bozeman Trail crosses the Yellowstone just west of Big Timber. The trail was more or less abandoned in 1868 after 6 years of bloody skirmishing between Native Americans, who began to envision the end of their traditional lives, and settlers, who envisioned acres of new lives and land free for the taking.

US 191 ends at **Big Timber,** which was named by William Clark for a large stand of cottonwood trees where either the Boulder River or Big Timber Creek (it's not clear which) flows into the Yellowstone River. On their way east from the Pacific Ocean, the Corps of Discovery chopped down a cottonwood tree here to make a pirogue.

Big Timber is a quaint town with a small park and tree-lined streets along which tidy houses sit. The **Crazy Mountain Museum** (http://sweetgrass.mtgen web.org/museum.html) displays items reflecting the history of Sweet Grass County and surrounding area, including fossils, dinosaur bones, and Indian artifacts. The museum celebrates its summer opening each year on Memorial Day with music, food, and a sneak preview of the current season's new exhibits. The Sweet Grass County Fair is in July or August, and at the Bull-a-Rama, in late May, you can watch the region's top bull riders defy death in the ring. If fishing is your bag, several guides are available in Big Timber to take you along the Yellowstone or Boulder Rivers.

From Big Timber you can reach Scenic Routes 11 and 23 near Livingston or take Scenic Route 12 south from Big Timber into the Absaroka-Beartooth Wilderness Area.

APPENDIX:
FOR MORE INFORMATION

Tourism Information

Travel Montana
301 South Park
PO Box 200533
Helena, MT 59620-0533
(800) VISIT-MT (800-847-4868) or
(406) 841-2870
TDD: (406) 841-2702
www.visitmt.com

Montana Indian Reservations

General Information about Montana's
Indian Nations: http://visitmt.com/
places_to_go/indian_nations/

Blackfeet Reservation
Browning, MT
(406) 338-7406 or (406) 338-7181
www.blackfeetnation.com

Crow Reservation
Crow Agency, MT
(406) 638-7272
www.crownations.net

Flathead Reservation
Pablo, MT
(406) 675-2700 or toll-free:
(888) 835-8766
Tourism Information: (406) 675-0160
www.cskt.org

Fort Belknap Reservation
Harlem, MT
(406) 353-8473
www.ftbelknap-nsn.gov

Fort Peck Reservation
Poplar, MT
(406) 768-2300
www.fortpecktribes.org

Little Shell Chippewa
Great Falls, MT
(406) 452-2892
State-recognized nation without a
designated reservation in Montana.
The tribe is currently petitioning for
federal recognition.
www.littleshelltribe.com/index.shtml

Northern Cheyenne Reservation
Lame Deer, MT
(406) 477-6284
www.cheyennenation.com

Rocky Boy's Reservation
Box Elder, MT
(406) 395-4282
www.rockyboy.org

USDA Forest Service

Beaverhead-Deerlodge
National Forest
Supervisor's Office
420 Barrett St.
Dillon, MT 59725
(406) 683-3900
www.fs.usda.gov/bdnf

Madison Ranger District
5 Forest Service Rd.
Ennis, MT 59729
(406) 682-4253

Pintler Ranger District, Philipsburg
88 Business Loop
Philipsburg, MT 59858
(406) 859-3211

Wisdom Ranger District
PO Box 238
Wisdom, MT 59761
(406) 689-3243

Wise River Ranger District
Box 100
Wise River, MT 59762
(406) 832-3178

Bitterroot National Forest
Supervisor's Office
1801 N. 1st St.
Hamilton, MT 59840
(406) 363-7100
www.fs.usda.gov/bitterroot

Custer National Forest
Supervisor's Office
1310 Main St.
Billings, MT 59105
(406) 657-6200
www.fs.fed.us/r1/custer

Ashland Ranger District
Box 168, US 212
Ashland, MT 59003
(406) 784-2344

Beartooth Ranger District
HC 49, Box 3420
Red Lodge, MT 59068
(406) 446-2103

Sioux Ranger District
Box 37, Main and First Streets
Camp Crook, SD 57724
(605) 797-4432

Flathead National Forest
Supervisor's Office
650 Wolfpack Way
Kalispell, MT 59901
(406) 758-5208
www.fs.fed.us/r1/flathead

Swan Lake Ranger District
200 Ranger Station Rd.
Big Fork, MT 59911
(406) 837-7500

Gallatin National Forest
Supervisor's Office
Box 130
Bozeman, MT 59715
(406) 587-6701
www.fs.fed.us/r1/gallatin

Big Timber Ranger District
Box 1130, 225 Big Timber Loop Rd.
Big Timber, MT 59011
(406) 932-5155

Bozeman Ranger District
3710 Fallon St., Suite C
Bozeman, MT 59718
(406) 522-2520

Gardiner Ranger District
Box 5, 805 Scott St.
Gardiner, MT 59030
(406) 848-7375

Hebgen Lake Ranger District
PO Box 520
West Yellowstone, MT 59758
(406) 823-6961

Livingston Ranger District
5242 US 89 South
Livingston, MT 59047
(406) 222-1892

Kootenai National Forest
Supervisor's Office
31374 US 2 West
Libby, MT 59923
(406) 293-6211
www.fs.fed.us/r1/kootenai

Cabinet Ranger District
2693 Hwy. 200
Trout Creek, MT 59874
(406) 827-3533

Libby Ranger District
12557 Hwy. 37
Libby, MT 59923
(406) 293-7773

Rexford Ranger District
949 US 93 North
Eureka, MT 59917
(406) 296-2536

Lewis and Clark National Forest
Supervisor's Office
1101 15th St. North
Great Falls, MT 59405
(406) 791-7700
www.fs.fed.us/r1/lewisclark

Augusta Information Station
Box 365, 405 Manix St.
Augusta, MT 59410
(406) 562-3247

Belt Creek Ranger District
4234 US 89
Neihart, MT 59465
(406) 236-5511

Judith Ranger District
Box 484, 109 Central Ave.
Stanford, MT 59479
(406) 566-2292

Musselshell Ranger District
Box 1906, 809 2nd St. Northwest
Harlowton, MT 59036
(406) 632-4391

Rocky Mountain Ranger District
1102 Main Ave. Northwest
Choteau, MT 59422
(406) 466-5341

White Sulphur Springs Ranger District
Box A, 204 W. Folsom
White Sulphur Springs, MT 59645
(406) 547-3361

Lolo National Forest
Supervisor's Office
Building 24, Fort Missoula
Missoula, MT 59804
(406) 329-3750
www.fs.fed.us/r1/lolo

Missoula Ranger District
Building 24, Fort Missoula
Missoula, MT 59804
(406) 329-3814

Seeley Lake Ranger District
3583 Hwy. 83
Seeley Lake, MT 59868
(406) 677-2233

**Shoshone National Forest
Supervisor's Office**
808 Meadow Ave.
Cody, WY 82414
(307) 527-6241
www.fs.fed.us/r2/shoshone

**Clarks Fork, Greybull, and
Wapiti RDs**
203A Yellowstone Ave.
Cody, WY 82414
(307) 527-6921

Montana State Parks

**Montana Department of Fish,
Wildlife & Parks**
Parks Division
1420 E. 6th Ave.
Helena, MT 59620
(406) 444-2535
http://fwp.mt.gov

*For information about Blackfoot-
Clearwater Wildlife Management Area,
Painted Rocks, Placid Lake, Salmon
Lake:*

MT Dept. FWP, Region 2
3201 Spurgin Rd.
Missoula, MT 59804
(406) 542-5500

*For information about Bannack,
Beaverhead Rock, Holter Lake,
Lewis and Clark Caverns, Missouri
Headwaters:*

**MT Dept. FWP, Region 3
Helena Area Resource Office**
930 Custer Ave. West
Helena, MT 59620
(406) 495-3260

*For information about Ackley Lake,
Bear Paw Battlefield, Giant Springs,
Sluice Boxes, Smith River:*

MT Dept. FWP, Region 4
4600 Giant Springs Rd.
Great Falls, MT 59405
(406) 454-5840

*For information about Chief Plenty
Coups, Cooney Reservoir, Greycliff
Prairie Dog Town:*

MT Dept. FWP, Region 5
2300 Lake Elmo Dr.
Billings, MT 59105
(406) 247-2940

*For more information about Fort Peck
Lake or Rock Creek (by Fort Peck):*

MT Dept. FWP, Region 6
54078 US 2 West
Glasgow, MT 59230
(406) 228-3700

*For information about Medicine Rocks,
Pirogue Island, Rosebud Battlefield,
Tongue River Reservoir:*

MT Dept. FWP, Region 7
352 I-94 Business Loop
Miles City, MT 59301
(406) 234-0900

*For information about the Boulder
River Road:*

Montana's state flower, the bitterroot. Tom Kilmer

Sweet Grass County
(406) 932-3011
Visit www.co.sweetgrass.mt.us for a
direct link to road conditions

Park County
(406) 223-2860 or 222-2860
(after 3 p.m.)
www.parkcounty.org

Chambers of Commerce

Anaconda
(406) 563-2400
www.anacondamt.org

Baker
(406) 778-2266
www.bakermt.com

Bigfork
(406) 837-5888
www.bigfork.org

Big Sky
(406) 995-3000
www.bigskychamber.com

Big Timber
(406) 932-5131
www.bigtimber.com

Bitterroot Valley (Hamilton)
(406) 363-2400
www.bvchamber.com

Bozeman
(406) 586-5421
www.bozemanchamber.com

Browning
(406) 338-2344
www.browningmontana.com

Choteau
(800) 823-3866
www.choteaumontana.com

Columbus
(406) 322-4505
www.stillwatercountychamber.com

Dillon
(406) 683-5511
www.beaverheadchamber.org

Drummond
(406) 288-3297
www.drummondmontana.com

Ekalaka
(800) 346-1876
http://custer.visitmt.com

Ennis
(406) 682-4388
www.ennischamber.com

Eureka
(406) 889-4636
www.welcome2eureka.com

Gardiner
(406) 848-7971
www.gardinerchamber.com

Glasgow
(406) 228-2222
www.glasgowmt.net

Hamilton
(406) 363-2400
www.bvchamber.com

Hardin
(800) 346-1876
www.thehardinchamber.org

Harlowton
(800) 527-5348
www.harlowtonchamber.com

Havre
(406) 265-4383
www.havremt.com

Lewistown
(406) 535-5436
www.lewistownchamber.com

Libby
(406) 293-4167
www.libbychamber.org

Livingston
(406) 222-0850
www.livingston-chamber.com

Malta
(406) 654-1776
www.maltachamber.com

Miles City
(406) 234-2890
www.milescitychamber.com

Missoula
(800) 526-3465
www.missoulacvb.org

Philipsburg
(406) 859-3388
www.philipsburgmt.com

Red Lodge
(406) 446-1718
www.redlodgechamber.org

Saco
(800) 653-1319
www.sacomontana.net

Seeley Lake
(406) 677-2880
www.seeleylakechamber.com

Swan Lake
(800) 886-2303
www.swanlakemontana.org

Three Forks
(406) 285-4753
www.threeforksmontana.com

Troy
(406) 295-1064
www.troymtchamber.org

Virginia City
(800) 829-2969
www.virginiacity.com

West Yellowstone
(406) 646-7701
www.westyellowstonechamber.com

White Sulphur Springs
(406) 547-2250
http://meagherchamber.org

National Parks, Monuments & Recreation Areas

Big Hole Battlefield
PO Box 237
Wisdom, MT 59761
(406) 689-3155
www.nps.gov/biho

Bighorn Canyon NRA
Visitor Center, Box 458

Fort Smith, MT 59035
(406) 666-2412
Visitor Info: (307) 548-5406
www.nps.gov/bica

Glacier National Park
Park Headquarters
West Glacier, 59936
(406) 888-7800
www.nps.gov/glac

Little Bighorn Battlefield
USDI Park Service
PO Box 39
Crow Agency, MT 59022
(406) 638-3217
www.nps.gov/libi

Yellowstone National Park
PO Box 168
Mammoth, WY 82190
(307) 344-7381
www.nps.gov/yell

Bureau of Land Management

Dillon Resource Area
1005 Selway Dr.
Dillon, MT 59725
(406) 683-8000
www.blm.gov/mt/st/en/fo/dillon_field_office.html

Judith Resource Area
920 NE Main St.
Lewistown, MT 59457
(406) 538-1900

Lewistown Field Office
920 NE Main St.
Lewistown, MT 59457
(406) 538-1900

National Wildlife Refuges

Bowdoin NWR
194 Bowdoin Auto Tour Rd.
Malta, MT 59538
(406) 654-2863
www.fws.gov/bowdoin

Charles M. Russell NWR
PO Box 110
Lewistown, MT 59457
(406) 538-8706
www.fws.gov/cmr

Red Rock Lakes NWR
27650B S. Valley Rd.
Lima, MT 59739
(406) 276-3536
www.fws.gov/redrocks

Swan River NWR
922 Bootlegger Trail
Greatfalls, MT 59404
(406) 727-7400
www.fws.gov/bentonlake/swanRiver

INDEX